GREAT CA

THE PHILADELPHIA CAMPAIGN

June 1777 - July 1778

David G. Martin

DA CAPO PRESS
A MEMBER OF THE PERSEUS BOOKS GROUP

Cataloging-in-Publication data for this book is available from the Library of Congress.

ISBN 0–306–81258–4

First Da Capo Press edition 2003
Maps by Robert L. Pigeon III

Published by Da Capo Press
A Member of the Perseus Books Group
http://www.dacapopress.com

Da Capo Press books are available at special discounts for bulk purchases in the U.S. by corporations, institutions, and other organizations. For more information, please contact the Special Markets Department at the Perseus Books Group, 11 Cambridge Center, Cambridge, MA 02142, or call (800)255–1514 or (617)252–5298, or e-mail j.mccrary@perseusbooks.com.

1 2 3 4 5 6 7 8 9—07 06 05 04 03

THE PHILADELPHIA CAMPAIGN

A sketch of George Washington at the end of the Revolutionary War. Washington suffered several losses during the Philadelphia campaign, but his iron refusal to give in kept the army in the field and eventually paved the way for total victory.

GREAT CAMPAIGNS SERIES

The Atlanta Campaign
The Chancellorsville Campaign
The Gettysburg Campaign
The Little Bighorn Campaign
The Philadelphia Campaign
The Peninsula Campaign
The Wilderness Campaign

Contents

Maps

Sidebars

Stylistic Note:

To simplify matters several ahistorical conventions have been adopted in this work:
1. The identities of British units are in *italics*.
2. Times have been rendered on a 24-hour basis.

Preface to the Series

*J*onathan Swift termed war "that mad game the world so loves to play." He had a point. Universally condemned, it has nevertheless been almost as universally practiced. For good or ill, war has played a significant role in the shaping of history. Indeed, there is hardly a human institution which has not in some fashion been influenced and molded by war, even as it helped shape and mold war in turn. Yet the study of war has been as remarkably neglected as its practice commonplace. With a few outstanding exceptions, the history of wars and of military operations has until quite recently been largely the province of the inspired patriot or the regimental polemicist. Only in our times have serious, detailed and objective accounts come to be considered the norm in the treatment of military history and related matters.

Yet there still remains a gap in the literature, for there are two types of military history. One type is written from a very serious, highly technical, professional perspective and presupposes that the reader is deeply familiar with the background, technology and general situation. The other is perhaps less dry, but merely lightly reviews the events with the intention of informing and entertaining the layman. The qualitative gap between the last two is vast. Moreover, there are professionals in both the military and academia whose credentials are limited to particular moments in the long, sad history of war, and there are laymen who have more than a passing understanding of the field; and then there is the concerned citizen, interested in understanding the phenomena in an age of unusual violence and unprecedented armaments. It is to bridge the gap between the two types of military history, and to reach the professional and the serious amateur and the concerned citizen alike, that this series, GREAT CAMPAIGNS, is designed. Each volume in GREAT CAMPAIGNS is thus not merely an account of a particular military operation, but it is a unique reference to the theory and practice of war in the period in question.

The GREAT CAMPAIGNS series is a distinctive contribution to the study of war and of military history, which will remain of value for many years to come.

CHAPTER I

Too Many Plans

*I*n the fall of 1776, British commander-in-chief Sir William Howe turned the war in America in England's favor with his skillfully run campaign that captured New York City. By avenging the loss of Boston the previous year, Howe secured an important prize that provided a key port for the British navy. More significantly, New York City furnished an ideal base for future operations against the middle and northern colonies. Howe's command, cooperating with a reinforced British army in Canada, posed half of a double threat that the undermanned and disheartened Colonial armies were ill prepared to face.

Howe was well aware of the advantage he had gained, and on 30 November 1776 wrote to London with a plan to exploit his success. His immediate goal was to secure New Jersey and provide support for the state's loyalists. The remnants of Washington's ragtag army were fleeing across the Delaware and could be dealt with later. New Jersey could be secured for the winter with a string of fortified posts stretching from Perth Amboy to Trenton, while the main portion of the army would winter in New York. Foundations for a movement into New England would be laid by sending General Henry Clinton to occupy Rhode Island. This expedition would have the additional advantage of keeping Sir Henry Clinton occupied for the winter. Clinton was Howe's second-in-command and had been continually besieging his superior with plans and suggestions on how to run the war. Howe did not care much for his ambition and techniques, and was looking forward to sending him off on detached duty.

Howe had more ambitious plans for the coming year of 1777. His basic strategy was to send out three large armies, one each towards Boston, Albany, and Philadelphia, that would collectively "strike such terror through the country that little resistance would be made to the progress of H. M. arms in the provinces of New England, New York, the Jersies, and Pennsylvania." These three forces would capture American supply sources, disrupt their communications, and occupy their chief recruiting areas, thereby destroying the Colonists' will to fight. This in turn would encourage the Loyalists to take control of local, state and national governments in a movement that would bring an end to the armed rebellion.

The details of Howe's plans were as follows. Clinton would be reinforced to 10,000 men so that he could use his base in Rhode Island as a springboard for an expedition "into the country towards Boston" that would hopefully recapture the original seat of the Colonial rebellion. A second force of 10,000 men, presumably to be led by Howe himself, would march north from New York to meet an invading column that Howe had heard was going to be sent south from Sir Guy Carleton's army in Canada. The two forces would meet near Albany and in the process separate New England from the rest of the rebellious colonies. Washington's army in Pennsylvania would be kept in check by a 5,000-man garrison to be stationed in New York City and a "defensive army" of 8,000 men under Lord Charles Cornwallis, which was to occupy New Jersey. Cornwallis would be ordered to "keep the southern army in check, by giving a jealousy to Philadelphia, which I propose to attack in autumn, as well as Virginia, provided the success of the other operations will admit an adequate force." Howe's strategy was well thought out and showed good promise for leading the war towards a successful conclusion, even if he was overly ambitious as to the number of campaigns he could wage before the end of the year.

Howe was well aware that the implementation of his campaign strategy would be dependent on receiving substantial reinforcements from England. Lord Germain, the British secretary of state for the American colonies since 1775, was understandably aghast on 31 December when he received Howe's request for 15,000 more men. He had strained to reinforce both Carleton and Howe before the previous year's campaign, and there was little money and few troops available to provide new reinforcements. Germain felt that perhaps 3,000 new recruits could be raised and some 4,000 new German mercenaries could be hired for service in America, but not all could be sent to Howe. In addition, he did not favor Howe's strategy of attempting to garrison all the ground that his forces occupied. Instead, he thought that the war could be won by maintaining large field armies that would demoralize the Americans into submission by winning victory after victory. He also felt that Howe had a big enough army to defeat any Colonial force opposed to him, provided that he did not fritter away his strength in garrisons and detachments. For these reasons Germain did not endorse Howe's plan when he replied on 14 January 1777, though he did remark that the general's plans seemed "well digested."

Howe must have sensed that his first plan might be considered too ambitious and that he would be unlikely to obtain the level of reinforcements he requested. In mid-December he developed an alternate plan that could be more readily carried out with the forces he had on hand. He sent this second campaign strategy to Germain on 20 December. Howe now suggested that the proposed attack on Boston should be delayed until more troops could arrive from England. He felt that 2,000 men should be enough to hold Rhode Island, and that 4,000 should garrison New York City. Only about 3,000 men would be sent north from Manhattan "to act defensively upon the lower part of Hudson's River to cover Jersey on that side, as well as to facilitate in some degree the approach of the army from Canada." Howe then proposed using his primary force of 10,000 men for an expedition against Philadelphia. He rightly judged that the

Sir William Howe

Sir William Howe (1729-1814), the British commander-in-chief during the Philadelphia campaign, came from an aristocratic family with a strong tradition of military service—his oldest brother George (born 1724) was a brigadier general killed at Ticonderoga in 1758, and his older brother Richard (1726-1799) was a distinguished Royal admiral. The family owed its high connections to the fact that Sir William's grandmother was the mistress of King George I. This made Sir William and his brothers the illegitimate uncles of King George III.

William attended Eton and began his military career at age 17 as a cornet in the *Duke of Cumberland's Light Dragoons*. In the next decade he rose steadily in rank, becoming Lieutenant Colonel in the *58th Foot* in 1759. He served with distinction in the victories at Quebec in 1759 and Montreal in 1760, and by the close of the Seven Years War was recognized as one of the army's most promising young officers. As a result, his promotions continued in the years before the Revolution. He was named colonel of the *46th Foot* in Ireland in 1764, and became lieutenant governor of the Isle of Wight in 1768. He was promoted to major general in 1772.

When the shooting broke out in 1775, Howe was sent to Boston and commanded the troops that won the costly British victory at Bunker Hill on 17 June. Four months later he succeeded to command of the army at Boston, replacing General Thomas Gage. In April 1776 he was formally named commander-in-chief of the British army in America (excluding Canada), and he was knighted the same year. He masterminded the successful campaign

invading force from Canada would require all summer to reach Albany. In the meanwhile, his own command could be gainfully employed in an attempt to defeat Washington's diminished army and capture Philadelphia. That town was the Colonists' capital and largest city and he felt strongly that the seizure of Philadelphia might persuade the Colonists to sue for peace. He also argued that "the principal army should act defensively on that side where the enemy's chief strength is located." If all went well, he could achieve his objective and still move north in time to meet the Canadian invasion at Albany.

Howe's second plan was much more to Germain's liking, especially since it would require a minimum number of reinforcements. On 3 March 1777, the American secretary against New York City (June-October 1776) that included victories at Long Island (27 August) and White Plains (28 October). After occupying New Jersey as far as Trenton, his troops were defeated by Washington's ragtag army at that city (26 December 1776) and Princeton (3 January 1777). These losses were psychologically important to the Colonial cause, and forced Howe to withdraw his outposts to New Brunswick and Amboy. Later in 1777 the general led the successful campaign against Philadelphia, including the victories at Brandywine (11 September) and Germantown (4 October). He had hoped that the capture of the Colonial capital at Philadelphia might bring an end to the war. When it did not, he asked to be relieved, and was replaced in May 1778 by Sir Henry Clinton.

Howe continued in the army after the war and held a number of various commands. He was pro-moted to lieutenant general in 1782, and became a full general in 1793. He became the fifth viscount Howe when his brother Richard died in 1799, and was named Governor of Plymouth in 1805. He died in 1814 after a long illness, leaving no children.

Howe had a swarthy complexion, and was about six feet tall. He somewhat resembled George Washington, and like Washington suffered from very bad teeth. Both General William and his brother, Admiral Richard, were noted for their bravery and sensibility, but they were by nature so taciturn and reserved that it was difficult to know them well or judge their abilities fully. Nevertheless, William was very popular with his troops, and the good-bye party he was given before leaving Philadelphia (the famous Mischianza of 18 May 1778) was one of the grandest affairs the city has ever seen.

---

replied to Howe that the king had approved his "proposed deviation from the plan which you formally suggested, being of the opinion that the reasons which have induced you to recommend this change...are solid and decisive." However, Germain added that Howe should expect no more than 2,500 fresh troops as reinforcements.

It was mid-April by the time Howe received approval of his 20 December plan. By then the situation in his theater had changed drastically from conditions under which he had formulated his strategy four months earlier. Soon after Howe had dispersed his troops into various garrisons in central New Jersey, Washington had boldly crossed the Delaware to gain victories at Trenton (26 December 1776) and Princeton (3 January 1777). These American successes had revived the

New York City at the time of the Revolution. British troops occupied the city from 1776-1783.

flagging spirits of the Colonists and completely changed the nature of the war in the middle colonies. Howe had to withdraw most of his troops to New York City, and Washington established a winter camp at Morristown, 25 miles to the east. Instead of having strong outposts on the Delaware poised to cross over to Pennsylvania in the spring, Howe had to set up his pickets at Amboy and Brunswick on the outskirts of New York Harbor.

This sudden turn of events caused Howe to become much more cautious and pessimistic about his plans for the coming campaign. On 20 January, he had written Germain that he would need another 20,000 reinforcements in order to secure the capture of Philadelphia. On 9 March he received Germain's 14 January letter giving limited support to his original 30 November campaign plan, so he again revised his strategy. On 2 April he wrote Germain to suggest that he take 11,000 men to invade Pennsylvania; 4,700 would be left to defend New York, and 2,400 would be stationed in Rhode Island.

Howe's 2 April plan contained three significant changes from his revised plan of 20 December. Firstly, his force

General Sir William Howe won his campaign when he captured Philadelphia, but his failure to cooperate with Burgoyne's expedition may have cost Britain the war.

stationed at New York would be entirely on the defensive, and would no longer be directed to head north toward Albany to meet or cooperate with any force coming down from Canada. This change would be significant because, unknown to Howe, General John Burgoyne had just received formal instructions to form an army of 7,000 men in Canada and "proceed with all expedition to Albany, and put himself under the command of Sir William Howe." Due to Germain's lack of specific orders to Howe and the awkward time lag in sending communications across the Atlantic, Howe was not expecting to cooperate actively with any potential invasion from Canada, and was directing all attention in the other direction, towards Philadelphia.

This focus is all the more apparent in Howe's second major alternation to his campaign plans. On 2 April he proposed to abandon New Jersey and proceed against Philadelphia by sea. He had two reasons for suggesting this approach: a genuine apprehension of the difficulty of crossing the Delaware in the face of Washington's army, and a desire to avoid maintaining a 100-mile-long line of supplies and communication from New York across New Jersey to the Philadelphia area. A seaborne movement, such as that successfully executed at New York the previous year, would advance him to a base much closer to Philadelphia. Howe's reasoning was sound, but his plan would admittedly carry his army totally out of supporting range on any invasion coming from Canada.

In the 2 April letter Howe also advised Germain that, due to a lack of strength, his army might not proceed as quickly as he had at first hoped. In addition, he noted that "it is probable the campaign will not commence as soon as your Lordship may expect." This third alteration to his revised 20 December plan was also quite significant, since he had earlier intended to capture Philadelphia in time to be able to turn north towards Albany by autumn. A later start in the drive on Philadelphia made it still more unlikely that he would be able to provide any aid to Burgoyne's expedition coming from Canada.

When Howe received approval of his 20 December plan in mid-April, he set about planning the details of his independent campaign against Philadelphia. Meanwhile, Germain did not show any concern for Howe's strategy or timetable until 18 May, when he wrote to Howe that he should plan to complete his Philadelphia campaign in time "to cooperate with the army ordered to proceed from Canada." For some strange reason Germain did not expedite the letter, with the result that it took almost three months to reach Howe! Consequently, Howe did not get this important missive until 16 August, when the campaign was already well under way. The general was by then unable to change his plans and could not send any significant force to cooperate with Burgoyne without jeopardizing the success of his own campaign. The results would be deadly for Burgoyne's expedition.

It indeed seems strange to us today that Germain did not make more of an effort to coordinate Burgoyne's and Howe's expeditions. Burgoyne appears to have been expecting to meet at least part of Howe's army at Albany, but it was not until August that Howe received any positive directions to make such a move. In July Howe had received a copy of

Lord George Germain, British secretary of state for the American Colonies, erred in not explaining Burgoyne's campaign objectives more clearly to Clinton.

Germain's 26 March campaign directive to Burgoyne, but there was no cover letter to detail what Howe's role should be. Given this situation, Howe proceeded to plan his own campaign with minimal consideration for Burgoyne's "private show," which Howe felt was draining troops, supplies, and attention from his own campaign.

To be certain, neither Germain nor Howe felt before the campaign that Burgoyne should be in any danger, since the Canadian force was deemed to be strong enough to achieve its objective. In fact, Burgoyne developed contingency plans to come to help Howe if the latter met unexpected difficulty in Pennsylvania! The only contingency plan Howe drew up to help any force coming from Canada was that he would follow Washington closely in the unlikely event that the main Colonial army headed north from Pennsylvania.

In the last analysis, there were two principal causes for the lack of unity in the British plans for 1777. The primary cause was the fact that military strategy was being plotted at two separate locations, London and New York. As commander-in-chief in America, Howe set about establishing his own goals and objectives, subject only to general guidelines received from London. Meanwhile, Germain and the king developed their own strategy for the army in Canada, without specific regard for Howe's plans. Clearly, the British would have fared better if they had possessed just one office to coordinate the nation's strategy, whether at London or through unifying the American and Canadian commands on the other side of the Atlantic.

The second cause hindering the British effort was an offshoot of the first—neither Howe nor Germain took special care to keep the other speedily and accurately informed of their plans and intentions. Germain, of course, was much more guilty on this count than Howe, though Howe would later be too focused on his own goals, as will be seen. The British communication problem was exacerbated by transmission difficulties in this pre-telegraphic age. It took from one to three months to send a message or plan across the Atlantic, and at least two months to send a message and get a reply. This meant that letters and replies were constantly crossing each other during the critical planning stages for the campaign. In addition, neither Howe, Germain, nor Burgoyne were able to make their plans on the basis of precise data from other theaters. Consequently the British were not able to coordinate the movements of their two principal armies in America in the critical year of 1777.

CHAPTER II

The Spring Campaign in New Jersey

Neither side was particularly anxious to renew operations at the beginning of spring in 1777, when seasonal rains turned New Jersey's roads into quagmires. After his defeats at Trenton and Princeton, Howe had been forced to withdraw his garrisons in New Jersey to points closer to New York, and set up encampments at Amboy, Brunswick, Raritan Landing and Bonhamtown. When Washington established his winter quarters in mid-January at Morristown, 25 miles west of New York, Essex County and northern Middlesex County became a no-man's land that was constantly being raided by foraging parties and scouting expeditions from both sides. Washington's greatly depleted army of less than 4,000 men was much too weak to conduct any large scale attacks on the enemy, and the Americans had enough problems trying to obtain adequate food and supplies to get through the winter. All Washington could do was watch the enemy closely while he waited for spring and reinforcements.

Howe was also waiting out the winter, and had no intention of attacking the American camps even though he greatly outnumbered the enemy. His scouts had informed him of the natural strength of Washington's position behind the Watchung Mountains, and the aggressiveness of the American scouting parties had effectively disguised the numerical weakness of Washington's army. Howe also showed a traditional British disdain for conducting a winter campaign, where losses due to the weather would probably be heavier than those from combat. Howe understood that any losses he suffered would be much more difficult to replace than Washington's would be for the Americans, and he wanted to conserve all his strength for the coming campaign against Philadelphia. Lastly, he was well aware that any move to press Washington would simply drive the enemy to seek a new camp farther from New York, a move that would lengthen his own fragile supply lines. In view of these considerations, Howe was content to wait until the weather improved before taking the field.

As the weather started to improve, both sides began organizing stronger raids against enemy forward posts. The most successful of these was an attack Cornwallis conducted against Major General Benjamin Lincoln's command at Bound Brook, less than 10 miles northwest of Cornwallis' large camp at Brunswick. Cornwallis was already annoyed at the American raids on the camp of his *33rd Regiment* at Bonhamtown, so he decided to make a retaliatory attack against Bound Brook. Before dawn on 13 April he led a 2,000-man force across some poorly guarded forts on the Raritan River and surprised Lincoln's men at breakfast. The Americans were routed but most managed to escape before their retreat was cut off; their losses amounted to a few killed and wounded, and 30 men and 3 cannon captured. The British gathered up what supplies and booty they could (including 100 sheep and cattle) before they were compelled to withdraw by the arrival of Greene's Division, which rushed to the scene from its camp at Basking Ridge, 12 miles to the north.

The principal outcome of the Bound Brook affair was a decision by Washington to pull in most of his forward outposts in order to avoid suffering any more surprise attacks. He also wanted to keep his army more concentrated in order to counter Howe's movements in the anticipated spring offensive. Washington's primary concern was that Howe might march north up the Hudson Valley towards Albany, so he sent a makeshift division of eight newly raised regiments

Major General Benjamin Lincoln commanded one of Washington's divisions until he was detached to Gates' command in July 1777.

to reinforce General Israel Putman's command in the Hudson Highlands west of West Point.

The arrival of spring brought a much needed influx of recruits into the American camps. The previous September Congress had authorized the raising of 76,000 new Continental troops, and fresh regiments were at last beginning to arrive, even though most were greatly under strength. By 21 May Washington's army had grown to a strength of 7,363 officers and men "fit for duty and on duty," a force that was at last large enough to be able to take the field. The army was divided into five divisions led by Major Generals Nathanael Greene, Adam Stephen, John Sullivan, Benjamin Lincoln, and William Alexander (more commonly known as Lord Stirling). Each division had two brigades. During the spring Washington also began to receive the munitions his force badly needed. In March alone two ships from Europe brought almost 19,000 muskets, 1,000 barrels of gunpowder, and other supplies for the American cause. After Washington began receiving his share of the shipments, Major General Henry Knox, the army's chief of artillery, was able to write his wife that the army "was well supplied with arms and ammunition of all kinds." Even so, many units were still short on equipment and ammunition.

During May, Washington's scouts brought in more and more evidence that Howe was at least beginning to prepare to move out. A number of Hessian troops arrived at Perth Amboy from Newport, and many of the troops previously quartered in private homes and barracks were moved to tents in open camps. Most significantly, Howe in early May began to transfer his sick, wounded, and many of his camp followers to New York. Howe also was gathering transports and flat boats, and even had a pontoon train newly arrived from England, an apparatus that would render the Delaware much less of an obstacle.

These indications persuaded Washington to prepare to take to the field, and on 20 May he broke up his winter camp at Morristown. His decision was to advance most of his command to the Watchung Mountains near Bound Brook in order to be better able to react to any British movement. This new position also dominated the lower country between Brunswick and Amboy. Washington's men were in position and constructing defensive works by 31 May. As a precaution, Sullivan sent Smallwood's Brigade and Hazen's command to Princeton in order to guard the army's far right. After reaching Bound Brook, Washington was gratified to see more fresh troops join his army—New Jersey militia were enlisting in large numbers, several Rhode Island regiments were en route from Peekskill, and Benedict Arnold was successfully gathering Pennsylvania militia.

Howe was indeed getting ready to begin the campaign. He had not been anxious to take the field until he received needed reinforcements and new equipment. Due to the weather, his supply convoys had not been able to leave England until April, so they did not begin to reach New York until late May. His equipment began to arrive on 24 May, and the last of his reinforcements arrived on 7 June. Howe then ordered his troops to pack up their tents and winter gear, preparations that consumed the next four days.

When Howe at last ordered his troops to break camp, he did not embark them to go by sea to Philadelphia, as he had written Germain on 2 April that he intended to do. Instead, he headed west towards Washington's army. His goal appears to have been to try to lure Washington out of his defensive position and then force him to make some critical error that might bring about the destruction of the Colonial army. Such a victory would make Howe's attack on Philadelphia much easier to carry out, since he would not have to face an intact American army on either side of the Delaware. It is also possible that he decided to put his army in the field to keep his men from getting restless while he waited for the rest of his naval transport to arrive. Even so, Howe's decision to begin the campaign on land in central New Jersey instead of embarking immediately for Philadelphia remains difficult for us to understand today. It is but one of several such critical choices he would make during the campaign.

Howe began his campaign on 11 June by moving most of his troops in New York to Amboy. After joining the large garrison there, the combined command marched to join the rest of the army at Brunswick the next day. From here his 18,000 man force marched west in two columns, Cornwallis toward Brunswick and Von Heister toward Middlebush (near Somerset Court House). Howe's goal was probably to draw Washington down from his strong position at Bound Brook; if possible, he also hoped to cut off Sullivan's command at Princeton. Some authorities believe that Howe may have been trying to make a direct march to Coryell's Ferry on the Delaware, but this seems unlikely in view of the fact that Howe had over 1,000 cumbersome wagons with him and did not have the boats or pontoons necessary for crossing the Delaware.

Washington was aware of this, since he had heard reports that Howe had left his heavy baggage and pontoons in New York. He correctly deduced that Howe did not intend to advance far into New Jersey, so he held his principal force where it was. His chief reaction to Howe's advance was to withdraw Sullivan's Division from its exposed position at Princeton to Rocky Hill and Trenton to a safer post at Flemington, 15 miles to the northwest. As a precaution, he ordered his troops to load up all their baggage, and Major

General Thomas Mifflin was directed to gather boats on the upper Delaware in case the army had to retreat again to Pennsylvania. At the same time Congress ordered Arnold to move to Trenton, and a call went out for more New Jersey militia to mobilize. Meanwhile Washington held his army ready to move should Howe march to attack him or begin moving to the north or south.

Washington's refusal to move from Bound Brook left Howe in an awkward situation. He felt that Washington's position was too strong to assault, and it was becoming increasingly difficult for him to hold his own advanced position due to constant attacks on his outposts and convoys by Colonial riflemen and militia. He kept his men busy for a couple days building redoubts at Somerset and Middlebush. He then decided to try to entice Washington to move by sending his baggage trains back to Brunswick, giving the appearance that he was lightening his column for a dash on Philadelphia. When Washington still declined to react, Howe early on the night of the 19th made a hasty withdrawal to Brunswick, perhaps trying to lure Washington into conducting too hasty a pursuit, one that the British might turn on and overwhelm. When Washington again refused to move, Howe began withdrawing from Brunswick to Amboy on the 21st.

Washington was perplexed by Howe's sudden withdrawal, but did not fall for the ploy. On the evening of the 21st he directed Sullivan to make a feint towards New Brunswick while Maxwell took 1,500 men in a limited advance towards the enemy's right flank. The next morning he also directed Greene to fall on the enemy's rear as they retired, but at no time did he order the whole army to advance as Howe hoped.

Washington's advance began well enough on the 22nd. Morgan led the way and conducted a successful dawn attack on the Hessian guard over the Raritan bridge at Brunswick. Greene and Wayne then joined the attack, and together they drove the British rear guard out of Brunswick as far as Piscataway. Here they had to stop for lack of support. Sullivan had received his orders too late to help, and Maxwell had not received his at all (the courier simply disappeared or deserted). The British army then was free to continue unmolested in its march to Amboy, and even tauntingly burned all the houses and barns they passed.

Howe had his entire command safely reconcentrated at Amboy by nightfall on 22 June. Washington came up with his advance guard at 0600 the next day to survey the British lines and found them to be stronger than he anticipated—both flanks rested on waterways and the line between was well guarded by Redcoats. In addition, Howe had set up his pontoon bridge to provide access to Staten Island, if needed.

Though Howe had failed to engage Washington's army, he at last succeeded in drawing the Americans out of their strong position at Bound Brook. Washington was actually apprehensive of his ability to maintain an advanced position, and even released most of his Jersey militia on 23 June. Nevertheless on 24 June he moved his troops towards the strengthened British position at Amboy. Stirling's Division and a few other units were posted about five miles from Amboy at Metuchen Meeting House, while Washington stationed his headquarters and the rest of his command at Quibbletown, five miles behind Metuchen.

Washington's movement provided just the opening that Howe was looking for. At 0100 on 26 June he led his troops out of Amboy in two parallel columns. Cornwallis led one towards Woodbridge and Vaughn took the other towards Bonhamtown. Howe's goal was to destroy Stirling's command and then cut off Washington from Bound Brook and his escape route to the west. The British march proved to be a difficult one due to their heavy uniforms, the increasing heat of the day, and Colonial snipers.

Howe's two columns rejoined just before attacking Stirling's camp, which was strongly situated and well provided with artillery. Stirling for some reason chose to stay and fight the superior enemy force rather than withdraw. He further endangered himself by not taking full advantage of his defenses; instead he formed his men in parade ground order to meet the British advance. One observer noted that Stirling "was in no hurry to retreat, but preferred engaging for awhile.

Wherein he made a wrong choice, for he had been nearly cut off by the right column under Lord Cornwallis." Cornwallis had indeed tried to take advantage of the situation by slashing into Stirling's lines in an effort to cut off the Americans' retreat. He might have succeeded had his troops not been so hot and tired. Cornwallis did manage to take captive about 70 Americans along with 3 French-made cannons in the Colonial rear guard, but the rest of Stirling's force escaped successfully. Both sides suffered about 100 battle casualties in this engagement that is known as Flat Hills but should more properly be called Metuchen Meeting House.

Cornwallis pursued Stirling for five miles towards Westfield, where he halted. Meanwhile, Washington had learned of Howe's advance when he heard the guns being fired in a skirmish at Woodbridge. He at once understood Howe's intentions, and retired as quickly as he could to the mountains near Bound Brook.

Howe came up later in the day to examine Washington's line, and determined that it was too strong to attack. The two armies now held the same relative positions they had occupied a month earlier, and nothing at all had been gained from two weeks of campaigning. Disappointed in his hope to defeat Washington in battle or lure him into making a costly strategic error, Howe determined to return to Spanktown on the 27th, and reached Amboy on the 28th. He then moved all his troops to Staten Island, and New Jersey was completely evacuated by 30 June.

CHAPTER III

New York to Head of Elk

Upon returning to New York following the end of his inconclusive campaign in New Jersey, Howe began loading supplies for his naval campaign against Philadelphia. He himself had already transferred his headquarters to the fleet's flagship, the *Eagle*, on 24 June before he began his second foray into New Jersey. The embarkation process was a laborious one, and it would be three weeks before the expedition would at last be ready to sail. In the meantime he set many of his restless troops to work at strengthening New York's defenses. His unrushed embarkation seems strange in view of the fact that it was getting to be midsummer and he still had not accomplished anything of note for the year. Some sources suggest that he may have been awaiting the arrival of still more shipping and supplies. Whatever his reasons, Howe certainly was in no hurry to get underway in an effort to accomplish all the goals he had outlined earlier to Germain.

Howe may also have been delaying in order to await the arrival of his second-in-command, Henry Clinton, who was still on his way from London. Clinton was going to take command at New York while the rest of the army moved against Philadelphia, and Howe probably wanted to brief his subordinate personally before taking to the field. Clinton arrived on 5 July and was dismayed to see that Howe was still not ready to start his campaign. He was also discouraged to observe how dispirited many of Howe's troops were over their lack of success since the fall of Trenton.

What disturbed Clinton the most was the news that Howe

was planning to move against Philadelphia by sea. Howe's 2 April plan had not reached London before Clinton left for New York, and Clinton now heard his commander's full campaign plans for the first time. He at once understood that Howe's strategy would radically change the situation in New York and New Jersey. Howe would be abandoning most of New Jersey and would be moving too far afield to give Burgoyne help or receive any from him. Clinton was also concerned that Washington might ignore Howe's expedition for the moment and turn east to "murder" the garrison left in New York.

Clinton argued long and hard in an effort to get Howe to change his plans, but was not able to do so. The situation was not helped by the fact that the two generals did not get along very well. Clinton had been Howe's second-in-command during the 1776 New York campaign, and had continually aggravated his superior with criticism and suggestions for alternate lines of strategy. The two also disagreed in their basic operational strategies, as Howe preferred to take and hold geographic objectives and Clinton preferred to seek and destroy enemy armies. In fact, Clinton's lengthy arguments against a seaborne movement to Philadelphia only strengthened Howe's resolve to conduct the campaign on his own terms. In the end, Howe simply informed Clinton that "he had sent home his plan, it was approved, and he would abide by it." The actual fact of the matter was that Germain and the king had approved Howe's 20 December 1776 proposal to move against Philadelphia, but Howe had not yet received their 18 May response to his 2 April letter proposing that the movement be made by sea.

Howe had embarked most of his 13,000 infantry by 9 July, but he still did not order his force to set sail. Apparently he decided to heed the advice of several of his subordinates that he should wait for information on Burgoyne's progress. Satisfactory news finally came on 15 July, when a dispatcher arrived from Burgoyne stating that he was preparing to attack Ticonderoga. Howe's departure may also have been delayed by unfavorable winds that blew for several days at mid-month.

Admiral Richard Howe, brother of General William Howe, commanded the British fleet stationed in North America from 1776-1778. Both Howes were Whigs, and attempted to conduct peace negotiations while directing the war.

The next day, 16 July, Howe sent a confused message to Germain that showed just how cloudy the general's thinking was. If Washington moved north "preventing a junction between this and the northern army," as he appeared to be doing, there would be no cause for alarm. Howe would simply reinforce Clinton's reserve in New York, and Washington would "no further affect my proceeding to Pennsylvania." If Washington moved against Burgoyne while Howe was at sea, he had no doubts that Burgoyne could fend for himself. And if Washington moved north only to retard Burgoyne's advance, "He may soon find himself exposed to attack from this quarter" (that is, by Clinton's force at New York). Howe offered no alteration of his plan to move against Philadelphia by sea. Strangely, he even reduced Clinton's garrison of New York by a brigade before he left instead of reinforcing it as he had promised Germain. Apparently he wanted to make sure that his own expedition succeeded regardless of what happened elsewhere. Clinton would only have 7,000 men (all but 1,000 of them provincials and Hessians) to defend New York and cover New Jersey and the lower Hudson.

Washington had not been as elated as his troops when he learned on 1 July that the enemy had withdrawn to Staten Island. He realized how weak and ill supplied his troops were, and was all too aware that British strength and naval superiority gave them the option of moving to any point from Boston to Savannah. On 3 July, he withdrew his forces to Morristown in order to be better able to march towards the Delaware or the Hudson should Howe head for either of those goals.

When news began to reach Washington of Burgoyne's advance towards Ticonderoga, he came to the conclusion that Howe's most likely line of advance would be up the Hudson to join Burgoyne. If Howe headed up the Hudson he would have a jump on Washington and would be able to overwhelm the American defenses in the Hudson Highlands before help would be sent. This reasoning led Washington to warn General Israel Putnam, his commander in that district, to be on the alert. He also sent Sullivan's Division to Pompton, 16 miles northeast of Morristown, so that it could march more speedily to Putnam's aid if needed. Washington asked New York Governor George Clinton to call out his militia, and notified General Philip Schuyler, commander of the troops facing Burgoyne, of his concern that Howe might take possession of the Highlands, a move that "would be most fatal to our interests" because it "would effectually bar all mutual assistance of our two armies." Washington's preoccupation with conditions in the Hudson Valley brought criticism from Quartermaster General Thomas Mifflin and other Philadelphians who feared for the safety of Philadelphia.

Washington's concern for Putnam's command intensified on 10 July, when he received a dispatch from Schuyler that Ticonderoga had been evacuated. The greatest obstacle to Burgoyne's advance had been lost, and nothing but Schuyler's force could slow the British down now. If Howe moved north, both Putnam and Schuyler would be in trouble. This apprehension persuaded Washington to take most of his command north via Pompton Lakes and Smith's Clove, Orange County, in the vicinity of West Point. He felt that this was the best place from which to oppose Howe should the British head north. If by chance Howe moved by land across New Jersey towards Philadelphia, Washington trusted that

George Washington was hard pressed to win victories with amateur soldiers fighting against British and Hessian professionals. His greatest asset was his refusal to give up.

the local militia might slow the British enough to allow his own army to reach the Delaware ahead of the British. If Howe left New York by sea for Philadelphia, Washington would have to rely on maritime scouts in order to rush troops to the threatened points as soon as possible.

The bulk of Washington's army had been in Orange County for about a week when Washington heard on 22 July about the intense British naval movement near Sandy Hook. His information proved to be correct, as Howe finally had his fleet ready to cast anchor. The convoy, commanded by the general's brother, Admiral Richard Howe, headed out to sea from Sandy Hook on 23 July. It consisted of a total of 267 vessels, the largest fleet ever to sail in American waters. The Howes divided their forces into two columns. The flagship *Eagle* (64 guns) and the frigate *Liverpool* (32 guns) led the way, while the *Augusta* (64 guns) and the *Iris* (50 guns) guarded the center. The rear of the flotilla was brought up by the *Nonsuch* (64 guns) and two armed schooners, the *Swift* (16 guns) and the *Dispatch* (16 guns). In addition, nine frigates "sailed around the fleet at some distance" and brought in a few captured enemy ships as prizes.

Washington received confirmation of Howe's departure on 24 July, and was gravely concerned as to the Britisher's destination. He wrote a friend that "the amazing advantage the enemy derive from their ships and the command of the water keeps us in a state of constant perplexity and the most anxious conjecture." Washington judged that Howe's most logical goal would be Philadelphia, but his greatest fear was that the enemy might head for New England. What was most clear was that Howe was not going to move up the Hudson, a conclusion that allowed Washington to begin moving his army towards the Delaware. He sent his light horse at once to Philadelphia, and started Stephen's and Lincoln's Divisions for Trenton, which was the most suitable point from which to move to Philadelphia or points to the north, wherever Howe would land his troops. He himself followed with the rest of the army after dispatching General Wayne to take command of the Chester County militia.

As Washington marched south, evidence began to accumulate that Howe was heading towards Philadelphia. Washington was near Flemington on the 25th when he received a report that 70 British ships had been seen the previous day off Egg Harbor, near Atlantic City. The British goal seemed to be to round Cape May, 30 miles south of Egg Harbor, and then head north up the Delaware Bay to a point at or near Philadelphia. Even so, Washington could scarcely believe that Howe was sailing away from Burgoyne, and he still suspected the British fleet might double back to New York. He wrote to General Horatio Gates three days later that Howe's abandoning of Burgoyne was "so unaccountable a matter that till I am fully assured it is so, I cannot help casting my eyes continually behind me."

Washington was confident his troops could reach Philadelphia before Howe's, if indeed the capital was the enemy's destination. Greene's Division reached Coryell's Ferry on the evening of 28 July, while Stephen's and Lincoln's Divisions were four miles upstream at Howell's Ferry. Sullivan's Division was at Morristown bringing up the army's rear. In view of the decreased threat against the Hudson Highlands, Washington directed Putnam to prepare to send two of his brigades south to Pennsylvania.

At about 0930 on 31 July Washington received an important message from Philadelphia that the British fleet had been seen passing Cape May, at the entrance of Delaware Bay, on the 30th. The general promptly issued orders for his men to proceed to the capital, and directed Sullivan specifically to march by the shortest route possible. He calculated that his leading divisions should reach the city the next evening, well ahead of any British troops.

Washington proceeded to the capital ahead of his troops, accompanied only by his staff. He did not stop in the capital, but instead rode past it to "look for a proper place to arrange the army." He was at Chester, located on the Delaware 15 miles southwest of Philadelphia, on the evening of 1 August when a disturbing message arrived from lookouts on Cape May in New Jersey. They reported that a British fleet of at least 228 boats had left Cape May at 0800 on 31 July and was not heading up the Delaware, but had gone out to sea.

This news caused Washington great anxiety—Howe had forsaken the best sea route to Philadelphia and could be headed anywhere. Indeed, his naval movement may have been only a feint to draw Washington away from New York and the Hudson Highlands. To deal with this possibility, Washington halted most of his command at the Delaware, sent Sullivan's Division back to Orange County, and returned the two brigades he had borrowed from Putnam's command on the Hudson. He certainly did not relish the thought of marching across New Jersey yet another time. The general wrote his brother on 5 August that his men were "more harassed by marching and counter-marching than by anything that had happened to them in the course of the campaign." Captain John Clinton of the 3rd Virginia wrote on 17 August that his men were exhausted because "we have made a complete tour of the Jerseys."

Washington remained in Philadelphia until 5 August, when he rejoined his troops that were encamped in eastern Bucks County. A lack of news about Howe's progress was greatly distressing. He wrote one friend that the enemy "keep our imaginations constantly in the field of conjecture. I wish we could out fox on their object. Their conduct really is so mysterious that you cannot reason upon it so as to form any certain conclusion."

By 7 August Washington felt that the British might be moving against eastern Long Island, so he started his troops marching towards Coryell's Ferry on the Delaware. His occupation of Coryell's would put the army "near enough to succor Philadelphia should the enemy, contrary to appearances, still make that the object of their next operation, and will be so much more conveniently situated to proceed to the northward, should the event of the present ambiguous and perplexing situation of things call them that way." Camps were soon set up along the upper Neshaminy River, a few miles west of Coryell's Ferry (modern Lambertville).

Additional reports received on 10 August changed Washington's estimation of Howe's goal. The enemy fleet was then reported to be some distance south of the Delaware Capes and heading south, news that suggested they were heading for Charleston, South Carolina. Since there was no way that his army could march south to oppose Howe in the deep South, Washington decided to await more definite news of Howe's progress. When no reports arrived over the next 10 days, he and his generals decided on 21 August to move north against Burgoyne. Because such a move would leave Philadelphia defenseless, the commander sent one of his new aides, Colonel Alexander Hamilton, to secure Congress' approval for his plan. Washington also was concerned about entering the Northern Department, which "has long been considered as separate and in some measure distinct." Congress wisely voted that "General Washington was to act as circumstances might require."

As Washington prepared to march back to New York on 21 August, he received startling news that the British fleet had been seen a week earlier at the entrance of Chesapeake Bay. This probably meant that the enemy was headed farther south, since they surely would have been spotted already if they had headed north up the Chesapeake. Even so, Washington could not afford to have most of his army in New York if

Howe were indeed still in the Chesapeake. He temporarily suspended his move to the north, and was rewarded the next day with definite news that the British fleet had been seen on the Eastern Shore opposite the mouth of the Patapsco River (Baltimore). Howe was heading towards the upper Chesapeake in order to invade Central Pennsylvania or attack Philadelphia from the west!

The astonishing news of Howe's whereabouts ended three weeks of anxious indecision for Washington. It was now clear that he had to march southwest past Philadelphia in order to meet the enemy, and he at once began issuing the necessary orders. Sullivan was ordered to march from eastern New Jersey "with all convenient speed" to rejoin the main army, which would march "tomorrow morning very early towards Philadelphia and onwards." In addition, Brigadier General Francis Nash was to take his newly raised North Carolina brigade along with Proctor's artillery command to Chester.

As the army neared Philadelphia, Washington was persuaded by some of his officers to march his command through the capital in a show of force. He was at first reluctant to do so because not all his troops were well equipped and they certainly were not uniformly clothed. Perhaps he agreed to conduct a parade through Philadelphia in order to show Congress exactly how much he needed all the supplies he had been begging for. In preparation, he directed his men to burnish their arms and wash their clothes so that they would put on their best appearance for the citizens and Congress. He also instructed that every man should wear a "green sprig, emblem of hope" in his hat.

The army left its camps on the Neshaminy River at 0400 on 23 August and reached Germantown that evening. The parade through Philadelphia was scheduled for Sunday morning, 24 August. The day opened with heavy rains, but the skies cleared by 0700. The troops were carefully drawn up about a mile out of town before marching down Front Street to Chestnut and then up to the Common. The army's wagons were sent by a different route, and none of the command's camp followers were permitted to join the procession. The troops were to march in strict discipline, and anyone who dropped out of the ranks would be punished with 39 lashes.

The army's order of march was carefully drawn up in a campaigning column. First came a subaltern with 12 Light Horse, then an entire troop of horse, followed by 2 mounted regiments (Baylor's and Beard's). Next came "a company of pioneers with their axes, etc., in proper order." General Nathanael Greene and his staff led the infantry, whose vanguard was a full regiment 12 men deep. Lincoln's and Stirling's Divisions followed, with light artillery batteries interspersed. The column's rearguard was formed by one of Stirling's regiments, which marched 150 yards behind its brigade. Washington himself was mounted on his best horse and rode with his staff near the head of the column.

The army put on a reasonably impressive show as its 16,000 men took almost 2 hours to pass the reviewing stand. To John Adams the army appeared "extremely well armed, pretty well clothed, and tolerably disciplined." Nevertheless, he continued, "Much remains to be done. Our soldiers have not yet quite the air of soldiers. They don't step exactly in time. They don't hold up their heads quite erect, nor turn out their toes exactly as they ought. They don't all of them cock their hats; and such as do, don't all wear them in the same way." Another observer noted that the men "though differently dressed, held well burnished arms and carried them like soldiers, and looked, in short, as if they might have faced an equal number with a reasonable prospect of success."At the completion of the parade the army marched over the floating bridge on the Schuylkill and encamped at Darby. The force continued to proceed to the southwest the next day. Most of the infantry pitched camp on the 25th near Naaman's Creek, while Washington accompanied his staff and light cavalry to Wilmington. His goal was to locate the British landing site as soon as possible, and then determine their goal and line of march. He planned to use his cavalry to harass the enemy's advance and gather up all the cattle and supplies they could in order to keep them from the enemy's hands. The bulk of the infantry would be kept several miles to the rear in order to avoid bringing on a general engagement prematurely. Washington hoped that he would not have to fight until he found the time and place best suited to success.

Howe's destination in the upper Chesapeake had been as much a surprise to his troops as it had been to the Americans. When the British fleet was rounding Cape May on 30 July, Captain Andrew S. Hammond of the *Roebuck*, which had been patrolling Delaware Bay, recommended that Howe disembark his men at Reedy Island, located about 12 miles south of Wilmington and about 35 miles from Philadelphia. Much to Hammond's amazement, Howe replied that he would not sail up Delaware Bay but would instead enter Chesapeake Bay.

Howe's apologist, Troyer Steele Anderson, suggests that the general may have originally planned to sail up Delaware Bay but turned to his alternate course when he learned Washington was en route to Philadelphia and so would soon be in position to contest his landing. However, Howe's writings and other sources suggest that he was influenced mostly by reports that the Colonists had prepared floating batteries, river obstructions, and fire boats to block the passage of the lower Delaware. In addition, he was aware that forts and other defenses had already been prepared on the south side of Philadelphia. A movement up the Chesapeake, Howe felt, might catch the Americans unaware and would allow him to avoid all the enemy's prepared defenses. He also had hopes of cutting Washington and his capital off from the important American supply sources west of the Susquehanna.

Whatever were his reasons for doing so, Howe's decision to sail up the Chesapeake instead of Delaware Bay is yet another of the great enigmas of the campaign. There were in reality no riverine defenses in the Delaware below Philadelphia, and the American fleet there consisted of only four ships and two floating batteries. Howe would actually have met more difficulty trying to navigate the Delaware's meandering channel than he would have received from any American defenses. Another point of consideration is that the move to the Chesapeake made it much more difficult, if not impossible, for him to keep contact with his garrison in New York or

The Philadelphia Campaign, Fall 1777

Washington Forms Camp
20 Dec.

Whitemarsh

Valley Forge

Schuylkill

Germantown
4 Oct.

21 Sept.

Palli

River

West Chester

White Horse
16 Sept.

Darby

Brandywine

Fort Mifflin

Chadd's Ford

11 Sept.

Chester

Fort Mercer

Creek

British Occupy Philadelphia:
26 Sept.

N

British Land
25 Aug.

Wilmington

Delaware River

Elkton

British Movements

Colonial Movements

0   5   10

MILES

Chesapeake
Bay

Burgoyne's force coming down from Canada. Lastly, it should be noted that Howe's plan to try to cut off Philadelphia from its supply bases west of the Susquehanna was not well thought out, since there was plenty of food and supplies available from Lancaster, Reading, Allentown, and other towns to the north of the capital.

To make matters worse, Howe's voyage from the mouth of Delaware Bay to the upper Chesapeake did not go as smoothly as Howe had hoped. His voyage around the Virginia capes took much longer than planned because of calm and contrary winds. Then, as the fleet sailed up the Chesapeake, it reached water so shallow that the ships were scraping bottom. Luckily for the British, the thick mud could not hold their boats, and they were able to slide through the low spots until pilots were found who could lead them back to the main channel.

Because of these delays, the British fleet did not reach the upper stretches of the Chesapeake until the fourth week of August. Howe and his brother surveyed the shoreline on the 23rd, and they determined to make a landing on the 25th at Head of Elk (so named for being at the mouth of the Elk River). By then most of the British troops had been aboard ship for almost seven weeks and were suffering terribly from the summer's heat, cramped quarters and a lack of fresh food. In addition, the conditions of the voyage had killed or disabled most of the horses that had been brought along.

The lead elements of Howe's fleet dropped anchor in the Elk River opposite Cecil County Court House on the "distressingly hot" morning of Monday 25 August. The first landing party consisted of a reinforced brigade (*1st* and *2nd Light Infantry*, *1st* and *2nd British Grenadiers*, and the Hessian and Anspach jägers) that was loaded onto flat-bottomed boats. Only four companies of local American militia were on hand to oppose the British landing, and they promptly fled without firing a shot. Howe sent his light infantry to occupy Head of Elk, four miles distant, and landed most of his troops later in the day. The sea weary troops made flimsy huts from fence rails and corn stalks, only to be drenched by a heavy thunderstorm that broke that night. Curiously, the camp at Head of Elk was farther from Philadelphia than the army would have been had it landed at New Castle, below Wilmington on Delaware Bay. The army was also 10 miles farther from Philadelphia than it had been while encamped at Amboy before the campaign started.

Washington located the British camp personally on the morning of 26 August when he rode southwest out of Wilmington with General Greene and a large cavalry force in an attempt to find the enemy. Upon climbing Gray's Hill, Washington spotted Howe's camp some two miles distant, but was unable to determine its size. After reconnoitering the area, the party was overtaken by a thunderstorm that drove Washington and his staff to seek shelter in a farmhouse. Washington's aides urged him to leave the house for fear he would be ingloriously captured by an enemy patrol, as General Charles Lee had been captured at Basking Ridge on 13 December 1776. His staff guarded the house nervously throughout the stormy night. It turned out that the owner of the house was a Tory, and that Washington was indeed lucky to be able to ride off unscathed the next day. He later admitted that he had not acted prudently at the time.

There is no doubt that the bad weather aided Washington's escape from possible trouble. Howe had planned to begin his march inland at 0300 on 26 August, but the movement was delayed by the same storm that had driven Washington to seek shelter in the Tory farmhouse. Nor was Howe able to use his cavalry as he would have liked. Some 170 horses had died during the long sea journey and another 150 were so "miserably emaciated" that they would not be suitable for use for some time. There were consequently no mounts for the cavalry or the infantry officers, and no teams to pull the ammunition and supply wagons. In addition, Howe found his men to be so shaky from the voyage that they needed a few extra days in order to regain their land legs. As Howe himself put it on the 27th, "Since the heavy rain continues, and the roads are bottomless, and since the horses are sick and stiff, we had to countermand the order to march."

The weather turned better on the 28th, and Howe at last put his army into motion. He formed his command into two columns. The Hessian General Knyphausen led the right column across the Elk River and occupied Cecil Court House. The left column was led by Cornwallis, who marched into Elkton, which consisted of "about 40 well built brick and stone houses." An American force of 1,000 men under Colonel Patterson and the Philadelphia Light Horse was easily driven out of town towards Gray's Hill, from which they were later dislodged by the British advance guard. Howe took up his headquarters in the same Tory house that Washington had sought shelter in two days before. He was pleased to find

Elkton "storehouses full, consisting of molasses, Indian corn, tobacco, pitch, tar and some cordage and flour" that the Colonists had neglected to remove or destroy. Perhaps these supplies would deter his troops from all the pillaging they had undertaken. Indeed, he had already been forced to execute two soldiers and whip five others for looting.

Howe's army rested for the next five days as his agents purchased or commandeered enough local horses to serve his calvary and wagon train. A large number of cattle and sheep were also taken in, as the troops were extremely (and understandably) hungry for fresh meat. One foraging expedition brought in "261 head of horned cattle and 586 sheep and 100 horses," while another grabbed 350 sheep, 55 horned cattle, and 204 horses. The foragers encountered minimal opposition from American forces. Washington had returned to Wilmington on the 26th and reported to Congress that he was unable to advance his army "till their arms are put in order and they are furnished with ammunition, both having been greatly injured by the heavy rain that fell yesterday and last night." Because of the muddy roads and Washington's lack of aggressiveness, there were only a few skirmishes before the end of the month. Howe reported that "the chasseurs encountered a body of the rebel infantry" on 29 August and the next day "the Welsh fusiliers fired a few platoons into a body of rebel cavalry of about 200."

Howe at last found time at the end of the month to reply to Germain's much delayed dispatch of 18 May, which he had received on 12 August while still at sea. In this dispatch, Germain gave approval to Howe's seaborne movement to Philadelphia with the significant condition that Howe give proper support to Burgoyne's expedition. Howe's late receipt of this proviso put him in an awkward position for several reasons—he had started out with no concern for cooperating with Burgoyne; his late start from New York made it all the more difficult to observe his instructions; and he was in the middle of his own campaign, the success of which was still in doubt.

These considerations led Howe to compose a carefully

worded yet revealing reply to Germain on 30 August. He at first stated straight out that he would not be able to cooperate with Burgoyne because of the lateness of the season. He was also explicitly critical of Germain's delay in sending direct instructions to cooperate with Burgoyne. Furthermore, Howe claimed that Germain's failure to send the reinforcements he had requested made it unlikely that his campaign on Philadelphia would bring an end to the war. In reality, Howe was brought to this conclusion by the fact that only a few loyalists had rallied to his cause after he landed on the Chesapeake. He had hoped on beginning the campaign that the presence of a strong British force in the middle colonies would embolden large numbers of Tories to assert themselves and take control of their local governments.

By 1 September the stage was at last set for the first great battle of Howe's campaign. Washington, after weeks of anxious indecision, had posted his troops ably along the Delaware and was in position to be able to put a shield in front of Philadelphia after he correctly determined that Howe was still aiming for the capital. Howe, despite his delays and somewhat questionable strategy, had rightly judged that Washington would come forward to defend Philadelphia, just as he had with New York the year before. The British general certainly had few reasons to doubt that this campaign would be any less successful than that of the previous year.

CHAPTER IV

Brandywine

General Howe was not ready to move against Philadelphia until a week after his weary command landed near Head of Elk on 25 August. It took him that long to bring his supplies ashore, refresh his men, and replace the 320 horses that had died or been disabled during the long voyage from New York. Once the newly obtained animals were shod. Howe formed his command into two columns for the purpose of foraging better and gave them orders to move out. The southern column, led by Knyphausen, left its camp at Cecil Court House at 0500 on 2 September and marched to Buck Tavern, located near the present Chesapeake and Delaware Canal. The northern column, led by Cornwallis and accompanied by Howe, decamped at dawn the next day and marched along the lower road to Christiana by way of Aiken's Tavern (modern Glasgow, located five miles east of Elkton). Howe's immediate goal was to have his two columns meet at Aiken's before continuing on. However, Cornwallis' column arrived there first and Howe decided to move on through the thickly wooded countryside instead of waiting for Knyphausen.

Cornwallis' advance corps consisted of 293 Hessian and Anspach jägers, commanded by Lieutenant Colonel Ludwig von Wurmb, and was supported by some light infantry and two "amusettes" (small field pieces). The column was proceeding cautiously near Cooch's Bridge on Christiana Creek when it was struck at about 0900 by heavy fire from enemy riflemen concealed in the woods. This Colonial force was a large contingent of Brigadier General William Maxwell's

Weapons and Tactics

Battlefield tactics at the time of the Revolution were centered entirely around the capabilities and limitations of the musket. The musket of this period was a heavy smoothbore weapon that fired a round lead ball at a moderate distance (up to 100 yards) at a reasonable rate of fire (2 or 3 times a minute). The standard musket used by the British (the famous "Brown Bess") did not differ significantly from American versions and the French pieces that were supplied to Colonial troops in such heavy numbers (the French musket came in 15 variations produced from 1717 to 1797, with the later Charleville models being the most popular). The "Brown Bess" ("Bess" may have been a corruption of the "buss" from "blunderbuss") was about 39 inches long and weighed 13 pounds. It fired a one ounce ball from a .75 inch bore. Muskets had very limited range, and seldom killed beyond 150 yards; most fighting was done at 50-80 yards.

Musket fire was remarkably inaccurate; one source estimates that less than 10 percent of the shots fired in combat actually struck someone. Muskets had no sights, and were fired while simply pointed in the enemy's general direction. Loading and firing was done in a complicated series of motions ordered step by step by the line officers (the British employed 12 motions, a number reduced by Von Steuben in his new drill system

for Washington's army). Nor would the weapon always discharge properly. Flints were fragile and could easily be dislodged from the hammer; British flints reportedly lasted about 10 firings and American ones about 50. Powder was often unpredictable, and the weapons were useless in the rain (as occurred at Warren Tavern during the Philadelphia campaign). Iron ramrods for loading the ball and charge down the barrel had only recently been introduced, and the weapons were useless if their ramrods were lost, bent, or fired by mistake. In addition, the musket tube could foul easily after only a few firings.

The unpredictability and short range of the musket governed the battlefield tactics used during its heyday, which stretched from the early 1700s through the Napoleonic wars. Emphasis was placed on moving closely packed formations of foot soldiers into good range of the enemy. Volume and speed of fire mattered more than accuracy. Usually troops would exchange only a few volleys before one or the other side began to waver. Then the side with the upper hand would make a bayonet charge to carry the field, such as the British did at Birmingham Hill during the Brandywine battle. The key element of Von Steuben's training at Valley Forge was to teach the American troops to maneuver and fight in dense formations that would enable them to match the British firepower. This training took a considerable time to master, since formations were usually three men deep with file closers (who would step up to replace casualties). It is remarkable that Washington's men learned the essential elements of linear drill in only three months before Monmouth.

During the war, several Colonial units (such as Morgan's command in the Monmouth campaign) carried hunting rifles of the Davy Crockett variety. These guns were longer than the common musket and had greater range (200-300 yards) because of rifling in their barrels that gave a spin to the projectiles. Riflemen were very effective as scouts and skirmishers but could not stand up to British line troops for the simple fact that their rifles were not equipped with bayonets. The American riflemen were routed every time the British infantry closed in with their bayonets (Bunker Hill, Long Island, and the opening stages at Princeton). This fostered a dread of British bayonets that was heightened by the ferocity of "No Flint" Grey's bayonet night attack on Wayne's men at Paoli.

British light infantry and the German jägers were especially trained for skirmishing and often carried lighter muskets such as the fusil or carbine. Originally each British battalion had one light infantry company and one grenadier company (grenadiers were larger and stronger men whose job was to throw grenades; by the time of the Revolution the grenades were no longer used, though the grenadiers remained elite troops). By the time

of the Philadelphia campaign, the British had detached their light infantry and grenadiers into special consolidated battalions. Detachment of grenadier and light infantry companies left the foot battalions with only 8 companies each, depleting their firepower against the American battalions which could theoretically field 640 musket men to a British battalion's 448.

Use of artillery during the war was limited, except at forts and during sieges, by primitive field carriages and lack of training, particularly among the Americans. Guns had a range of from 800 to 1,200 yards, but because of ammunition problems were not generally effective beyond 400 yards. The principal projectile was solid shot, which could break up enemy formations but seldom caused many casualties; grape and case shot were better anti-personnel weapons. The characteristic of the guns used by both sides were largely the same since the Americans used so many captured British pieces. Principal sizes used in the field were 3-, 6- and 12-pounders, though the British also had howitzers and some 24-pounders. Because the guns had to be dragged into position by trail ropes, they were not a significant element of battlefield linear tactics. Field artillery did not play a significant role in any battle of the Philadelphia campaign, except for the battery Greene established on Comb's Hill during the battle of Monmouth. It succeeded at creating a raking fire on the advancing British lines and broke up more than one attack on the American center.

It should be noted that the heavily wooded terrain in America prevented the use of cavalry, and indeed linear tactics in general, on the scale they were use in Europe. Only a few battles, such as the British attack on Birmingham Hill at Brandywine and the late afternoon's fighting at Monmouth, were fought in "traditional" style by lines of infantry blazing away at each other. The lessened role of artillery and cavalry also prevented the "combined arms" tactics of the Napoleonic era—cavalry was never used to force the infantry to form "squares" which were in turn mowed down by artillery.

Cavalry and dragoons (mounted infantry) also played only a minor part in the campaign. The British had difficulty securing sufficient houses for both their supply wagons and mounted troops, particularly after most of their horses became incapacitated or died due to the strenuous voyage from New York at the beginning of the campaign. Consequently they used what few mounted troops they had primarily for scouting and carrying messages. Their shortage of cavalry and dragoons was especially felt after Brandywine, when a determined pursuit might well have routed the confused and fleeing American army. Washington also had a shortage of cavalry. The greatest service the American horsemen performed was done by the scouts who watched Howe's movements,

particularly during his movement to Whitemarsh in early December.

Finally, mention needs to be made that most of the American troops were young tradesmen and farmers by occupation, and not frontiersmen as is often thought. Such troops did not respond favorably to discipline, which was fairly lax until Von Steuben arrived, and units were depleted quickly since their terms of enlistment were up. Congress had difficulty creating a continuous standing army, especially because of poor supplies and irregular rate of pay.

British troops on the other hand, tended to come almost entirely from the poorer elements of English society. The King's soldiers led a hard existence with continuous drill, poor food, and heavy penalties for minor offenses. There was little hope of promotion, and the social gap between the common soldiers and their officers was much greater than in the American army. A private's pay of eight pence per day was subject to numerous required deductions, that kept the men so poor that, as one historian has put it, they had no choice but to become "chronic thiefs." If a soldier lived out his lengthy term of enlistment he would be eligible for a pension and perhaps some farmland in Canada. Most, however, did not serve their full time in the field and would instead be sent back to England because of illness or wounds, and would finish their term on reserve or recruiting duty.

newly formed "Corps of Light Infantry," which Washington had created on 28 August for the purpose of observing the enemy. The command had an original strength of about 720 (120 officers and non-coms, and 100 picked men from six different brigades) Maxwell had sent forward to be "constantly near the enemy and to give them every possible annoyance." After being alerted to the British advance the previous day, Maxwell had 450 of his men ready for action near Cooch's Bridge on 5 September.

The jägers formed battle line as soon as the action started, and Wurmb brought up his two field pieces. He then sent a column to envelop Maxwell's right, and supported the movement with a bayonet charge. Maxwell withdrew, only to be attacked again as the affair degenerated into a running fight. The Americans eventually fled to Washington's main camp at White Clay Creek, having suffered about 40 killed and wounded. The British, who lost about 30 men in the affair, pursued them for some distance before returning to occupy Iron Hill. The action, also known as the engagement at Iron Hill, was one of the first in which American troops fought under the newly made "Stars and Stripes."

Knyphausen's column came up too late to join in the fight, having been delayed by the large herd of cattle it was driving. During the day, its flankers brought in an additional 500 head of cattle, 1,000 sheep and 100 horses. After his two columns were reunited, Howe chose to go into camp instead of pushing on farther. He needed to bring up more provisions from the fleet, and the last of his infantry, two brigades under Grant, did not arrive from Elkton until 6 August. He also needed to gather still more horses, since most of the animals that had survived the sea voyage broke down on the march to Iron Hill.

Washington's command was largely inactive while Howe was camped near Iron Hill. Greene's and Stephen's Divisions had occupied a position on White Clay Creek on 28 August, and Washington was waiting for Howe to move forward and attack him on ground more favorable to the Americans. When the British declined to advance, Washington held a Council of

War that decided on 6 August to move most of the army from Wilmington to Newport, located northeast of White Clay Creek on the main road to Philadelphia. Washington also moved his headquarters to Newport, leaving Maxwell's light infantry as the only American force remaining on the southwestern side of Red Clay Creek.

Later in the evening of the 6th Washington received word that the British had "disencumbered themselves of all their baggage, even to their tents, reserving only their blankets, and such part of their clothing as is absolutely necessary." Howe was indeed preparing to move out at last, intending to make "a speedy or rapid movement" towards Philadelphia. Unbeknown to Washington, Howe had also broken contact with his fleet and had sent it back to sea with orders to sail up Delaware Bay and make an attack on Philadelphia by water simultaneously with his land attack from the west.

In response to Howe's preparations, Washington on the morning of 7 September also ordered his command to strip for action. Surplus clothing and baggage was to be sent north of Brandywine Creek, and the army's cooks were directed to prepare a two days' supply of cooked rations. Later in the day Washington concentrated his entire command at Newport, where he ordered his men to "build abatises and dig entrenchments ready to oppose their advance." His position behind Red Clay Creek was not a bad one, blocking the direct overland route to Philadelphia. He was hoping that Howe's army of approximately equal size to his would attack him there, though he heard that the enemy might march instead to the Delaware.

Howe had other intentions than what Washington anticipated. Long before dawn on 8 September he set his command in motion under a magnificent display of northern lights. Once again he formed his command into two columns—Cornwallis led 12 British and 3 Hessian regiments of about 8,000 men, and Knyphausen led around 6,000 men in 9 British and 4 Hessian regiments. Howe had learned of Washington's strong position near Newport late the previous day from six deserters from Washington's dragoons who had come in eager to sell their horses for the high bounty Howe's agents were offering. Howe accepted the deserters' story as true, and decided to send only a token force towards Newport. He took most of his command to the left, marching by way of White Clay Creek and Newark. By the end of the day he had covered 12 miles, easily outflanking Washington's lines.

Washington's active scouts were aware of Howe's march by 0300 on 8 September, not long after the British began moving. The American camps were soon buzzing with activity. "The General (alarm) was beat and all tents struck. All regiments were paraded, the men properly formed with an officer at the head of every platoon, and after wheeling to the right, we remained under arms until 9 o'clock. The alarm guns were fired and the whole army drawn up in line of battle, on the east side of Red Clay Creek, with General Greene's division on the right."

Washington's men were eager to fight, and became dismayed when only a few enemy troops appeared "on a high hill about three miles west of Newport, who show themselves very freely." Later in the day Washington unsuccessfully sent Weedon's Brigade of Greene's Division forward to provoke an attack. The British declined to fight, since they were posted only "by way of decoy and to amuse our troops." A reconnaissance conducted in the evening found all British troops gone from the American front. Only then did Washington realize what had happened—that Howe had stolen a march on him and moved past his right flank.

Washington was left with no choice but to withdraw to a new position closer to Philadelphia. His clear choice was to form behind Brandywine Creek, which runs southward from West Chester to the Delaware at Wilmington. Brandywine Creek furnished an excellent position at which to block the British drive on Philadelphia, since it was wide enough and broad enough to hinder British movement, and it could be crossed only at its fords, many of which had relatively steep banks.

Washington had his army on the march to Chadd's Ford, located 10 miles north of Wilmington, at 0200 on 9 September.

After arriving there that afternoon, he held a Council of War in his headquarters at the Benjamin Ring house, which was about a mile east of the ford. After he expressed his intention to stay and defend the Brandywine line, Sullivan and several other generals expressed a concern that Howe would "try to come around our right flank" rather than conduct a frontal attack. Washington then called in several local farmers and interrogated them about the fords on the Upper Brandywine. One particular informant stated emphatically that there was no good ford for eight miles past Buffington's, and this was reachable only by a "long circuit through a very Bad Road." Taylor's Ford, the crossing he referred to (modern Copesville), was a full 12 miles from Washington's headquarters. This evidence from the locals strengthened Washington's resolve to remain at Chadd's Ford, and persuaded him that it was necessary to protect the creek only as far as Buffington's, which was located near the junction of Brandywine's East Branch and West Branch, about four miles northwest of Chadd's.

Washington had his army positioned behind Brandywine Creek by midday on the 10th. He formed his center at Chadd's Ford, which actually consisted of two crossings— one located at Chadd's Ford, a short distance south of the present U.S. 1 highway bridge, and the other at Chadd's Ferry, located 300 yards south of Chadd's Ford, near the mouth of Harvey Run. Two divisions, Greene's two Virginia brigades and Lincoln's Pennsylvania command (now led by Wayne while Lincoln was on detached duty with Schuyler) were posted on a rise south of Harvey Run. Greene was on the left, near Chadd's Ferry, and Wayne was on the right near Chadd's Ford, supporting Proctor's Pennsylvania artillery, which was placed on a hillock north of the road to the ford. The center was backed up by Stephen's Division, which formed near the present Bullock Road and Ring Road.

Washington was less concerned with his left, where the hills along the creek's eastern bank furnished a stronger defensive position. The natural strength there allowed him to hold that part of the line with Major General John Armstrong's division of Pennsylvania militia, about 1,000 strong. Armstrong took up position on both sides of Wilson's Run, overlooking Gibson's Ford, and also guarded Pyle's Ford farther downstream. Washington requested General Rodney to bring the Delaware militia up to support Armstrong's left, but Rodney refused to take his command out of their state.

Washington knew that his right formed more of a problem. He placed Sullivan's Division at Brinton's Ford, the next crossing about a mile upstream from Chadd's. Sullivan's line contained an artillery detachment and was supported by Stirling's Division, stationed about 1,000 yards to the rear. The upstream fords as far as Buffington's were to be guarded by detachments from Sullivan's Division. Sullivan sent his Delaware regiment to Painter's Ford, just over one mile upstream from Brinton's. One battalion of Hazen's "Canadian" regiment was sent to guard Wistar's Ford, another mile upstream from Painter's, and Hazen's other battalion was posted at Buffington's Ford, about a mile upstream from Wistar's. Washington by his dispositions was hoping that the enemy would strike at either Chadd's or Brinton's Fords. If they tried to cross farther north, Washington apparently planned to shift his reserves (Stirling and Stephen) to meet the threat first. (Note: The names of the different fords are given variously in both Revolutionary and recent accounts of the battle. The names used here are those preferred by Christopher Ward in his history of the war.)

A number of American units patrolled the western side of Brandywine Creek prior to Howe's anticipated approach. The largest of these was Maxwell's battalion of light infantry, reinforced by a battalion of 200 local Chester County militiamen. Maxwell's principal position was astride the main road west of Chadd's Ford. The far right of the American line was screened by a Pennsylvania militia detachment under Major James Spear, which was posted in front of Buffington's Ford near the confluence of the Brandywine's East and West branches. The front between Spear's and Maxwell's commands was scouted by various probing parties sent out by Greene and Stirling.

Major General John Sullivan was acquitted of charges of misconduct at Long Island and Brandywine. He was transferred to Rhode Island in early 1778 and did not participate in the Monmouth campaign.

While Washington was forming his troops, Howe was marching his army north towards Kennett Square. On 8 September he had outflanked Washington's position near Newport by marching 12 miles from Iron Hill past White Clay Creek and through Newark. The next day Knyphausen's column reached Kennett Square, located eight miles east of Chadd's Ford, and encamped "on a hill near Kennett's Tavern." Cornwallis' column was delayed by bad roads and then the coming of darkness, and had to encamp on the 9th at Hokesson Meeting House.

At about 1730 Howe received reliable information from his scouts concerning Washington's dispositions—about 3,000 Americans were east of Brandywine Creek and most of their army was concentrated at Chadd's Ford. Howe at once determined to conduct a flank march, the same strategy he had successfully used to defeat Washington at the battle of Long Island on 27 August 1776. He would send a part of his force under Knyphausen to front Chadd's Ford while Cornwallis took most of his men on a march around the enemy right. To carry out his plan, he had Cornwallis' column on the road at 0500 on 10 September. He issued his battle orders upon reaching Kennett Square at 1000, only to be confronted by his officers with the complaint that the move would be "impossible since the men, and even more the horses, were completely exhausted." Howe was probably also persuaded to delay his attack because he needed more precise information on the location of Washington's right and how to bypass it.

Howe delayed his movement for a day and permitted his troops to rest the remainder of the 10th. Cornwallis' troops went into camp north of Kennett's Tavern, and pickets were sent out to scout the Americans' position. There were minor clashes all day with Washington's scouting parties as each side tried to investigate the other's position. Howe used the rest of the day to fine tune his plans. He transferred the *1st* and *2nd Brigades of Foot* to Knyphausen's column, giving it a strength of 6,825 (see Order of Battle). Cornwallis' column would number 8,241, including a number of pioneers who were to clear the road of obstructions. Most of the army's supply wagons were to accompany Knyphausen. Cornwallis' troops warily observed a number of empty wagons join their column. Empty wagons were always needed to carry the wounded, a sure sign of pending battle.

Howe took personal command of Cornwallis' column, and led the troops out of camp at 0500 on 11 September. They marched out of Kennett Square via Union Avenue and then headed north through the open countryside under cover of a dense fog. His goal was some six miles away at Jeffries' Ford, a deep but passable crossing on the East Branch of Brandywine Creek about a mile north of Washington's northernmost detachment at Buffington's Ford.

Knyphausen's Division broke camp at Kennett Square soon after sunrise (0546), about an hour after Howe moved out. He was ordered to march east towards Chadd's Ford, and sent in advance of his infantry a 496-man vanguard consisting of the *Queen's Rangers*, a detachment of riflemen, and a squad of the *16th Light Dragoons*. The main body of his column consisted of the *1st* and *2nd British Brigades*, the *Hessian Brigade*, and then the artillery, baggage and cattle herd. The *71st Regiment* served as the column's rear guard.

Howe's columns were not the only troops in motion that morning. Shortly before dawn Maxwell had been sent forward towards Kennett Square in order to determine Howe's intentions. Maxwell proceeded to Kennett Meeting House, about three miles from Chadd's Ford, and sent some cavalry vedettes to scout the road ahead. The vedettes rode forward a mile to Welch's Tavern (modern Longwood) and went inside to refresh themselves, perhaps waiting for the heavy fog to lift. About 0900 they received a rude surprise when they spotted Knyphausen's cavalry approaching less that 100 yards away. The Americans hastily fired a few shots and bolted unceremoniously out the tavern's back door, leaving their horses behind. The battle of Brandywine had begun.

The British vanguard halted at the tavern long enough for all the rest of the column to take to the road. The *Queen's Rangers* then moved forward again. They had not gone more than half a mile when they were struck by a volley from a company of Maxwell's infantry under Captain Charles Porterfield. Porterfield had taken up a protected position on a hill just west of Old Kennett Meeting House (modern Harroton) with orders to harass the enemy's advance and then fall back to another similar position. After firing their volley, the Americans withdrew hastily about half a mile to a hill 700 yards east of the meeting house, where they formed behind a fence. The *Queen's Rangers* pursued in haste and were preparing to smash into Porterfield's men when they received "a close and destructive fire" from another American infantry company formed in a concealed position. The musketry stopped the *Rangers* in their tracks and they quickly withdrew, leaving 30 casualties on the ground.

While the British regrouped, the two American companies withdrew to a third preassigned position farther up the road to Chadd's Ford. When the enemy approached too cautiously to fall for this trap, the American light infantry fell back to a hill less than 200 yards west of the ford. Here Maxwell was waiting with the rest of his command behind a light breastwork.

Knyphausen's vanguard halted to deploy when it came up, since it was not strong enough to tackle Maxwell's entire command by itself. Before long Knyphausen himself came up to take charge of the situation. He sent the *Queen's Rangers* to scout for any American ambuscades on the north side of the road, and brought up four artillery pieces, supported by the *28th* and *49th Regiments*, to be positioned on a hill opposite Maxwell's center. He also dispatched the dragoons and the *1st Battalion* of the *71st Regiment* to move around the Americans' left flank and strike it in the rear.

A short while later, before all his troops were in position, Knyphausen became concerned about his left flank and sent the *4th Regiment* towards Brinton's Ford. The unit was spotted by the Americans posted on the other side of the creek, and Sullivan at once sent a detachment with a cannon down to the ford to fire on the British regiment. Before long "a pretty hot fire of musketry" was being exchanged. The affair lasted about 15 minutes until two British cannons came up, whereupon Sullivan's detachment "retired to their former ground."

Knyphausen by then had his troops formed opposite Maxwell's center. He opened fire with his artillery (two heavy guns and two 3-pounders), and sent the *28th Regiment* forward to seize a hill right behind Maxwell's left. The threat forced the Americans, who "had been shouting Hurrah! and firing briskly," to begin withdrawing towards the ford. The British *23rd Regiment* came up to press the attack, and the advancing troops linked up with the men of the *71st Regiment* who had been working their way through the woods on Maxwell's left. Maxwell tried to reform his men, only to see a fresh Hessian battalion come charging on the double against his right. Since he was on the verge of being cut off from the ford, Maxwell ordered a full retreat.

The last of Maxwell's men crossed the creek about 1000 as Knyphausen's troops pushed forward towards the water under American artillery fire. One Hessian officer noted how "the balls and grapeshot were well aimed and fell right

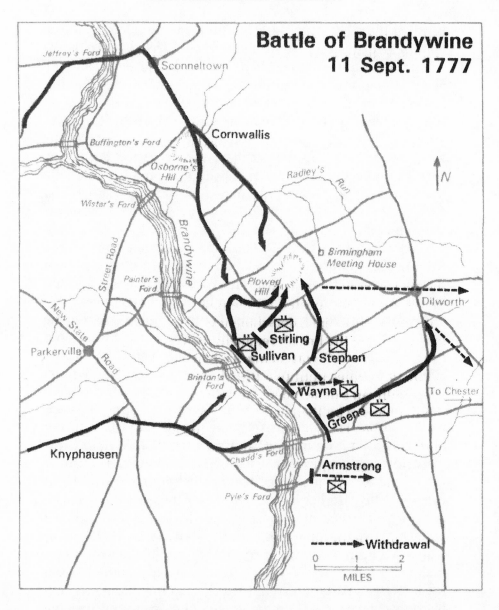

among us." Nevertheless, "the cannonade had but little effect, partly because their battery was placed too low." Soon Knyphausen brought up his own artillery to counter the Americans and cover his infantry as they formed on the high ground near the creek. The British *1st Brigade* (minus the *4th Regiment*) went into position on the right opposite Chadd's

Ferry, with the *Queen's Rangers*, Ferguson's riflemen, and the *1st Battalion* of the *71st Regiment* guarding its open downstream flank. The *Hessian Brigade* moved up near Chadd's Ford. The approach to Brinton's Ford was held by the *4th Regiment*, and the line between there and the *Hessian Brigade* was held by the British *2nd Brigade*. Knyphausen kept his dragoons and the *2nd Battalion* of the *71st Regiment* in the rear to guard his wagons and to act as a reserve. The morning's engagement drew to a close at about 1030 as Knyphausen's troops ceased firing and took cover in their new positions. The Americans likewise stopped firing except for occasional cannon shots, and the heavy smoke that had filled the valley began to dissipate.

Washington and Green watched Knyphausen anxiously for the rest of the morning, expecting the enemy to attack across the creek at any moment. Their anxiety was increased by confusing reports they were receiving that a British column was possibly moving north from Kennett Square towards their right. The first such report had come in early in the day, and Washington had sent Major John Jamison of Bland's Dragoons to investigate. At about 0930 a report came in from General Sullivan, posted at Brinton's Ford, that Major Jamison had "come from the right of the army" and assured him that "I might depend there was no enemy there." Half an hour later a contrary report came in from the battalion stationed at Wistar's Ford that a large body of the enemy was moving to the right.

Washington was confused by these conflicting reports, and at 1120 sent a message to Colonel Theodorick Bland, commander of the dragoons posted on the east side of Painter's Ford, to pay "vigilant attention to the movements of the enemy." Particularly, Washington wanted him "to gain satisfactory information of a body confidently reported to have gone up to a ford seven or eight miles above this." Bland replied by noon that he had indeed seen an enemy column headed north on the "valley road" towards Trimble's Ford on the West Branch of the Brandywine. At about the same time a confirming message was received from Lieutenant Colonel

James Ross of the 8th Pennsylvania of Wayne's Division, who apparently had undertaken to send a scouting party of 100 men across the creek. Prefaced "Great Valley Road, Eleven O'Clock A.M.," Ross's message stated "a large body of the enemy from every account 5,000, with 16 or 18 field pieces, marched along this road just now. This road leads to Taylor's and Jeffries' ferries on the Brandywine and to the Great Valley at the Sign of the Slip on the Lancaster Road to Philadelphia." Ross had evidence that Howe was with the enemy column, and reported that his small command was skirmishing with the British rear guard.

Washington did not show alarm at these reports, which clearly showed that Howe had split his command and was sending one portion of it on a march to the north. He could not for the moment determine whether the British column was trying to move around his right by a circuitous march, or was heading for his supply depot at Reading. The column's disposition did not matter, Washington decided, as he was convinced that Howe had made "a terrible blunder" to divide his command. He would take advantage of the situation by boldly sending Greene, Maxwell and Armstrong across the creek to attack the enemy force opposite Chadd's Ford, while the rest of the army moved against the rear of the enemy column moving up the Great Valley Road.

Washington issued the necessary orders for his attack, and soon his advance troops were heading across the Brandywine. Sullivan sent the 3rd Maryland Regiment across at Brinton's Ford, and it at once began skirmishing with the *4th British Foot*. At the same time Maxwell ordered his light infantry to cross at Chadd's Ford one more time. His eager men "pushed over with his corps, and drove them from their ground with the loss of thirty men left dead on the spot, among them a Captn of the 49th, and a number of Entrenching Tools with which they were throwing up a Battery."

Just as Washington's entire force was preparing to move, more news arrived concerning the British march up the Great Valley Road. During the morning Colonel Patterson Bell of the 8th Chester County Militia, temporarily attached to Maxwell's command, had sent Major James Spear to scout the "upper country" above the fords of the Brandywine. Spear was a native of the district and knew it well. He had investigated the area and then reported to Sullivan, who forwarded his news to Washington: "I saw Major Spear of the militia who came from a Tavern in the Forks of the Brandy-wine. He came thence to Welchs Tavern and heard nothing of the enemy about the Forks of the Brandywine and is confident they are not in that Quarter. So Colonel Hazen's information must be wrong."

Washington had to evaluate this new information quickly. According to Hazen's and Ross's reports earlier in the day, a large column of the enemy had marched north from Kennett Square on Great Valley Road. On the other hand, Spear reported that none of the enemy had crossed the West Branch of the Brandywine. When Spear himself arrived at headquarters, Washington interrogated him and decided "that the movement of the enemy was but a feint, and that they were returning to reinforce Knyphausen at Chadd's Ford." Since it would be disastrous under these conditions to leave his prepared positions and assault Knyphausen, Washington canceled his attack orders and recalled Maxwell's and Ramsey's commands.

Washington's regiments returned to their former positions and resumed their wait for the British to attack. Around 1400 more messages arrived hinting that the situation on the right was perhaps not the way Washington had interpreted. First Major John Skey Eustace of Sullivan's staff rode up with a report that the enemy definitely had the "intention to turn our right flank." Eustace was dismayed when "Gen'l. Washington and Gen. Knox laughed at my intelligence and sent me back to Gen. Sullivan without an answer." A short while later, Thomas Cheyney, a local farmer, arrived at headquarters to report that the British were across the creek and on their way to attack. He had gone out on his own to look at the enemy column and was fired on by them; he had escaped only because his horse was much faster than theirs. Washington was not certain about whether or not to believe Cheyney because he could have been a Tory spy bearing a false tale. This mistrust exasperated Cheyney and made him shout, "If Anthony Wayne or Perse Frazer was here, they'd know whether I'm to be believed... My life for it. You're mistaken. By hell! It's so. Put me under guard till you can find out it's so!"

This confusing situation was soon resolved when a courier from Sullivan arrived with two messages. One was from Colonel Bland, commander of the dragoons. Writing at "a quarter past one o'clock," Bland stated, "I have discovered a party of the enemy on the heights, just on the right of the two Widow Davis' who live close together on the road called the Fork Road, about a half a mile right of the [Birmingham] Meeting House." The second message was a later report from Sullivan that "Colo. Bland has this moment sent me word that the enemy are in the Rear of my Right about two miles coming down, there is, he says, about two Brigades of them. 2 of clock P.M. he also says he saw a Dust Rise back in the country for above an hour."

Howe indeed had succeeded in deceiving Washington, and now had his column across the Brandywine in the rear of Washington's right. As reported by some of Washington's scouts, Howe had marched north from Welch's Tavern on the Great Valley Road that morning. Other American scouts, however, had somehow missed the British column by arriving just before or after the enemy marched by a given point. It was their reports that so confused Washington as to Howe's movements and intentions.

Howe's column had crossed the West Branch of the Brandy-wine at Trimble's Ford, and then proceeded on a winding three mile march to Jeffries' Ford, located a mile north of Washington's far right at Buffington's Ford. Washington was not guarding Jeffries' because his local informants had told him that there were no good crossings for several miles above Buffington's. The locals were right, since Jeffries' was a deep ford with water up to a man's waist, and was difficult to reach. In this case, though, Howe had much more accurate local topographical information than did Washington. As soon as Howe had landed near Head of Elk, a Chester County loyalist named Curtis Lewis had come into camp to volunteer his help as a guide. Lewis "rendered them essential services" by explaining the location of the fords on the Brandywine and by leading them directly to Jeffries' Ford, which Howe's active scouts believed to be loosely guarded or not guarded at all.

Howe's advance guard, 250 picked troops from the jägers, light infantry and the *42nd Regiment*, were cautious when they approached Jeffries' Ford. They found that the crossing was indeed deep; more importantly, no American troops were on hand to oppose them. While the infantrymen dried themselves off, Captain Johann Ewald proceeded with some mounted jägers to scout the road ahead. He proceeded a short distance and was alarmed to come upon a narrow winding defile over a thousand paces long, "where a hundred men could have held up either army the whole day." After consulting with Cornwallis, Ewald proceeded gingerly up the defile. The pass was clear, "left wide open for us."

Cornwallis at once began moving his troops through the pass, which was such a bottleneck that the men could pass only four abreast. The regiments were reformed at Sconneltown, and then moved a mile southwest to Osborne's Hill, where they were given a chance to rest from their 15-mile march while awaiting the remainder of the column. A number of local farmers came out to view the show. "In a few minutes the fields were literally covered with them... their arms and bayonets being raised shone bright as silver, there being a clear sky and the day exceedingly warm." One Quaker youth noted that Cornwallis made "a brilliant and martial appearance," while Howe "was a large and portly man, of coarse features. He appeared to have lost his teeth, as his mouth had fallen in." The other British officers were mostly unimpressive, being "rather short, portly men, well dressed and of genteel appearance, and did not look as if they had ever been exposed to any hardship, their skins being white and delicate as is customary for females who were brought up in large towns and cities."

While Cornwallis' men were rested, Captain James

Major General William Alexander preferred to be known by his adopted title "Lord Stirling." He was an able division commander during the Philadelphia campaign.

McPherson led his company of the *42nd Regiment* on a reconnaissance down the Forks Road (now Birmingham Road). It was this unit that Bland had seen at 1315 when he alerted Sullivan and Washington.

Washington acted promptly when he received Bland's disagreeable news, and sent orders to his two reserve divisions, Stirling's and Stephen's, to march to Birmingham Meeting House, located three miles due north of Chadd's Ford but about twice that distance by road. When the size of Howe's column was confirmed a short while later, Washington ordered Sullivan to move towards his right rear to oppose the threat. Only Wayne and Maxwell, with Proctor's artillery, would be left to face Knyphausen at Chadd's. Greene's Division was withdrawn slightly and would act as a reserve, to face Howe or Knyphausen if needed. Washington remained with Greene for the moment.

Stirling and Stephen reached Birmingham Meeting House in good order and formed on a hill to its southwest called Plowed Hill or Birmingham Hill. Stirling took the left of the line and Stephen formed on the right. The far right flank of the position was watched by the 3rd Virginia of Woodford's Brigade, which was stationed on the northeast side of the road in a woods near the meeting house. Overall, the American line was a good one, especially since it had woods covering both flanks and it was perpendicular to the expected British line of advance. Indeed, when Howe studied the line from Osborne's Hill, he curtly observed that "the damn rebels form well."

Sullivan had a much more difficult time reaching the right than Stirling and Stephen did. He later complained that "I neither knew where the enemy were, nor what route the other two divisions were to take, and of course could not determine where I should make a junction with them." Nevertheless, Sullivan did not hesitate to march "the most direct road for the enemy." As he headed northwest on a line parallel to the creek, he ran into Hazen's regiment, which had been guarding Wistar's and Painter's Fords. Hazen was retiring because the enemy had crossed the creek and "were close upon his heels," so he readily joined Sullivan's force. Soon afterwards the column made contact with some enemy troops, probably one of Cornwallis' scouting parties. In order to avoid a fight, Sullivan turned to the right and headed for a 262-foot-high hill that was nearby (near present day Street Road). From the top of the hill Sullivan at once saw a double problem—his men were in advance of Stirling's and Stephen's line about one half mile to the east, and they were dangerously close to the British line of attack, whose drums could be plainly heard a short distance to the north.

Sullivan promptly rushed over to Birmingham Hill, where he took command as senior general. As the three division commanders held a conference, they saw Howe's troops advancing to attack from the northwest. They decided to hold their position, and Sullivan sent for his division to join them from the hill on the left. The arrival of Sullivan's men forced an awkward reshuffling of the American line just as the British attack was about to strike. Sullivan directed his units to form on the left end of the hill, which forced Stirling to shift from the left to the center, as Stirling sidled to his right. Stephen was pushed farther to the right, with the result that Weedon's Brigade had to be moved behind the woods where the 3rd Virginia was posted, a position which gave the brigade no line of fire on the enemy's advance.

Unlike the Americans, Howe took his time forming his men

up for his attack. Indeed, had he not rested them for an hour on Osborne's Hill before attacking, he might have reached Birmingham Hill ahead of any enemy units. As it was, Howe wanted to have his lines perfectly arranged before beginning his advance. He formed his units in two lines, with the *3rd British Brigade* held in general reserve. The front line consisted of the *British Guards* on the right, the *British Grenadiers* in the center, and the British light infantry and Hessian jägers on the left. The second line was formed by the *Hessian Grenadiers* on the right and the *British 4th Brigade* on the left. Howe formed his battle plan while he ate lunch and leisurely studied the American lines through his spyglass. He would simply attack straight ahead while his light infantry worked its way into the enemy rear through the woods east of the meeting house.

All was ready a little after 1600. The grenadier band played the famous "Grenadier March" and then began beating a cadence. The disciplined ranks proceeded slowly down Osborne's Hill and over a stream bed. At first their only opposition was a number of fences that had to be climbed or knocked over. Potential difficulty arose when several units began to drift apart due to the terrain and heavy ground cover. In order to maintain a continuous front, Howe brought up his *Hessian Grenadiers* from the second line and placed them between the *British Guards* and the *British Grenadiers*. At the same time he sent the *4th British Brigade* to extend the front line to the left, to meet some American troops he saw moving in that direction.

All was ominously silent as Howe's veterans slowly advanced. The first firing arose on the British left, where the jägers ran into an American outpost stationed in an orchard. Soon afterwards the main British line came within range of Sullivan's artillery, which opened up with a deafening roar. Their fire was so destructive that the British center for a time had to stop and seek shelter.

The British were fortunate that their extended front line now overlapped the Americans on both the right and the left. On the British right, the *British Guards* were never in range of the American artillery, and the *Hessian Grenadiers* were able to escape the deadly barrage by drifting to the west. These two brigades struck the left of the American line before Sullivan's regiments were properly in position. It seems that Sullivan's senior brigadier, Preudhomme de Borre, had insisted on assuming the post of honor at the right end of the American line and was even moving his 2nd Brigade in that direction until he was stopped and directed to return to the left. Meanwhile, the division's 1st Brigade was rushing into position after its march from the hill one half mile to the left. Its lead regiment, Colonel John Stone's 1st Maryland, had just moved over the crest of Birmingham Hill and was filing through a narrow lane when it unexpectedly ran into the *Hessian Grenadiers.* Stone had to order a quick countermarch, and the shaken unit withdrew to the top of the hill, leaving 23 of its men dead in the lane.

What already was an awkward situation deteriorated when Stone was thrown from his horse and temporarily disabled. His regiment, deprived of their leader, broke for the rear, so throwing the other three regiments of the brigade into confusion. Soon the entire brigade was streaming back over the hill right into the lines of de Borre's Brigade, which was just coming up. Many of de Borre's officers and most of his men assumed that a general retreat had been ordered, and the command began to melt away. Among the first to run was General be Borre, an act for which he received so much censure that he felt it necessary to resign three days after the battle. Lieutenant Colonel Samuel Smith of the 4th Maryland vainly attempted to stem the tide and was able to hold only 30 of his regiment's 220 men in line. General Sullivan rode down from the hill to try to recall his men "but all in vain; no sooner did I form one party than that which I had before formed would run off."

Only one of Sullivan's units, Hazen's "Canadian" regiment, was able to keep its integrity during all this confusion. Hazen, who was at the front of de Borre's Brigade, simply pulled his command to the right, away from the stampede. He then headed his men up the hill, where they at length made contact with the 1st and 3rd New Jersey Regiments on the left of

Stirling's Division. They arrived just in time to help drive the oncoming *Hessian Grenadiers* back from the top of the hill.

On the left end of the British line, the light infantry managed to escape the American artillery fire by advancing towards Marshall's 3rd Virginia Regiment and keeping that unit between themselves and the cannons. The Britishers had observed that the American artillerists were not firing in that direction in order to avoid hitting Marshall's men, who were then posted in an orchard in advance of the Birmingham Meeting House.

As the light infantry advanced, they picked up elements of the British vanguard, which had been forced to seek shelter from the intense American fire. The leading light infantry company then encountered Marshall's main line, which fired a volley and fell back to a strongly built stone wall around the meeting house. The British decided that this line was too strong to attack head on, so their various companies began working their way around the meeting house enclosure as best they could. One company, though, was covered by a stone wall and a hedge running alongside the road, and had to run a gauntlet in front of the Americans. One by one the light infantry companies regrouped behind the meeting house. As they began to climb Birmingham Hill on the other side of the road, they "had a glimpse of the enemy line as far as the eye could reach to the right and left." Since they were not numerous enough to continue the attack by themselves, the men were "compelled to throw ourselves on our knees and bellies, and keep up a fire from the slope of the hill."

It was now the crisis of the battle. Cornwallis saw that his light infantry was pinned down on the left and that the *Hessian Grenadiers* had been repulsed after their initial success on the right. To give them both relief, he directed his two battalions of *British Grenadiers* to assault Sullivan's center. The troops advanced to within 40 paces of the American line where they received such a heavy volley from Stirling's line that they had to halt and hit the ground for cover. Within minutes they were ordered to fix bayonets, whereupon they rose and "ran furiously at the rebels." Stirling's line held gallantly until it began to receive heavier fire from the *Hessian Grenadiers* on its left and the British light infantry on the right. Generals Stirling and Conway managed to keep their line from breaking but could not keep it from being pushed off the hill.

The rest of the American line was faring no better. On the left, the *Hessian Grenadiers* renewed their assault and pushed back Hazen's out-manned regiment. On the right, several companies of British light infantry worked their way behind Scott's Brigade and forced it to give way from the hill. Scott managed to withdraw in fairly good order, though, and formed a new line slightly to the rear. Meanwhile, the battle continued to rage in the center as Stirling's troops even attempted several limited counterattacks. For 50 minutes the Americans here held off the British in some of the heaviest fighting of the war until they were at last forced to withdraw.

Stirling's withdrawal left only one organized American command on Birmingham Hill, Woodford's Virginia brigade of Stephen's Division. As already seen, Woodford had been moved to the far right when Sullivan's command came up from the left at the start of the battle. Woodford now brought up his men in order to give the rest of the army time to reform. They held on long enough for Marshall's 3rd Virginia Regiment to withdraw from the forward post at the meeting house, which had been bypassed by the enemy during their advance. Woodford managed to get an order through for the unit to withdraw, and it marched out "in good order," reaching Woodford's line by marching around the rear of the hill. The maneuver, though, cost the unit dearly, as it lost 6 officers and 75 men from a strength of 150 while moving past and through the British lines. The regiment's commander, Colonel Thomas Marshall (father of future Chief Justice John Marshall) emerged unscathed but had to walk after his horse was killed.

Woodford's command held valiantly until it was blasted by a British battery that had been brought forward to the newly captured hill. The first British salvo wounded several officers and killed so many men and horses in Stephen's only battery that its two guns had to be abandoned. In a short while Woodford himself fell wounded, and a charge by the British light infantry forced his command to fall back. Woodford's withdrawal also forced Scott's supporting line to pull back still farther.

Sullivan and Stirling used the time bought by Woodford to form Stirling's troops on a 400-foot-high hill about a mile southeast of the Birmingham Meeting House. Stirling's men were still in relatively good order in spite of having been heavily engaged at Birmingham Hill. Conway's Brigade and two cannons were drawn up near a right angle in Forks Road (near the present crossing of Wyle Road and Birmingham Road) and Stirling's two New Jersey regiments, along with Hazen's regiments, formed on a lower hill 700 yards to the east. The remains of Sullivan's Division were being reformed by Colonel Smith of the 4th Maryland some two miles to the rear and were in no position or shape to help any more that day.

Stirling's men had just taken their positions when Stephen's two brigades withdrew from the edge of Birmingham Hill. Stirling tried to give cover for Scott and Woodford to march by, but was prevented by an unexpected British attack. It seems that during Howe's advance, two of his units—the jägers and the *2nd Battalion Light Infantry*—had been delayed from entering the battle by the swampy ground around Radley Run. They finally came up after Birmingham Hill was captured, and were eager to enter action. They saw their opportunity when Stephen was making his withdrawal past Conway's position. The two fresh British commands pitched into Stephen's flank and totally routed the weary Americans. Lafayette happened to ride up at this critical juncture and "did all he could to make the men charge at the point of a bayonet...but the Americans, little used to this sort of fighting, did not care to do so, and soon this brigade fled like the rest of the army." For his efforts, Lafayette told his wife later, "the English honoured me with a musket ball, which slightly wounded me in the leg."

Conway's men retreated so quickly that they left their two cannons behind. At the same time the *33rd British Regiment*

Washington's headquarters at Chadd's Ford, now preserved in Brandywine State Park. Washington spent too much time here during the battle and should have been with his troops on the right at Birmingham Hill.

drove back Stirling's left. A few American troops tried to form 400 yards to the rear, but they, too, were easily driven back by the British advance. In the next few minutes Sullivan valiantly attempted to rally the Colonists at two more locations closer to Dilworth, with an equal lack of success. The British pursuit might have been even more successful had most of Howe's right wing (*1st British Grenadiers, Hessian Grenadiers,* and *British Guards*) not become so entangled in some thick woods south of Birmingham Hill that they were effectively out of the battle.

The British easily pursued the defeated Americans past Dilworth, which was located about two miles southwest of Birmingham Meeting House and about two and one-half miles northeast of Chadd's Ford. After passing Dilworth, they

African-American Troops in the Revolution

One of the first Americans to die in the struggle for American independence was an African-American, Crispus Atticus, one of the three men killed at the "Boston Massacre" of 5 March 1770. When armed hostilities broke out between the Colonies and their mother country, thousands of African-Americans served in the ranks of the Continental Army. It has been estimated that about 5,000 African-Americans served in the American armed forces during the Revolution. Many were free blacks who volunteered for service, while many others were slaves sent as substitutes for their masters. Some others were runaway slaves who sought the security and protection of the army as a means of escaping bondage. The use of black troops was a hot political issue, particularly in the South. Slavery was recognized in all the Colonies at the start of the war, and the status of black citizens, let alone that of African-American troops, was a thorny one in almost every state.

In 1775 South Carolina unsuccessfully attempted to persuade the Continental Congress to discharge all black troops. Neither Congress nor General Washington at first favored the use of African-Americans troops, but by the end of 1775 the pressures of the war forced Washington to authorize the recruiting of blacks. The next year Congress approved the reenlistment of black troops in the Continental Army, but said nothing of original enlistments or service in the various state militias.

By 1777 only Rhode Island, New York and Maryland were authorizing the recruitment of regiments of black slaves. The nation's growing manpower crisis persuaded Congress in 1779 to attempt to enlist slaves in the South by paying owners $1,000 per man. The plan failed when planters in South Carolina and Georgia refused to accept it. Upper South states came to accept the idea of blacks in service; in 1781 Maryland raised 750 black troops for service in white regiments, and Virginia began granting freedom to all African-American troops who served and were honorably discharged. It is interesting to postulate if other states would have

halted to reform upon seeing a fresh American line in the fields west of the Forks Road.

The troops that the British spotted south of Dilworth were the two brigades of Greene's Division. It will be recalled that Washington had held Greene in reserve behind Chadd's Ford when he had sent Sullivan, Stirling and Stephen to the right at 1400. When he heard the battle begin on that flank between 1600 and 1630, he was hesitant to release Greene, since taken similar measures if the war had lasted longer.

A report dated 24 August 1778 showed 755 African-Americans serving in 14 regiments of the New York Continental Line. If these were typical regiments, blacks formed about 10 percent of their strength. Washington's army at mid-war is thought to have contained about 50 African-Americans per battalion (regiment), and one author estimates that 700 blacks participated in the Monmouth campaign. At least two regiments, one from Rhode Island and one from Massachusetts were composed entirely of black troops led by white officers. The Rhode Island regiment, commanded by Colonel Christopher Greene, fought with exceptional bravery at the battle of Newport on 29 August 1778.

Army life for the African-American troops, particularly former slaves, was usually quite onerous. Because of their low social position in society at large, blacks often found themselves assigned the army's most undesirable tasks such as cook, team master, orderly, etc. At other times blacks were impressed into duty as conscripted labor to construct defenses and forts. Still, they appreciated military bounties and pay, attained status by their service, and had no incentive to desert.

Due to their recruitment policies, the British did not seek to raise black troops in the American Colonies. Their policy towards the blacks consisted principally of encouraging slaves to escape their masters as a means of weakening the Colonists' economy. They offered freedom to all American slaves who would serve the Crown, but in practice British officials treated all American blacks as booty to be confiscated for resale, particularly in the West Indies. Lord Dunmore, royal governor of Virginia, took almost 1,000 slaves with him when he left the state in 1776, and the British reportedly took over 5,000 slaves with them when they evacuated Charleston on 14 December 1782. At that time Lieutenant Colonel James Moncrieff may have sent as many as 800 "liberated" slaves to his personal estates in the West Indies. He was not the only British officer to get rich from the war in this manner.

Knyphausen's guns had opened up at the same time and his troops were threatening an attack. By 1700 Washington realized that the worse danger was on the right, because he had to keep his withdrawal route open to Philadelphia at all costs. He released Greene to move north, and his troops moved so fast that they covered 4 miles in 45 minutes.

Washington rode with his staff ahead of Greene's column, and was dismayed to see the number of fugitives streaming

View of Chadd's Ford in the early 1800s. Knyphausen's artillery was emplaced on the wooded hill to the right.

down the Forks Road; the battle on the right clearly had not gone well. As Greene's leading regiments came up, they calmly opened their ranks to let the fugitives pass through. Meanwhile, Washington held a conference with Sullivan and Greene and decided to form Greene's two brigades in some fields near present day Harvey Road, about a mile south of Dilworth. Muhlenberg was to form on the left of Forks Road in order to meet the British advance head on, while Weedon took up a position farther to the left in order to strike the enemy flank at an angle.

When the British saw Greene forming his division, they stopped near Dilworth to reform, as already noted. The first unit to resume their advance was the jägers, who headed east on the Dilworth Town-Thornton Road in order to outflank

Greene's right. Luckily for the Americans, this move was seen by Count Casimir Pulaski, who promptly gathered "as many of the scattered troops as he could find at hand...and by an oblique advance upon the enemy's front and right defeated their object." Meanwhile, the *2nd Battalion Light Infantry* and the *2nd British Grenadiers* were joined near Dilworth by Agnew's *4th Brigade*, which had not yet been engaged. Their combined force had about as many men as the defending Americans.

Once again the British marched forward to attack in parade ground order. Weedon's men, who now held a concealed position on the right flank of the English advance, held their fire until the enemy was almost on top of them. Their first volley was devastating and felled almost all the officers of the *46th* and *64th Regiments*. Despite losing 47 of its 312 men, the *64th* pressed on "enduring the utmost steadiness a very heavy fire." Muhlenberg's Brigade on Weedon's right gave the British an equally hot reception and brought their advance to a halt for half an hour. At length the British brought up two 6-pounder cannons and began blasting at Greene's right flank, whereupon the Americans began to withdraw. By then it was near nightfall, and the British "were too much exhausted to be able to charge or pursue."

While the battle was coming to a conclusion near Dilworth, Wayne and Knyphausen continued to spar with each other across the Brandywine. Wayne's principal position after Greene left was in support of Proctor's artillery, about 600 yards northeast of Chadd's Ford. Proctor had four guns (one 6-pounder, two long 4-pounders, and one 5 1/2-inch howitzer), and there was one 6-pounder still posted upstream at Brinton's Ford. Wayne also had at his disposal Maxwell's light infantry, which was stationed at Chadd's Ford, and Armstrong's militia, which was still posted downstream near Gibson's Ford. The total American strength in this sector was about 5,000, facing 7,000 under Knyphausen.

Knyphausen was under orders from Howe to assault whatever troops were in front of him as soon as he heard steady fire from Cornwallis' attack. When he heard Cornwallis' artillery open up between 1600 and 1630, he let loose his own guns and began his preparations to attack; it is said the blasts of the guns were heard all the way to Philadelphia. Knyphausen had decided to cross Chadd's Ferry rather than Chadd's Ford because the latter was too close to the American cannons and was also rumored to be blocked by logs. In order to assist his crossing, he quietly moved four cannons near the bank of the Ferry. The attack was to be spearheaded by the *5th* and *4th Regiments* of infantry, even though the *4th* was a mile away at Brinton's Ford and would require additional time to come up. The two regiments were to be supported by the *2nd Battalion* of the *71st Regiment*, the *Queen's Rangers*, and Ferguson's riflemen, followed by the remainder of the wing (the rest of the *1st Brigade* and *2nd Brigade*, plus Stirn's *Hessian Brigade*).

Knyphausen completed his preparations by 1700, and ordered his artillery at the Ferry to open up. Their blasts rightfully concerned Washington as he rode north ahead of Greene's Division, a move that deprived Wayne of his reserves. Knyphausen's bombardment lasted for about 15 minutes, then the infantry attack began. The first man into the stream, oddly, was Knyphausen's second-in-command, Major General James Grant. Grant luckily escaped being hit, but many of his infantrymen were not so fortunate.

The two lead regiments ignored their casualties and completed their crossing successfully. They then headed for Proctor's artillery position, aiming to come up on it from the rear. Knyphausen at this point ordered his artillery to cease fire for fear of hitting his own men. The British succeeded in their movement and came in below the battery to capture all its guns; its crew unceremoniously departed rather than put up a futile hand-to-hand fight. While this engagement was occurring, the *Queen's Rangers* and *2nd Battalion* of the *71st Regiment* easily marched to Brinton's Ford and captured the lone American cannon there.

Knyphausen's primary thrust was along Chester Road (Route 1) which was defended by Maxwell's command. He sent most of his infantry in that direction, and easily began pushing Maxwell back. Wayne became concerned that the enemy might cut off his line of retreat, and had no choice but to rush the two brigades of his own division to Maxwell's aid. They marched along the Ring Road to the Chester Road, and arrived just as the British were renewing their attack. The scene grew confused as darkness drew nigh—Colonel James Chambers of Wayne's leading regiment, the 1st Pennsylvania, fell wounded, and Lieutenant Colonel Perse Frazer of the 5th Pennsylvania was captured. Wayne's Division was still hold-ing on when darkness fell, and could have remained in its positions if Cornwallis' *British Guards* and *Grenadiers*—the units that had strayed to the south of Birmingham Hill while trying to pursue Sullivan—had not accidently, but most opportunely, come blundering through the woods upon the uncovered flank of the American center. Wayne withdrew to another hill, and successfully beat off one last British attack. Armstrong's militia was not so lucky. They did not reach the Chester Road ahead of the British, and had to fight their way to safety at the cost of a number of casualties.

Nightfall found almost the entire American command streaming east on the road to Chester. As already mentioned, Howe chose not to pursue because of their long march to the field followed by a three-hour-long heavily contested battle. Knyphausen's men were somewhat fresher, but he chose not to press a pursuit because of the darkness and the lack of an effective mounted force.

Howe had indeed planned and fought a masterful battle. He boldly divided his command in the face of an enemy of approximately equal size, and successfully conducted a lengthy flank march and flank attack. He handled his troops superbly, and the outcome of the battle was never seriously in doubt. The greatest criticism of British generalship during the day falls on Knyphausen, who failed to sustain his holding attack long enough to tie down Washington's troops all day, and then consumed too much time mounting his final attack, with the result that he was stopped by darkness rather than by exhaustion or any enemy forces.

Washington, on the other hand, rightfully deserves criticism on a variety of counts for what was one of his worst run battles of the war. His choice to form behind the Brandywine was not a bad one, but he failed to reconnoiter the creek properly and learn the locations of its fords, particularly those above Buffington's. He did not use his dragoons as aggressively as he could have to locate enemy columns, and clearly failed at interpreting the reports of his scouts accurately when they brought him news of Howe's flank march. He simply held too stubbornly to his hope that the British would attack him directly across the Brandywine, proving that he had not learned any lessons from Howe's successful flank march the year before at the battle of Long Island. Lastly, Washington's physical presence was strangely restricted for so important a battle. He spent most of the battle with his less engaged left wing, and was active at the front during only one portion of the late part of the battle, near Dilworth. If he had gone to the right with Stirling's command, Sullivan would have been with his men and might have prevented the embarrassing collapse of his division.

Final casualty figures for the Americans are difficult to determine, since they were not accurately reported at the time. General Greene estimated Washington's casualties at 1,200 to 1,300. A member of Howe's staff reported 400 Colonists were buried on the field by the victors. There was probably an equal number of wounded, and at least 400 prisoners (many also wounded). In addition, about 315 Americans deserted during this stage of the campaign. Washington also lost 11 cannons, 2 of which had been captured from the Hessians at Trenton. The British lost at least 89 killed, 488 wounded, and 6 missing; all but 40 of their casualties were British.

CHAPTER V

The Fall of Philadelphia

Washington did not attempt to rally his defeated men after the battle of Brandywine, but allowed them to make their way as best they could to Chester Bridge, twelve miles west of the battlefield. Fortunately for him, Howe organized no pursuit during the night, for there were few American units that retained any cohesion. Once the weary Colonists reached Chester Bridge they found Lafayette, wounded as he was, organizing a defensive line, and the situation began to improve. Washington and Greene rode in before midnight to help stiffen the line. Exhausted troops arrived from the battlefield all night, and towards morning the flow increased as men came out into the open after hiding all night to escape capture. Among these late arrivals was an entire regiment, the 7th Virginia, which had taken cover during the night in order to avoid the enemy. The unit had lost its colors, so its wounded Major John Cropper led his men with a red kerchief tied to a ramrod.

Strange to say, Washington's men were beaten, tired, disorganized and discouraged, but they were not demoralized. Most still carried their weapons, and were encouraged to see the number of men gathered at the bridge; Washington had feared his losses were much greater than the 10 percent that was finally reckoned. One American captain noted that "I saw not a despairing look, nor did I hear a despairing word. We had our own solacing words already for each other—'Come, boys, we shall do better another time'—sounded throughout the entire army." The spirits of the defeated troops may also have been lifted by the gill of rum Washington ordered to be issued to each man.

Washington's first concern was to gather in all the stragglers he could before they were captured, deserted, or otherwise disappeared; good soldiers were hard to find. He directed each brigade commander to send officers back as far as possible "on the roads leading to the places of action yesterday, and on any other roads where stragglers may be found, particularly to Wilmington, where 'tis said many have retired.... In doing this, they will proceed as far towards the enemy as shall be consistent with their own safety, and examine every house."

Washington was well aware that his army needed to be reorganized and reinforced, so he decided that there was no sense in trying to resist Howe a second time on ground east of the Schuylkill. At 0400 on 12 September he directed his men to march from Chester to Darby and then over the Schuylkill. From there they were to proceed to the Falls of the Delaware and Germantown, which would provide a central position from which to defend the Schuylkill and observe Howe's intentions. Greene's reliable command would march at the columns' rear in order to guard the wagons, and Maxwell would remain at Chester for another 24 hours to collect as many stragglers as he could. The wounded who still needed attention were sent to temporary hospitals in Trenton, Allentown and Bethlehem. Lafayette, who had traveled by barge from Chester to Philadelphia, was allowed by his surgeons to go by coach to Bethlehem.

Nor did Washington avoid the unpleasant task of notifying Congress of his defeat. Stopping at McIlvains, near Chester, he penned a summary of the battle to John Hancock. Hancock received the missive at 0400 and roused as many sleepy delegates as he could to an 0600 meeting. There they heard Washington's disturbing words, "I am sorry to inform you, that, in the day's engagement we have been obliged to leave the enemy masters of the field." Washington characteristically blamed no one for the defeat, though several congressmen would soon be criticizing Sullivan (who was already being investigated for his role in the defeat at Long Island) and Maxwell for their actions. Washington closed with words of unusual optimism: "Not withstanding the misfortune of the day, I am happy to find the troops in good spirits."

After adjourning for breakfast, the congressmen reassembled at 1000 with a resolve to continue the fight and bring still more reinforcements to shore up Washington's battered army. Orders were sent to Maryland, Virginia and New Jersey to forward still more militia. The hardest problem was getting more experienced line troops. After much discussion, Congress, with Washington's concurrence, ordered Putman to send 2,500 men from his command in the Hudson Highlands. Latest reports showed that Clinton's force at New York was not being aggressive, and Washington dearly needed experienced men and more muskets.

Washington's men remained at Germantown only two nights before they were once again ordered to move. Though Howe had not yet begun to advance the main body of his army, Washington was becoming concerned that the enemy might try to move around his right and trap him in the "pocket" formed by the Schuylkill and the Delaware. He was also wary that Howe might try to take the Colonists' supply base at Reading, located about 35 miles west of Germantown. These considerations led Washington to lead his army back to the west side of the Schuylkill and take up a position that would guard the route to Reading and still give him time to move to the defense of Philadelphia should Howe march directly on the capital. The American army broke its camp near the Schuylkill Falls at 0900 on 14 September and proceeded two miles north to cross at Levering's Ford. Their march westward brought them through Haverford to Buck Tavern, where they encamped. The next day they marched another 14 miles westward past modern Malvern. Here the army encamped with its head at White Horse Tavern (modern Planebrook) and its rear three miles behind at Warren Tavern. The little command faced south towards the recent Brandywine battlefield, only 10 miles to the south.

Howe was certainly surprised by Washington's movements. He had not actively pursued the Americans on 12 September, and instead allowed his troops to gather in the wounded and see to the burial of the dead. Most of the American dead were unceremoniously buried in a long trench in the yard of the Birmingham Meeting House, near the scene of the battle's heaviest fighting; Howe graciously invited Washington to send his doctors to care for the American wounded left on the field, and Washington accepted the offer. The only action Howe took on the day after the battle was to send the *71st Regiment* to occupy Wilmington. The rest of the army remained where they had closed the battle, in a line reaching from Dilworth to Chadd's Ford.

Howe rested and refitted his command for four days before he was ready to resume the campaign. On 15 September he issued orders for his troops to be ready to move out at dawn the next day, presumably for a march to the upper fords of the Schuylkill. During the afternoon he was meeting with Cornwallis at Village Green when the unexpected news arrived that Washington had come across the Schuylkill "with a firm intent of giving the Enemy battle." Howe was not about to decline the challenge, and adjusted his plans to march against the American force.

Howe divided his army into two columns for his advance, as was his custom. The eastern column, under Cornwallis, left Village Green soon after midnight and headed through Goshen Meeting towards White Horse Tavern. The western column, led by Knyphausen and accompanied by Howe, marched at dawn from Dilworth up the Wilmington Pike towards Boot Tavern. Knyphausen's vanguard encountered an American scouting party at Turk's Head and lost two men of the *33rd Regiment*, the first casualties in what would be a very strange day. After passing Turk's Head, Howe further divided his column, and sent Matthew's *Guards Brigade* up the Pottstown Pike, towards Indian King Tavern, marching west of and parallel to Knyphausen's column.

Washington learned of Howe's advance at about 0900 and decided to move forward to meet the enemy; he probably hoped to catch Howe's columns strung out in their march.

The Continental force marched slightly to the south to the crest of the South Valley Hills, and formed it along Indian King Road west of Paoli in a three-mile-long line stretching from Three Tuns Tavern west to Boot Tavern.

As soon as Howe learned of Washington's advance, he decided to continue on and attack, even though he was not certain of the American's precise position. Little did he know that his own three advancing columns were perfectly positioned to strike Washington's line.

The battle of White Horse Tavern (or Warren) began on the left of the American line at about 1300, when Washington sent out a number of cavalry and about 300 militia under acting Brigadier General Casimir Pulaski to scout and delay Howe's advance. Pulaski formed his command on the heights near Hershey's Mill, but Cornwallis spotted him and sent the *1st Light Infantry* to the attack. Much to Pulaski's dismay, his infantry "shamefully fled at the first fire." The militia had lost 12 killed and many wounded without inflicting a casualty on the enemy.

At about the same time, Knyphausen's advance guard, a party of jägers under Von Donop, ran into an American column under Wayne and Maxwell near Boot Tavern on the right of Washington's line. Von Donop was scouting the road ahead of his column and had to flee with some jägers when he unexpectedly came upon the American force. One eye witness observed that Von Donop "was almost cut off, but rejoined the vanguard again with all possible speed, after executing some maneuvers to his left." Knyphausen quickly brought up his grenadiers to reinforce the jägers, and the combined force advanced on the Colonists, who "had formed on high ground covered with a cornfield and orchards." An intense exchange of musketry followed, made louder by the arrival of some British light artillery. Finally the weight of British numbers forced Wayne and Maxwell to retire to a heavy woods.

Knyphausen's advance brought him to a commanding hill and forced Washington to withdraw to "a valley of soft wet ground, impassable for artillery." The Americans were definitely in for trouble, especially with the arrival of Matthews' column to strengthen Knyphausen's left. Washington was not interested in fighting on such unequal terms, and ordered a withdrawal to higher ground "on the other side of the valley." Just as he was beginning his retreat, Fate intervened to save the American army from disaster. The skies, which had turned cloudy and colder on 13 September, opened up in a tremendous downpour. Major Baurmeister of the Hessian troops wrote later that he could scarcely "give a description of the downpour which began during the engagement and continued until the next morning. It came down so hard that we were drenched and sank in mud up to our calves."

The heavy rain instantly rendered everyone's muskets useless, since the black powder in their gun pans was too wet to be ignited by flints. The British might still have attempted to carry the field by bayonet attack, but the wind blown rain made it too difficult to see, and the fields soon became too muddy to advance through. It was not long before everyone was drenched to the skin.

Washington took advantage of the confusion created by the storm to withdraw his soaked command slowly to the north. His men made their way as best they could through the mud and rain, and needed 9 hours to cover the 11 miles to Yellow Springs (Chester Springs). Exhausted by their march, they collapsed to sleep in the mud without their blankets, which had been lost at Brandywine. The British troops were not much better off that awful night, since their tents had been left with their fleet. Most had to seek what shelter they could find in the woods.

At Yellow Springs Washington was disheartened to learn that much of his troops' ammunition had been ruined by the storm. It seems that most of the American cartridge boxes were imperfectly designed, and their top flaps did not extend far enough to keep out the rain. As a result, thousands upon thousands of rounds were lost, and in some units there were not enough dry rounds to fire one volley. In order to replenish his ammunition, Washington had to move west toward Reading, where most of the munitions from Philadelphia had been transferred for safe keeping right after the defeat at Brandy-wine. His weary troops marched to Warwick Furnace and Reading Furnace on the 17th and were resupplied the next day from Reading, 20 miles to the northwest. Washington then turned back on the 19th for fear the British might move on Philadelphia in spite of the continuing bad weather and muddy roads. His command marched 12 miles to Parker's Ford on the Schuylkill, where the men crossed in water up to their chests. They then continued on without rest to cover another 17 miles before stopping at Richardson's Ford on Perkiomen Creek. Wayne's Division of 1,500 men, however, was left west of the Schuylkill near Warren Tavern to monitor and harass Howe's anticipated advance. Wayne was to be supported by Smallwood's command, and Maxwell was ordered to join them.

Meanwhile, Howe had shown no haste to move after the aborted battle at White Horse Tavern. Because of the muddy roads and continuing bad weather, he let his men rest most of the 17th. He saw little reason to rush towards Philadelphia because the Schuylkill was reported to be eight feet above flood level in its lower course and so would be uncrossable. His immediate concern was to reconcentrate his army. Corn-wallis occupied White Horse late on the 17th, and was joined by the rest of the army the next morning. On the 18th the reunited British army marched eight miles eastward into Tredyffrin Township, where it encamped near Centerville on the Swedesford Road.

Upon approaching Tredyffrin, Howe was informed by spies of a Colonial supply depot located nearby at Valley Forge. At mid-afternoon on the 18th, he decided to send three companies of light infantry north via the Gulph Road to capture and destroy the American base. The approach of the British column greatly startled two Colonial detachments that were desperately trying to remove the stores across the Schuylkill. The Americans, led by Light Horse Harry Lee and Alexander Hamilton, fled after the first British volley, and Howe's men were the easy victors of a bloodless battle. For their efforts, they gained possession of a great amount of supplies that included "3800 Barrels of Flour, Soap and Candles, 25 Barrels of Horse Shoes, several thousand tomahawks and kettles and entrenching tools and 20 Hogsheads of Resin." Howe was delighted at the cache and reinforced his raiding party the next morning for fear the Americans might try to recapture the depot. He ordered most of the supplies to be removed and the remainder to be burned, along with the forge and the other nearby buildings.

Howe intended to move forward towards the Schuylkill on 19 September, but decided to hold his position when he learned that Wayne's command was lurking somewhere in his rear. The British command spent most of the 19th gathering supplies and looking for Wayne. At length some spies reported that the enemy force was encamped in a wooded ravine southeast of Paoli, near the Lancaster Road in modern Malvern, less than four miles from Howe's camp in Tredyffrin. Howe at once began making plans to attack the exposed American position that night.

Wayne's command was indeed in an awkward position. As already noted, he had been left behind at Yellow Springs on 17 September when most of the rest of the army marched northwest to be resupplied at Reading Furnace. His instructions, confirmed by Washington on the evening of the 18th, were to try to cut off the enemy's baggage trains. For this effort he would be reinforced by Smallwood's Brigade, Maxwell's command, and Potter's militia. This was a risky assignment since the main army was a day's march distant, and Washington warned Wayne to be wary of "ambuscades."

When he sent his 18 September orders to Wayne, Washington was apparently planning to return to the Yellow Springs area in order to defend the Schuylkill line in advance of the river. The next day, however, he changed his mind and headed for Parker's Ford in order to form behind the river. Washington directed Maxwell and Potter to help defend the river line, but left Wayne and Smallwood south of the river to operate against the British baggage trains. Wayne was a native of the area, as were many of his men, and was expected to put his knowledge of the terrain and local roads to good use.

In accordance with his orders, Wayne marched his own command towards the British camps in Tredyffrin at dawn on 19 September. He was hoping to find the enemy on the move, so that he could strike their column, "but when we arrived within a half mile of their encampment found they had not stirred but lay too compact to admit of an attack with prudence." Wayne accordingly withdrew to a secluded camp two miles southwest of Paoli to await reinforcements, particularly Maxwell's command. Unfortunately, he was not aware that Washington had directed Maxwell to the north side of the Schuylkill. British patrols had intercepted several of Washington's dispatches, which had alerted Howe to Wayne's location and intentions.

Wayne felt secure in his position, close as he was to the enemy, and, while he patiently waited for Howe to break camp, took no unusual precautions beyond posting some pickets nearby. All was quiet until sometime between 2100 and 2200, when a Mr. Jones, "an old gentleman living near where we were encamped" came to Wayne's headquarters with evidence that the British were planning a night attack on the American camp. Wayne promptly increased his pickets and patrols, one of which soon reported British troops less than a mile away.

The British had indeed come close to achieving total surprise against Wayne. At about 2200 Howe had sent Major General Charles Grey with the 42nd and 44th Regiments, plus the 2nd Light Infantry and some dragoons, west along the Swedesboro Road towards Wayne's camp in a bold night attack. Grey was to be supported by the 40th and the 45th Regiments under Colonel Thomas Musgrave, who was to march at 2300 up the Lancaster Road to Paoli. The British force of 5,000 men was more than enough to deal with Wayne's 1,500.

The British plan of attack was an ingenious one. They had a pretty good idea of the location of the American camp, but did not know the disposition of the Colonial troops. That is

Mad Anthony Wayne

Anthony Wayne was perhaps the ablest of Washington's lieutenants during the Revolution. He was born on 1 January 1745 at "Waynesboro," located one mile east of Paoli, Pennsylvania, and followed in his father's footsteps to become a tanner. His real love, however, was the military, much to the dismay of his Quaker mother. His prewar career was otherwise undistinguished beyond the fact that he was elected to serve in the Pennsylvania legislature in 1774-1775.

Wayne was eager to serve when the Revolution began, and in January 1776 secured as appointment as Colonel of the 4th Pennsylvania Battalion. He saw his first service in the unsuccessful Canadian campaign, during which he won praise for his conduct at the battle of Trois Rivieres (8 June 1776). After commanding the garrison at Fort Ticonderoga, he won promotion to brigadier general on 21 February 1777 and took command of one brigade of the Pennsylvania Line at Morristown.

At the beginning of the Philadelphia campaign, Wayne was sent to Chester County to train recruits. His big break came on 11 August 1777 when he rejoined Washington to take command of both brigades of the Pennsylvania Line in place of Major General Benjamin Lincoln, who had been sent north to help Gates deal with Burgoyne. He handled his troops well at Brandywine, where he held Washington's left all day until overwhelmed by Knyphausen near sunset. His aggressiveness persuaded Washington to let him operate against Howe's rear after the battle, but Wayne camped too near the enemy and was himself overwhelmed by "No Flint" Grey's surprise night attack near Paoli on the night of 20-21 September. The defeat greatly tarnished his reputation and honor, so he demanded a court-martial, held in late October at Dawesfield in Whitpain Township. It acquitted him "with the highest honors" for his conduct at Paoli.

Wayne fought well at Germantown, even though his troops accidently collided with another division on the way to the front, and conducted himself well in the day long fight at Monmouth the next June. His greatest day came at the battle of Stony Point, New York (near West Point), on 16 July 1779, when he planned and executed a bold night attack that captured a strong British garrison. He was wounded in the head during the action, and later received a medal and the Thanks of Congress for his success.

Wayne remained in the New York theater in 1780, and dealt forthrightly with the temporary revolt of the Pennsylvania Line in early 1781. Later that year he was sent to Virginia to serve under Lafayette. Here he demonstrated his well known boldness at Green Spring on 6 July 1781—when he was awkwardly confronted by a greatly superior British force and judging that he could not safely retreat or hold his position, he bravely ordered an attack that startled the enemy and permitted his troops to withdraw safely. Wayne later served under Von Steuben at Yorktown. Despite valuable service in a number of capacities, he was not promoted to major general until he was brevetted with that rank on 30 September 1783, several weeks after the Treaty of Paris was negotiated.

Wayne was exhausted from the rigors of the war, and resigned from the army five weeks after his promotion. He experienced great difficulty adjusting to peacetime life. He served in the Pennsylvania legislature from 1783 until forced to resign by Quaker opposition in 1785. His attempts to run an 800 acre rice plantation in Georgia did not go well, and he was forced to mortgage his estate at Waynesboro until his creditors at length accepted the Georgia plantation as payment in 1791. In 1792 he was elected to the Georgia legislature but was disqualified because of ballot stuffing and questions over his residency.

Wayne happily returned to his first love, the military, when Washington appointed him commander-in-chief of the mismanaged American army in the Northwest Territory in 1792. He took the time to train his troops thoroughly at Pittsburgh, and successfully conducted a well planned campaign that defeated several hostile Indian tribes. The climax of the campaign came at Fallen Timbers, near Toledo, where his troops employed a bold bayonet charge on

20 August 1794 to rout the Indians, who could not stand up to "the sharp ends of the guns."

Wayne continued campaigning in the west despite the death of his wife and frequent attacks of gout. He died at Presque Isle, Pennsylvania, on 15 December 1796 at the age of 51. At his request he was buried at the base of the flagpole at the town's block house. His children removed his remains to the family burial ground at Radnor, Pennsylvania, on 4 July 1809.

Wayne was considered handsome, having brown eyes and dark hair waving above a high forehead. Though he was at times proud and arrogant, he possessed confidence, ability and an aggressiveness that was all too rare among his fellow Revolutionary War officers. His nickname "Mad Anthony" did not stem from recklessness (as Washington Irving later popularized him), but from the following incident that occurred in the winter of 1781. One of Wayne's neighbors, known as "Jemmy the Rover," had been arrested for desertion and appealed to the general to intercede on his behalf. When Wayne refused, Jemmy exclaimed, "Anthony is mad. He must be mad, or he would help me. Mad Anthony, that's what he is. Mad Anthony Wayne." Wayne was said to prefer the nickname "Dandy Tony" that he acquired for his careful dress and active social life (he reportedly had a mistress named Mary Vining whom he met in Wilmington two weeks before the battle of Brandywine).

why they approached in two columns, one from the north and one from the east. More significantly the British troops were directed not to fire their weapons and to rely solely on the bayonet. This tactic would conceal their own positions while those of the enemy would be made clear by the flash of the American guns. Major John Andre later explained that "No soldier was suffered to load; those who would not draw their pieces took out their flints. It was represented to the men that firing discovered us to the Enemy, hid them from us, killed our friends and produced a confusion favorable to the escape of the Rebels and perhaps productive of disgrace to ourselves. On the other hand, by not firing we knew the foe to be wherever fire appeared and a charge ensured his destruction; that amongst the Enemy those in the rear would direct their fire against whoever fired in front, and they would destroy each other."

Grey's advance proceeded very smoothly, and he took the added precaution of detaining all the civilians he passed, in order to maintain secrecy. Had it not been for the Mr. Jones who had reported the British intentions to Wayne, Grey might have achieved total surprise. The few American pickets he encountered were easily approached because the British had somehow acquired Wayne's password for the night, "Here we come and there they go." The pickets were then noiselessly slain by bayonets.

Grey's advance continued until he met one of the patrols Wayne sent out at Mr. Jones' prompting. The American general barely had time to form his troops before the British attack struck home. Because it had begun to rain, Wayne ordered his men to keep their cartridge pouches under their coats.

After passing Warren Tavern, Grey forced a local blacksmith to show the route to Wayne's camp (present Warren Avenue). The British light infantry led the way and surprised the innermost American pickets, killing most of them. Grey's men were now east of Wayne's position, and began forming at a right angle to the enemy line before beginning their final attack. Wayne responded by ordering his men to "wheel by

General Charles "No Flint" Grey acquired his distinctive nickname after he ordered his men to attack only with bayonets at Paoli.

subplatoons to the right," so putting his line on a parallel with the enemy's. He then intended to march up the Indian King Road and withdraw to the west towards Smallwood's camp near White Horse Tavern, three miles to the west.

Needless to say, Wayne's men were not able to complete their maneuvers before Grey's attack struck. The stoutest defense was put up on the right of the line by the 1st Pennsylvania, which fired a point blank volley that stopped Grey's men in their tracks. When the Pennsylvanians withdrew to reload, however, they were struck by an overwhelming bayonet charge. Soon the American line began to melt away as Wayne's troops fled west for safety. Many more fell dead or wounded and whole squads were taken prisoner.

The heaviest American losses occurred in Colonel Richard Humpton's 2nd Brigade. According to Wayne, Humpton was at first slow to react to his order to wheel to the right to face the enemy. Then, when the army began to march off to the left in order to withdraw, Humpton by mistake turned to the right and moved closer to the enemy, who were only 10 yards away. To make matters worse, Humpton's move placed his men between the American campfires and the enemy lines, so silhouetting them and making them easy targets for the British bayonet charge that followed. The light infantry led the way, supported by the *44th Regiment*, and hit Humpton's line on its right flank. Andre reported that the Englishmen "rushed along the line putting to the bayonet all they came up with, and, overtaking the main herd of fugitives, stabbed great numbers and pressed on their rear till it was thought prudent to order them to desist."

The scene was indeed a grisly one, punctuated by screams and the clashing of swords and bayonets more than by musketry. One British soldier observed "how the Americans were running about barefoot, and half clothed and in the light of their fires! These showed us where to chase them, while they could not see us. I stuck them myself like so many pigs, one after another, until the blood ran out of the touch hole of my musket." The *42nd Regiment* came up and began setting fire to the American huts containing some of Colonial troops who had sought shelter there. Some of these unfortunate troops were forced to flee the flames, only to be slaughtered while others decided to stay "choosing to suffer in the flames rather than be killed by the bayonet."

When Wayne saw the defeat of Humpton's command, he formed up his light infantry and one regiment to cover the retreat of what was left of his command, which was now scattered in flight over the countryside. Enemy pressure forced Wayne's rear guard to withdraw to the west towards White Horse Tavern and Smallwood's command, which had already begun marching towards the sounds of the fighting. Unfortunately Wayne's shattered units threw much of Smallwood's militia into confusion, making it difficult for the two generals to maintain even a minimum rearguard as the Americans retreated hastily towards Downington.

General Grey earned the colorful nickname "No Flint" for winning the battle solely by the bayonet. Musgrave's two regiments never entered the fight; their sole contribution was to ransack Wayne's nearby home at Waynesboro. Grey did not pursue the Americans far after his success, since he was under orders to return to Tredyffrin as soon as Wayne was defeated.

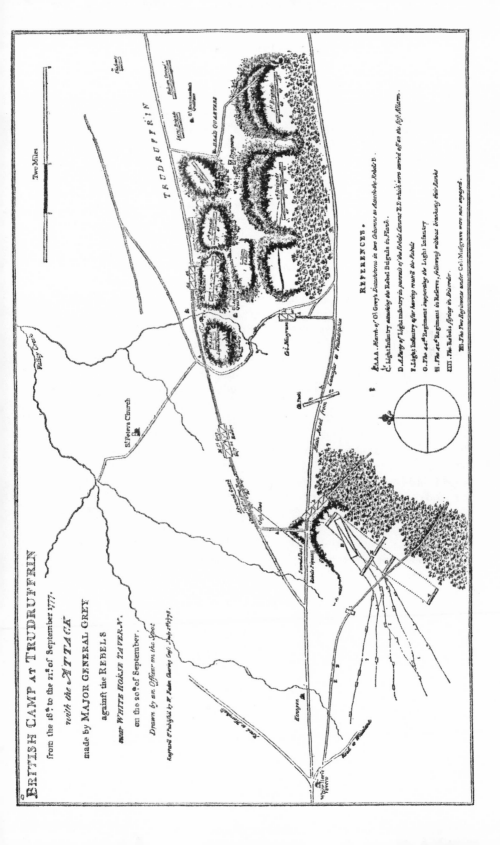

BRITISH CAMP at TRUDRUFFRIN

from the 18.th to the 21.st of September 1777,

with the ATTACK

made by MAJOR GENERAL GREY

against the REBELS

near WHITE HORSE TAVERN,

on the 20.th of September.

Drawn by an Officer on the Spot.

Two Miles

TRUDRUFFRIN

REFERENCES.

A A A A. March of Gen.l Grey's Detachment in two Columns to Lane to the Rebels. B.
C. Light Infantry attacking the Rebel Brigade in Front.
D. Lines of Light Infantry in pursuit of the Rebels course E.F. which were served upon on the left Alarm.
F. Light Infantry after having secured the Rebels
G. The 44.th Regiment supporting the Light Infantry
H. The 42.d Regiment in Reserve, following without breaking their Ranks
III. The Rebels flying in Disorder.
K. The Two Regiments under Col: Musgrave were now engaged.

The Paoli Massacre

On the morning of 21 September 1777, local Whig farmers found 53 mangled American bodies on the battlefield of Paoli—the British did not use musketry in the fight but relied solely on the bayonet, which can be a very messy weapon. The terrible condition of the bodies and the nature of the British surprise night attack soon led to the creation of rumors that the fight had been a "massacre," and that the British had attacked under orders "to give no quarter" and had bayonetted many of Wayne's men who were trying to surrender.

More recent analysis of the battle by historians on both sides of the Atlantic, however, has shown that the British troops were not unusually bloodthirsty in their attack at Paoli. The fact that there were only 53 Americans dead out of 1,500 engaged belies the battle as a massacre, and the fact that Grey carried off 71 prisoners—about 40 of them wounded—shows that there was no order "to give no quarters." Much of the Americans' resentment stemmed from their aversion to the bayonet as an "unfair" or "uncivi-

lized" weapon, and to the fact that Grey had employed a sneak attack in the middle of the night. This is not to deny, however, that the battle was fought savagely, particularly by the soldiers of the *42nd Regiment* who fired the American huts and burned or bayonetted a number of Wayne's men.

There is no question that the contemporary American public was stirred by news of the "Paoli Massacre," and numerous newspapers and recruiters used their anger to increase enlistments and animosity towards the enemy. This sentiment persisted long after the war, as shown by the following words from the burial marker erected to the slain on 20 September 1817: "Sacred to the memory of the Patriots who on this spot fell, a sacrifice to British barbarity...Here repose the remains of 53 Americans soldiers who were victims of cold-blooded cruelty in the well known massacre...The atrocious massacre which this stone commemorates was perpetuated by British troops under the immediate command of Major General Grey."

British losses in the affair were unusually light—one officer and six men wounded. Wayne's losses were heavy, including 53 killed and about 100 wounded; the British carried off 71 prisoners, 40 of whom were wounded. Wayne also lost eight wagons, but managed to extricate all four of his cannons.

Grey returned to Howe's camp at dawn, leaving the dead to be buried by the locals. Tradition relates that Wayne's casualties were interred in a common grave on a hill over-

Monument to the 53 American victims of the "Paoli Massacre." It was dedicated on 20 September 1817.

looking the battlefield, because the battle site itself was owned by a Tory who refused to allow American burials on his land. Grey had to leave many of his wounded prisoners in houses along the road beyond Paoli. True to the spirit of the day, Howe reported their location to Washington and urged him to send doctors to care for them, which Washington did.

After Grey rejoined Howe, the entire British army headed north on the Baptist Road towards Valley Forge and the Schuylkill. Knyphausen, who led the advance, turned west at Gulph Road, crossed Valley Creek, and continued on about three miles before stopping near the Fountain Inn in modern Phoenixville. The rest of the army encamped along the road between there and Cornwallis' rear guard on the hills east of Valley Creek at the site of the later American winter encampment. The British found the houses in this area to be full of military stores, which they plundered eagerly in spite of Howe's orders to the contrary. They also raped more than a

Anthony Wayne's residence at Waynesboro, near Paoli. Part of his family was captured here, but not harmed during the battle on 21 September 1777.

few farm girls, acts that greatly angered the local farm population regardless of their political leanings.

Howe's line of march confused Washington, who was uncertain whether the British would head next toward Philadelphia or towards his primary supply base at Reading. The American commander even rode down to Fatland Ford (about a mile east of Valley Creek's confluence with the Schuylkill) to view the enemy camps, but this observation did not help him decipher Howe's intentions. At length he was persuaded by Knyphausen's presence at Phoenixville that Howe was intending to cross the river there or farther upstream in order to threaten Reading or move against Philadelphia from the rear through a wide enveloping march.

Howe was soon aware that the Americans had moved their camp despite a Colonial ruse using fake campfires. On the 22nd the British commander sent out several patrols to learn Washington's new position and intentions. During the morning Sir William Erskine encountered no enemy troops as he led the *2nd Light Infantry* and some dragoons west on Nutt Road towards Parker's Ford. In the early afternoon some jägers were sent across the river at Gordon's Ford (Phoenixville), where they skirmished briefly with some militia before being withdrawn at dark. That afternoon Howe also ordered Cornwallis to send a few troops across at Fatland Ford (near Valley Forge), where no opposition was encountered. These patrols brought in exactly the information that Howe was waiting to hear—that there were no enemy troops south of the Schuylkill and Washington was defending the fords upstream from Phoenixville with militia only.

Howe interpreted the situation correctly, and made a masterful move at midnight on the 22nd—he simply moved all his men to Fatland Ford, whose northern approaches had already been secured, and marched them across, unopposed, in water scarcely a foot deep. The troops paused only briefly to dry their shoes before marching on towards Audubon. The entire army, including the trains, was safely across the river by 0600 on 23 September. They encamped by 1500 behind Stony Creek at Norristown, a position squarely between Washington's army and Philadelphia. Howe's strategy had indeed been superb. His move to Valley Forge forced Washington to choose between guarding his supply base at Reading or protecting the capital in Philadelphia. When Washington chose to move to the west to cover Reading, Howe promptly moved against Philadelphia, which was his preferred goal since he needed to link up with the supplies being carried by his fleet, which was working its way up the Delaware (see Chapter 7).

There was nothing that Washington could do now to save the capital. His troops were much exhausted from all the marching done since Brandywine, and their equipment was in poor shape. Many of the militia were unreliable, disheartened by the British successes at Brandywine and Paoli. One source believed that detachments, battle losses and desertions had lowered Washington's strength to 6,000, half of the force he had a month earlier. Washington's only option was to find

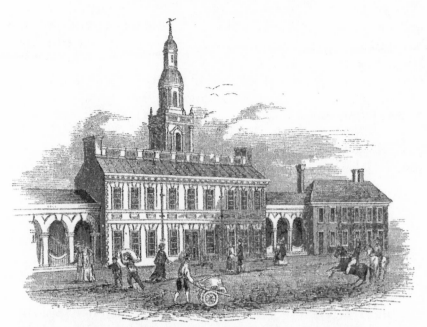

The State House ("Independence Hall") in Philadelphia. The American capital turned out to be a hollow prize for the British.

a secure camp and monitor enemy movements while he awaited reinforcements.

Howe was now totally in control of the campaign, and he knew it. He rested his men all day on the 24th, and the next day marched in two columns (one on Ridge Road and the other on Germantown Pike) to Germantown, 11 miles away. Their march was a peaceful one, as 12-year-old John Ashmead noted: "He beheld the host of twenty thousand men moving down Main Street; the order seemed to be complete; there swept before his eyes the grand army of Britain all marshalled by their dashing officers. Like a vast machine in perfect order, the army moved in silence, there was no display of colours, not a sound of music. There was no violence and no offense. Men occasionally dropped out of line, and asked for milk or cider."

Howe sent a few patrols out towards Philadelphia late on the 25th, but decided not to occupy the city formally until the next day, after his men rested and cleaned up for their

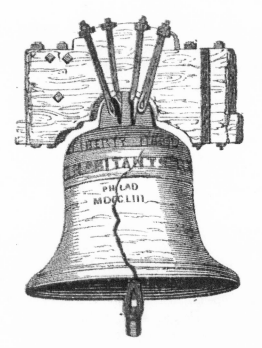

The famous Liberty Bell was taken to Allentown for safekeeping just before the British captured Philadelphia.

triumphal entry. The inhabitants of the city were in a great state of alarm for fear that the town would be plundered and burned, despite Howe's messages that they would not be disturbed if they remained "Quietly and peaceably in their own dwellings." Almost all of the capital's patriots had already left town, and numerous other concerned citizens slipped out that night. The length of Howe's campaign had given the government plenty of time to remove its records and stores, since it was expected that the capital would be lost eventually. Congress had already moved to York and the army's munitions were removed to Reading, as previously noted. The Liberty Bell was sent to Allentown for safety, and almost all the town's merchants had sent their goods elsewhere for safekeeping. Howe's prize would be unexpectedly barren when he at last arrived to claim it.

The morning of 26 September dawned brightly following a rainstorm the previous night. At 0830 Howe sent Cornwallis with the *British* and *Hessian Grenadiers*, two squadrons of the *16th Dragoons*, and some artillery, to take possession of

Philadelphia. Howe himself remained behind with the remainder of the army at Germantown in order to keep an eye out for Washington's army. Cornwallis' march was annoyed by occasional encounters with local militia, which kept the troops on edge. When he entered the Colonial capital, the column was greeted "amidst the acclamations of some thousands of the inhabitants, mostly women and children." A number of the town's prominent Tories came forward to embrace Cornwallis, who took formal possession of the city at 1000. Samuel Shoemaker was appointed mayor, and Joseph Galloway was named police commissioner. Both were supported by a detachment stationed at the State House and three armed camps set up on the outskirts of the city—the *Hessian Grenadiers* were stationed north of town, the *2nd Battalion British Grenadiers* encamped at Bettering House, and the *1st Battalion British Grenadiers* moved to the shipyards south of town. Cornwallis also set to work preparing batteries along the waterfront to deal with the American warships, which had withdrawn to New Jersey on the lower Delaware. The objective of Howe's campaign was now secure, just over two months after he sailed from Staten Island.

CHAPTER VI

Germantown

Washington was greatly embarrassed by the British occupation of Philadelphia on 26 September, but he also wisely understood that the loss of the capital did not mean the end of the war. Congress had simply moved to new quarters at York; he still held his supply base at Reading, and most importantly, his army was still intact, though diminished. It was also significant that he and his men were not demoralized by the loss of Philadelphia, which they had been expecting for some time. The course of the war had already shown that the enemy could seize and occupy large cities such as New York, but they could also be driven away eventually, as had happened in Boston. In no case had the British shown that they could take and hold large stretches of countryside. American morale was also improved on 28 September—two days after the fall of Philadelphia—by exaggerated news of a victory by Gates over Burgoyne at Freeman's Farm on the 19th. Washington issued a round of rum to his men and ordered a 13-gun salute to celebrate that the British invasion from Canada had at last been blocked. This gave Washington and his men a new appreciation of their role in Pennsylvania: they were contributing to Gates' victory north of Albany by keeping Howe occupied at Philadelphia.

Washington was also heartened by the fact that the arrival of various detachments and reinforcements increased his strength enough to take the offensive. The return of Wayne's experienced command of over 1,000 men and the arrival of Smallwood's Brigade of over 1,200 militia had encouraged him to march from Fagleysville to Pennypacker's (located on the east side of Perkiomen Creek) on 26 September, the day that Philadelphia fell. At Pennypacker's, the army was reinforced by McDougal's Brigade of 900 Continentals, which had been detached from Putman's command in the Hudson Highlands. These troops, plus a brigade of 800 New Jersey militia that was en route to the army after crossing the Delaware, increased Washington's effective strength to 10,000 men, about 7,000 Continentals and the rest militia.

Washington rested his men at Pennypacker's for three days while he told his generals what course of action to pursue. All agreed that a direct attack on Howe would be hazardous, but it might be advantageous to move closer to Philadelphia to see what opportunities might develop. Washington was also determined to support and strengthen the Delaware River defenses below Philadelphia, particularly those at Fort Mifflin (see Chapter 7). Because he feared that Howe might send a detachment up the Delaware, he directed General Philemon Dickinson to hold Trenton with his New Jersey militia until the supplies there could be removed to Bethlehem and Allentown, where Washington was also sending his sick and wounded (including General Lafayette).

Washington waited for Forman's New Jersey militia brigade to arrive on 29 September, and then marched southwest from Pennypacker's to Skippack, five miles distant. The army encamped here for three days, draining its supplies and militia reinforcements from as far as Lancaster. After reconnoitering the British positions near Philadelphia, the army moved on 2 October to Methacton Hill, near Worcester and less than 10 miles northeast of Howe's main camp at Germantown. The hill offered a perfect defensive position as well as an excellent observation post against the enemy.

Upon reaching Worcester, Washington set up his headquarters at the Peter Wentz farm on Schultz Road, which is still standing. Here on 30 October he shared with his leading generals the contents of two of Howe's letters that had been intercepted. The letters revealed that Howe had just sent a number of his regiments (about 3,000 men) to the New Jersey

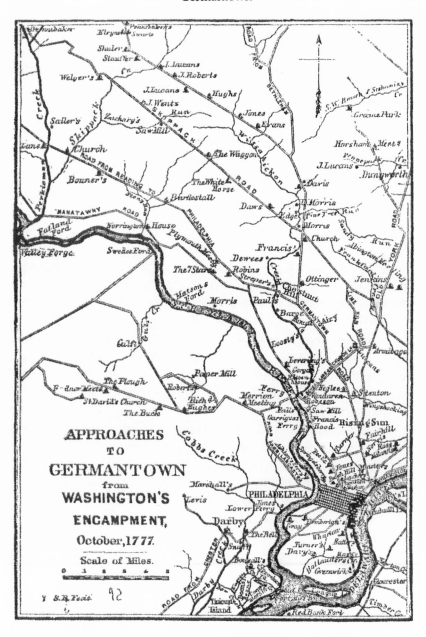

APPROACHES
TO
GERMANTOWN
from
WASHINGTON'S
ENCAMPMENT,
October, 1777.

Scale of Miles.

side of the Delaware in order to attack the American post at Billingsport (see Chapter 7). Since the British were still maintaining a strong garrison under Cornwallis in Philadelphia, five miles from Germantown, the time was ripe for an attack on Howe's reduced force.

Washington's generals were in unanimous agreement to make an attack on Germantown, and plans were accordingly drawn up. American scouts had determined that the British troops were encamped on a five-mile line that ran perpendicular to the Germantown Pike from Luken's Mill to the Schuylkill north of Wissahickon Creek. Washington planned to use the local road net to his advantage to strike the enemy line at four points simultaneously. The strongest column would consist of about 6,000 Continentals in Greene's, Stephen's and Douglas' Divisions, all under Greene's command. They were to march down the Limekiln Road and strike the right flank of the British line at the same time Washington would lead 3,000 Continentals in Wayne's and Sullivan's veteran divisions, supported by Stirling's newly reformed command (Nash's North Carolina Brigade and Maxwell's New Jersey militia) straight up the Germantown Pike against Howe's center at the Market House in Germantown. The two primary attacks would be supported by militia on their outside flanks—Armstrong was to lead his Pennsylvania militia up the Manatawny Road to distract the British left near the Schuylkill, and about 2,000 Maryland and New Jersey militia under Smallwood and Forman were ordered to advance through Jenkintown against the far right of the British line.

Washington directed his troops to depart their camps near Worcester at 1800 so that the attack would be made at dawn on 3 October. His orders for the advance route of each column and the ensuing attack were quite specific. Upon completing their march, he ordered "Each column to make their disposition so as to attack the pickets in their respective fronts precisely at five o'clock with charged bayonets, the columns to move on to the attack as soon as possible. The columns to endeavor to get within two miles of the enemy's pickets on their respective fronts by two o'clock and halt till four and make the disposition for attacking the pickets at the time mentioned." In order to avoid confusion that might lead to firing on friendly troops, every officer was to have a piece of white paper attached to his hat.

Carefully laid out as these plans were, they were as overly ambitious as Washington's December 1776 strategy at Trenton had been. They called for four separate columns to make a night march by different routes and converge on the enemy line in a coordinated dawn attack. Washington hoped that the various columns would keep in touch during their march, but this would prove to be difficult in the darkness and the unexpectedly heavy ensuing morning fog. In addition, the two left wing columns (Greene's and particularly the militia column under Smallwood and Forman) had complicated approach routes that would have been difficult to follow with guides even in the daylight. Above all it was necessary for the various columns to attack promptly and simultaneously. Any delays would permit Howe to shift his troops from one threatened point to another while he summoned reinforcements from Cornwallis' camps in Philadelphia.

Howe was informed by spies of Washington's preparations, which included the sending of his sick to Bethlehem and an order for his men "to leave their packs, blankets, and everything except arms, accoutrements, ammunition and provision." However, he greatly underestimated Washington's offensive capability (just as Rall had done at Trenton), and elected just to strengthen his pickets and send out a few additional patrols, which ranged as far northwest as Allen's Tavern in Mount Airy. Howe had no reason to fear for the left of his line, which was strongly posted above the steep banks of Wissahickon Creek. His center was also strongly held by numerous troops (the *2nd, 3rd* and *4th Brigades* of infantry) placed behind a line of light redoubts and artillery. The weakest part of the line was the far right, held by some light infantry and Von Donop's Hessians. Here the ground was more open and the British line was broken by Wingohocking Creek. The far right was fronted by a strong picket at Luken's

Mill, supported by the *Queen's Rangers*, and the entire right was supported by two brigades of *British Guards* posted near Howe's headquarters at the Logan House (Stenton).

Washington's march began as scheduled at 1800, led by Greene's command, which had the longest distance to cover in order to reach its pre-attack position. The column separated as planned after passing White House Church, where Greene continued on to the east while the troops behind turned right onto the Bethlehem Pike. The latter column, led by Washington, halted as planned at 0200 to form for the attack. Conway's veteran brigade of Stirling's Division was directed to lead the attack, supported by Sullivan on the right and Wayne on the left, with Stirling's other two brigades (Nash's and Maxwell's) in reserve.

Washington became concerned as 0500, the appointed hour for the attack, approached and no news came from Greene. When dawn finally arrived, Washington felt obliged to assume that Greene was on schedule, and ordered the attack to proceed as planned on his front. Conway's advance party, a body of dismounted horse led by Captain Allen McLane, struck the frontmost British picket at Mount Airy just at sunrise (0600) and easily pushed it back; the British officer in charge had learned of the Americans' presence nearby at 0300 but misjudged their number and intentions.

After overwhelming the British picket at Mount Airy, the Washington advance pitched into the *2nd Light Infantry*, led by Wayne's men, who were eager to avenge their defeat at Paoli. The American attack was aided by the early morning darkness and a heavy ground fog that together restricted vision to much less than one hundred yards. An officer in the English *52nd Regiment* noted the fierceness of the fighting immediately after his pickets were driven in. "We heard a loud cry, 'Have at the bloodhounds, revenge Wayne's affair' and they immediately fired a volley. We gave them one in return and charged.... We had no support nearer than Germantown a mile in our rear. On our charging they gave way on all sides but again and again renewed the attack with fresh troops and a greater force. We charged them twice till the battalion was so reduced by killed and wounded that the bugle was sounded to retreat. Two columns of the enemy had nearly got around our flank. But this was the first time we had ever retreated from the Americans and it was with great difficulty that we could get the men to obey our orders."

The light infantry was rescued by the *40th Regiment*, commanded by Lt. Colonel Thomas Musgrave, who marched quickly forward from his encampment at the Chew House. Musgrave's troops let loose several "well timed and heavy discharges" that halted the American advance and allowed the light infantry to reform. However, the light troops soon began to run out of ammunition and started giving way a second time. Musgrave, who had been sparing of his ammunition, covered their retreat as they rushed for the main British line at Market Square.

The American troops were overjoyed to drive the enemy back, and let out "repeated huzza's" when they came into possession of Musgrave's camp near Cliveden. From there they continued to press their advantage. Conway's troops led the way, with Sullivan following on the south side of the Germantown Pike and Wayne on the north side. Wayne's men were particularly exulted as they "pushed on with their bayonets and took ample vengeance" for Paoli.

The American advance pursued Howe's retreating light infantry for "two full miles" before they reached the main British line. By chance, General Howe happened to arrive at the front from his headquarters at Stenton just as the light infantry was being driven in: "Seeing the battalion retreating, all broken, he got into passion, and exclaimed, 'For shame, light infantry, I never saw you retreat before, form! form! it is only a scouting party.' However he was quickly convinced that it was more [when] the heads of the enemy's columns soon appeared. One coming through Beggarstown with three pieces of cannon in their front immediately fired with grape at the crowd that was standing with General Howe under a large chestnut tree. I think I never saw people enjoy a charge of grape before, but we really all felt pleased to see the enemy make such an appearance, and to hear the grape rattle about

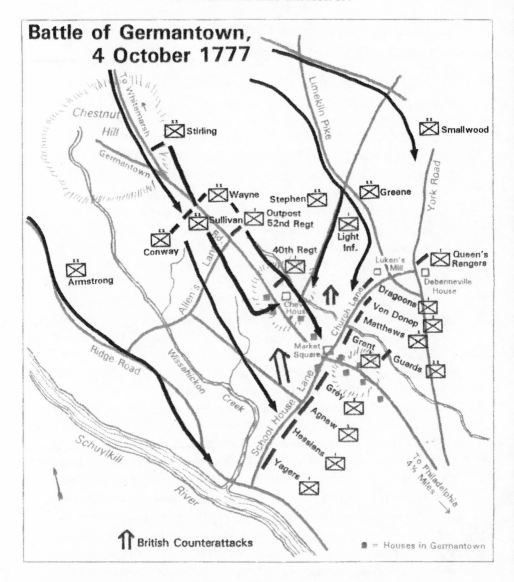

Battle of Germantown, 4 October 1777

Stirling
Smallwood
Wayne
Stephen
Greene
Sullivan
Outpost 52nd Regt
Conway
Light Inf.
Queen's Rangers
Armstrong
40th Regt
Luken's Mill
Debenneville House
Chew House
Dragoons
Von Donop
Matthews
Market Square
Grant
Guards
Grey
Agnew
Hessians
Yagers

To Whitemarsh
Chestnut Hill
Germantown
Limekiln Pike
York Road
Allen's Lane
Ridge Road
Wissahickon Creek
School House Lane
Church Lane
Schuylkill River
To Philadelphia 4¾ Miles

⬆⬆ British Counterattacks   ■ = Houses in Germantown

the commander-in-chief's ears, after he had accused the battalion of having run away from a scouting party."

The hurried American pursuit of the retreating British light infantry rushed right by Musgrave's *40th Regiment*, which had withdrawn towards the Chew House and could not be seen through all the battle smoke and morning fog. Musgrave at once realized that he was cut off from Howe's main line and promptly ordered his men to enter Cliveden, which was about 200 yards north of the Germantown Road. The house, built in 1760, had thick stone walls and was a veritable fortress. Six companies (about 120 men) followed their colonel, all closely followed by a strong American force. Washington's troops indeed would have contested Musgrave's occupation of the mansion had the British commander not "faced the regiment about and given them a fire which checked them enough for him to have time to get his regiment into the house and shut the door."

Musgrave rushed up the building's front steps and opened the heavy door for his men. Quickly he directed them to close the window shutters and barricade the doors on the first floor while he posted marksmen at the windows on the second and third floors. For awhile all grew quiet as Musgrave completed his defenses and the center of the battle shifted to the east towards Market Square. He could have remained safe and unnoticed in his fortress, but Musgrave boldly chose to reveal his presence when he directed his sharpshooters to open fire on an American column (the reserve troops from Washington's column) that was passing on the roadway nearby.

Musgrave's presence posed quite a dilemma to Washington, who happened to ride up soon after the British marksmen opened fire from their fort. Washington conferred with General Henry Knox, his chief of artillery, and several officers in front of the Bilmeyer House (still standing at 6505-07 Germantown Avenue) and even mounted a carriage block in front of the house to get a closer view of the enemy's position through his spyglass. Several officers thought it best to bypass Cliveden and join the intensifying battle farther east. Knox, however, successfully argued that they should not push on "leaving an armed fort in your rear."

Washington detached Maxwell's light infantry from his reserve and directed them to prepare to attack Cliveden. While they formed, it was decided to try to get the enemy to surrender first. Lieutenant William Smith, a deputy adjutant general, volunteered to undertake the dangerous mission, and bravely went forward under a flag of truce. He had

The Benjamin Chew House (Cliveden) was bravely held by the British **40th Regiment** *against numerous American attacks during the battle of Germantown.*

advanced only a short distance when he was struck by a bullet that shattered his leg. The wound was mortal and he died soon afterward.

As Maxwell's men began to open fire on Cliveden, Knox drew up four cannons (3-pounders and 6-pounders) immediately across the road from Cliveden, in the yard of present-day Upsala. Knox was determined to reduce the fort to rubble, but his guns proved to be too light to smash the mansion's three-foot-thick stone walls. Only one shot caused any significant damage, an early salvo that "burst open both the hall doors and wounded some men with pieces of stone that flew from the wall." Most of the succeeding shots, which were aimed at the building's upper stories, could do little more than knock off part of the roof and chip chunks off the house's western facade.

By now Maxwell had formed a firing line in a row of cherry trees that lined the mansion's entrance drive. His light infan-

General Henry Knox was a self educated artillery officer who served Washington well throughout the war. It was primarily on his advice that Washington ordered the attack on Cliveden during the battle of Germantown.

try suffered heavily from British fire as they approached the house in numerous charges; by the end of the fighting 56 of their number would be dead in front of the house. Most of their effort was concentrated on reaching the first floor windows and the shattered front door. The bravest troops who actually attempted to enter the house were quickly bayoneted by the British troops led by Captain Hains, Musgrave's commander on the ground floor.

When their attempts to enlarge the opening in the front door failed, the Americans decided to try to burn the house down. One attempt was made with a wagon loaded with hay found in one of the mansion's outbuildings, which was vainly pushed up to the mansion's side door. Another incendiary attempt was made by Major John White of Sullivan's staff, who sneaked up to the northern side of the house with a lighted torch. He leaned over to pick some twigs for tinder and fell mortally wounded by a British bayonet thrust through a window.

Another bold attempt to burn the house was made by Colonel John Laurens of Southern Carolina and a Frenchman, the Chevalier de Mandit du Plessis. Laurens grabbed some straw from the stables to use for kindling, and the two succeeded at sneaking up to a window in the mansion's first floor office. Du Plessis managed to break open a shutter, and

Cliveden

The Chew House, known as Cliveden, still stands today as an elegant memorial of the battle of Germantown and our Colonial past. It was erected by local craftsmen in 1763-1767 as a country house for Benjamin Chew (1722-1810), a Maryland born Quaker who came to Philadelphia to study and then practice law. Tastefully designed by Chew himself in Neo-Georgian style, the mansion has stone walls three feet thick that protected the British defenders well during the battle. The estate occupies an entire city block at 6401 Germantown Avenue, and included several outbuildings as well as a stone enclosure wall.

Chew was not in residence at the time of the battle in October 1778, but was living under "house arrest" with a friend near Trenton, New Jersey. Since Chew had been an important official in the pre-war Royalist government of Philadelphia (he had served as the state's attorney general and chief justice, among other posts), General Washington ordered him to be arrested ("detained" in modern parlance) for not signing a loyalty oath to the Colonial government. In the spirit of the day, however, Chew was permitted to live "with three or four servants" at the home of a friend in New Jersey, where he resided from September 1777 to June 1778. At the time of the battle, Cliveden was being cared for by a gardener and his wife; the wife found herself locked in the basement by the British troops during the fighting.

The house, as well as the estate, suffered considerable damage during the battle. The front door was smashed in by a cannon ball, plaster was broken in every room, furniture was broken, and powder stains were everywhere. In addition, parts of the roof were blown off, and the building's exterior, especially the front facade and the northwest side, received scars that can still be seen today. Reportedly a crew of several carpenters and craftsmen needed a full year to restore the building's woodwork. The estate's grounds were also a mess. All the cherry trees lining the entrance drive had been stripped of their bark and leaves, and there were numerous

had just climbed the window sill to throw a torch in when he was confronted by the pistol of a British officer who ordered him to surrender. Just at that moment an English private entered the study and fired at du Plessis, but missed and killed the British officer instead. Du Plessis thought it best to retire before he was bayoneted, and he escaped safely. Laurens was not so lucky. He was wounded in the shoulder near the house, and had to stop to consider whether he should fresh graves around the house. At least 16 American soldiers were buried in a communal grave near the front gate, and other Colonial and British casualties were probably buried near where they fell in the heavy fighting.

After surviving the battle, Cliveden was also fortunate to avoid a general conflagration of Colonial mansions that was ordered soon afterwards. It seems that the British were greatly annoyed that the local inhabitants had not warned them of Washington's approach before the battle. In retaliation, a colonel named Ayres ordered 17 large homes in the area burned. Cliveden was not on the list, due to its role in the battle and the fact that its owner was a Tory. Stenton, Howe's headquarters, before the battle, was not so lucky. Its owner, Dr. James Logan, was an active Patriot, so it was ordered to be destroyed. Two privates were sent to carry out the task, and began gathering straw to start the fire. While they were in the barn, a British officer rode up and asked one of the house servants if she had seen any deserters around. The quick thinking servant replied that there

were two deserters in the barn at that very moment. The officer had them arrested, despite their protestations that they had been sent to burn the house, and the mansion avoided its death sentence.

When Benjamin Chew returned from his house arrest in New Jersey, he thought it would be best to sell Cliveden because of continuing friction with the local Patriots. For this reason the estate was sold in 1779 to Blair McClenachan, a Philadelphia merchant, for $8,000. McClenachan owned the house for eight years until he fell into economic difficulty. Negotiations with the former owner resulted in McClenachan selling Cliveden back to Benjamin Chew in 1797 for $25,000.

Chew lived in the house until his death in 1810 at the age of 88. Cliveden then remained in the family for another five generations, until 1971. It was acquired by the National Trust for Historic Preservation in 1972, and still contains many of the original furnishings preserved by the Chew family. The estate is open to the public and hosts a reenactment of the battle each October.

stay where he was or try to run or walk to safety. He chose to walk back to his own lines, which he miraculously reached without further harm.

While the battle was raging around the Chew House, Wayne's troops reached Howe's main line a mile to the southeast and succeeded at pushing *Grant's Brigade* back from Market Square. In the heavy fighting, Wayne's horse was killed and he was slightly wounded on the left foot and left

Present-day photo of Cliveden.

hand. General Francis Nash and his aide Major James Wither-spoon (son of New Jersey's John Witherspoon, a signer of the Declaration of Independence and president of the College of New Jersey at Princeton) were not so lucky. As the two were bringing Nash's Brigade to help Wayne, they were struck by a British cannonball that came flying through the fog. The shot split Witherspoon's head, inflicting a mortal wound, and struck Nash in the thigh before it disemboweled the general's horse. As Nash lay on the ground he bravely covered his wound and called to his men. "Never mind me, I have had a devil of a tumble—rush on my boys, rush on the enemy—I'll be after you presently." His wound was also mortal, and he died five days later at Whitemarsh. He was buried in the Mennonite church graveyard in Kulpsville.

Wayne's capture of Market Square caused Howe to think seriously of abandoning the field. Before he would act, however, the British commander was astonished to see the Americans begin to withdraw from his front. Wayne's retreat was caused by the confusion of an accidental collision with

Greene's troops on the army's left. Greene's advance had begun well enough, even though he had been almost an hour late in establishing contact with the enemy, detachments of the *1st Light Infantry* and the *4th Regiment* that were posted on the Limekiln Pike two miles north of Luken's Mill. Greene stopped to form his troops along the Pike, with Stephen's Division on the right, McDougal's on the left, and his own in the center. The American force readily drove their British opposition back, but their formation into battle line so far from Howe's main line severely retarded their advance.

Unfortunately for the Americans, General Stephen's command on the right of Greene's line drifted to the right in the fog and lost contact with the British troops in the front. Stephen was then attracted by the din of the fighting at Cliveden and headed in that direction. Woodford's Brigade actually reached Cliveden and supported Maxwell's attacks on the mansion. Stephen's own brigade managed to get lost in the woods; Stephen himself was later cashiered under charges of drunkenness and misconduct in the battle. His command stumbled forward until they ran into a body of troops in their front. When they opened fire, they were unknowingly shooting at the rear of Wayne's command. When some of Wayne's men turned to return the fire, their attack on Howe's line lost all its impetus.

Wayne's line became disordered as some of his men turned to deal with Stephen and others attempted to continue the attack on Howe's lines. The situation became critical when many of Wayne's men began to run out of ammunition. A number went to the rear to seek a new supply, not to return, while others began calling to their comrades for more bullets and powder. Their cries were heard by Howe's troops, who at once understood the enemy's predicament and began a limited advance. Soon Wayne's entire line was in general retreat. Many of the Americans were demoralized by the noise of the fighting at the Chew House, which they interpreted as evidence that the enemy held the army's line of retreat.

Wayne's withdrawal exposed Sullivan's left, which fell under attack by the *5th* and *55th Regiments*. Sullivan's men were as tired and low on ammunition as Wayne's and were forced to withdraw along with Conway's. At this critical juncture Howe received much needed reinforcements that enabled him to press his advantage—troops began to arrive from Cornwallis' garrison in Philadelphia, and Knyphausen released Agnew's *4th Brigade* from the left wing, which was not being seriously threatened by an American militia force under Armstrong. Howe sent Agnew's *37th Regiment* to support Grey's *15th Regiment* near Market Square, and ordered the rest of Agnew's command (*33rd, 46th* and *64th Regiments*) forward to drive Sullivan's command from the area west of Germantown Pike.

Agnew's men experienced a bit of difficulty in conducting their advance. The right of their line was supposed to enter Germantown, but instead the entire command halted on the edge of the town to fire at a distant American column. To fill the gap in the British line, "No Flint" Grey led his *17th* and *44th Regiments* north into town. At the same time General Agnew rode ahead of his line to examine the streets along which he was supposed to proceed. Unexpectedly a force of about 100 Americans rushed out from behind the Mennonite meeting house at 6119 Germantown Avenue and shot Agnew in the back as he attempted to flee. The general died about 15 minutes later, and his body was removed by his staff to his former headquarters at the Wister House, known as Grumblethorpe (5261 Germantown Avenue), where his bloodstains can still be seen on the floor. Agnew and Lieutenant Colonel John Bird of the *15th Regiment*, who also fell in the battle, were initially interred in the Lower Burial Ground at Germantown Avenue and Logan Street. In May 1778, before evacuating Philadelphia, the British quietly reburied the two officers in the private burial ground of Dr. George De Benneville at Branchtown, for fear that the Colonists might desecrate the graves if they knew where they were.

Agnew's men continued on after the fall of their commander, and helped drive Washington's column back up the Germantown Road towards Chestnut Hill. The British counterattack drew Maxwell's men away from their assault on

Cliveden, and soon they, too, were caught up in the general American retreat. Musgrave's gallant band was at last relieved, though they had suffered only a few casualties and could have held on as long as their ammunition lasted. They had inflicted over 100 casualties on Washington's troops, and played a key role in the battle by deflecting Maxwell's Brigade and other troops from participation in the primary American attack on Howe's center.

The battle, however, was still not over. General Greene, not aware of the retreat of the troops on the Germantown Pike, was continuing to press his attack on the British right. After pushing the *1st Light Infantry* back along the Limekiln Pike, Greene ran into the main British position (*49th, 4th, 27th* and *28th Regiments,* supported by the *British Guards*) beyond Luken's Mill. McDougal's regiments on the left of Greene's line had difficulty keeping up with the advance, but Greene's own two brigades (Weedon's and Muhlenberg's) succeeded in denting the English line. One of Muhlenberg's units, the 9th Virginia, even managed to penetrate the enemy's line under cover of the fog and reached the vicinity of Market Square, where its men began plundering the deserted huts of the *1st Light Infantry.* Their joyful shouts attracted the attention of several British units, including the *Queen's Rangers* and a detachment of the *British Guards,* which soon mounted a counterattack. The first British volley felled many of the 9th's officers, and others were quickly dispatched with the bayonet. The survivors of the regiment had little choice but to surrender. They were for the moment locked up in nearby Market Square Church.

By now Greene was aware of Washington's retreat on his right and realized that he had no choice but to extricate his command as best he could. Despite pressure from the *British Guards* and *27th* and *28th Regiments,* he managed an orderly retreat with no significant losses other that the 400 men of the 9th Virginia. His retreat was aided by the several volleys he stopped to let loose on his pursuers, and by undue caution showed by the British General Grant, who failed to push his advantage.

Greene's withdrawal left Smallwood and Forman in an exposed position on the army's far right. They had advanced along a circuitous route and eventually established limited contact with a detachment of *Queen's Rangers* on old York Road. Had they arrived earlier, they might have drawn off some of the British troops that moved to confront Greene. As affairs developed, the two militia commands withdrew hastily when they saw Greene retire, and joined in the army's general retreat along Skippack Pike.

The last American troops to withdraw were Armstrong's militia, which had advanced until he reached the west side of the Wissahickon gorge, where he deployed his cannons and began an active but inconsequential skirmish with Von Wurmb's Hessians posted across the creek. The lack of vigor in Armstrong's attack enabled Knyphausen to send most of his troops north against Sullivan's right flank, as already mentioned. Armstrong continued his demonstration until 0900, when he received an order to march to the left to join Washington. He actually believed that the Americans were winning the battle, and was startled to run into a large force of the enemy after he followed Wissahickon Creek back to the Germantown Pike. He then withdrew and joined the army's retreat to the north.

The American retreat was by no means a rout, even though strong British forces pursued them on both the Bethlehem and Germantown Roads. The famous pamphleteer Thomas Paine, who was serving as a volunteer aide to General Greene, observed that "the retreat was extraordinary. Nobody hurried themselves. Everyone marched his own pace. The enemy kept a civil distance behind, sending every now and then a shot after us, and receiving the same from us." The army's rear guard was formed by Wayne's reassembled command, which was anxious to win back its honor. Wayne formed his men near Whitemarsh Church, just over seven miles from the battlefield, and fired a few cannon shots at the British advance as it came up. This ended the day's action, though the English dragoons continued their pursuit for a few more miles.

Washington ordered his men to retire up the Skippack Pike as far as their camps at Worcester where they had stayed the previous night. The weary troops, however, continued on another six miles to Pawling's Mills on Perkiomen Creek, which they reached about 2100. It had indeed been a long and terrible day for them—marching 14 miles in the dark to fight a fierce 5-hour battle, and then retreating 20 miles, all in the space of 27 hours. The American troops were certainly exhausted, but they were far from discouraged. Most, in fact, were heartened by the fact that they felt they had come very close to winning a pitched battle against the enemy—had it not been for the fog, Greene's late arrival, Stephen's drunkenness, or the lengthy attack on Cliveden, they thought they well might have won the day. Such a hard fought defeat increased their confidence in themselves and their leaders so that the army would be eager to fight again. As Washington ably put it, "Upon the whole it may be said the day was unfortunate rather than injurious. The enemy are nothing better by the events; and our troops, who are not the least dispirited by it, have gained what all young troops gain by being in such actions." The official report of American casualties for the battle lists 152 killed, 521 wounded, and more than 400 missing. The British, however, said they took 438 prisoners, and also claimed to have buried 300 slain Rebels. At least 17 were buried in a common grave just inside the main gate of the Cliveden estate. Besides Brigadier General Nash, the American officers killed included Colonels Jacob Engle, Matthew Boyd and Edward Buncumbe, plus two lieutenant colonels and four majors.

Howe's losses were over 500 of his 10,000 men engaged. He lost 4 officers and 66 men killed, 30 officers and 396 men wounded, and 1 officer and 13 men missing. Hessian casualties were about 25, including several killed. The number of British captured would have been much higher had the *49th Regiment* not recaptured three companies of light infantry that had been taken prisoner by Greene's troops near Luken's Mill.

British Generals and Generalship

British field generalship during the campaign was, with few exceptions, handled expertly from the army down to brigade level. Howe's flanking tactics at Brandywine and prompt defensive response at Germantown were carried out most successfully, and Clinton in 1778 skillfully completed his awkward withdrawal across New Jersey. With the advantage of such good leadership, it seems clear that defeat was due to a combination of other reasons—a severe shortage of troops, unexpected intervention of France after Burgoyne's surrender, poor planning in London, and a communications breakdown that allowed Howe to conduct the campaign on his own terms without regard for Burgoyne's needs.

The careers of Howe and Clinton are discussed in separate sidebars. It should be noted here that neither again held significant field command, though Howe would hold several important posts in Britain during the Napoleonic crises of the 1790s.

Howe and Clinton were greatly aided by a number of able professional officers, chief among whom was Charles Cornwallis (1738-1805). Cornwallis had extensive experience in the Seven Years War, and was already a major general when the Revolution began in 1775. He participated in Howe's successful 1776 campaign against New York, and was in overall (but not local) command of the troops Wash-ington defeated in Trenton and Princeton that winter. During the Philadelphia campaign, Cornwallis usually commanded one of the army's two grand divisions, and played a significant role at Brandywine and Germantown. As a reward, he was named Clinton's second-in-command in 1778. It was Cornwallis' troops who fought the battle of Monmouth, where he personally led at least one attack. Later in the war he conducted a very successful campaign in Georgia and the Carolinas, until he was eventually checked by Nathanael Greene. He is best remembered today for the unsuccessful Virginia campaign he conducted in 1781. Acting contrary to Clinton's orders, he attempted to catch Lafayette's command in Virginia, only to be cornered by a combined French and American force at Yorktown. His surrender on 10 October 1781 effectively ended the war's military operations, though the Treaty of Paris was not signed until almost two years later. After the war he won several significant battles in India, and served for a time as governor general of Ireland.

The most notable of the British brigade commanders in the campaign was perhaps Major General Charles "No Flint" Grey (1729-1807). He had extensive service in the Seven Years War, and in 1775 was serving as an aide to the King. He came to America with Howe in 1776, and commanded the British

3rd Brigade during the Philadelphia campaign. Grey received his colorful nickname for his successful night attack on Wayne's troops at Paoli on 21 September 1777, where he ordered his troops to attack with bayonets only. After fighting at Germantown and Monmouth, he was transferred to New England in late 1778 and conducted several raids there. He was then recalled to England, and was promoted lieutenant general in 1782 for the purpose of assuming overall command in America. However, because the war was speedily moving to a conclusion, the post was given instead to Guy Carleton, who was already at the front. In the 1790s he became a full general during Britain's confrontations with Napoleon, though he was, like Howe, too old to take the field.

Brigadier General Alexander Leslie (1740-1794), commander of the British *5th Brigade*, fought well during this campaign, but experienced difficulty during the other campaigns. Noted for his aggressiveness, he played a leading role in the battle of Harlem Heights but then led a poorly conducted attack at White Plains on 28 October 1776. In January 1777 he commanded a brigade encamped at Maidenhead (Lawrenceville), New Jersey, and did not detect Washington's army marching nearby on its way to battle at Princeton. His slowness to reach Cornwallis in January 1781 was a contributing cause to the British defeat at Cowpens. By the end of the war he held command of Savannah and Charleston with the "local rank" of lieutenant general.

Major General James Grant (1720-1806) was one of the most colorful British officers in the war. He fought against the Scots at Culloden in 1746 and then saw extensive service during the Seven Years War in the *77th Highlanders*. He was captured by the French following defeat near Fort Duquesne in 1758, and later fought against the Cherokees in Georgia in 1761. From 1764 to 1771 he served as Royal Governor of Florida. After the Revolution broke out, he returned to America with Howe in 1776 and commanded a brigade during the New York campaign. He greatly despised the American troops, and, appointed to command the British outposts along the Delaware late in 1776, haughtily assured Colonel Rall at Trenton that there was nothing to fear from the enemy. Not long afterwards Washington won his two victories at Trenton and Princeton within a week's time. Grant later performed efficiently as commander of the *1st British Brigade* at Brandywine and Germantown. The next spring he was largely responsible for allowing Lafayette to escape Howe's trap at Barren Hill, and during the height of the Monmouth campaign he failed to follow specific orders to help Cornwallis' rear guard. As a result he was detached from the army in America and sent to fight at St. Lucia in the West Indies. His good work there won him promotion to lieutenant general. Somehow he lived to the age of 86 in spite of his high life style and "immensely corpulent" body.

Baron Wilhelm von Knyphausen (1716-1800) was the efficient commander in chief of the German and Hessian troops during the campaign. He entered the Prussian army in 1734 at the age of 18 and rose to the rank of general in 1775. He was sent to America in the fall of 1776, and became the senior Hessian general in early 1777. Because of his high rank, there was concern in London that he might succeed to the post of British commander in chief if any misfortune befell Howe or then Clinton; for this reason London issued a "dormant commission" to the senior British officer in America, to be exercised if necessary to prevent Knyphausen from becoming commander in chief during an emergency.

Knyphausen commanded one of the British army's two grand divisions during the Philadelphia campaign, but did not play any significant role in action. At Brandywine, he led the holding action that primed most of Washington's army near Chadd's Ford while Cornwallis and Howe marched around the American right. He was not actively engaged at Germantown, and missed the fighting at Monmouth because his command formed the army's advance guard that was never called to the battlefield. He spent the remainder of the war on garrison duty in New York, where he held command briefly when Clinton went to Charleston in 1780. He retired in 1782 because of "bodily infirmity and the loss of an eye."

The most significant battlefield error by a British commander during the campaign was made by the Hessian Colonel Emil Kurt von Donop at Fort Mercer on 22 October 1777. He was a career officer who fought at Long Island and then had charge of the outposts along the Delaware at the time of the battle of Trenton; his suggestion to concentrate all the posts at Trenton was overruled by Howe. He commanded a foot regiment during most of the Philadelphia campaign before he was given a force of 2,000 Hessians to take Fort Mercer. He did not reconnoiter the ground well before beginning his attack and was deceived by the fort's apparent weakness. Nevertheless, he possessed such personal bravery that he went forward to lead the attack, where he received a mortal wound in the leg. He died in American hands soon after the battle.

CHAPTER VII

The Delaware Forts

The Philadelphia campaign had another aspect than the confrontation between Howe's and Washington's relatively evenly matched armies. Both opposing generals understood that Howe was faced with great difficulty in keeping his army supplied. Even if the British did manage to capture Philadelphia, Washington could prevent the English fleet from reestablishing contact with Howe's field army as long as American forces kept control of the Delaware River. The boldest aspect of Howe's landing at Elkton was the necessity to use that town as his base until he could reach Philadelphia. This decision forced him to rely on a tenuous supply line through Colonial territory, one that was vulnerable to enemy raids and required numerous troops to maintain. That is the primary reason why he had to post one battalion of the *71st Regiment* in Wilmington for most of the early portion of the campaign. The supply shortage also forced Howe to rely more than he desired on the impressment of animals and foodstuffs from local farmers. These foraging expeditions often turned to plundering forays (especially when conducted by the Hessians) and did little to win the support of the rural population, many of whom were neutral Quakers.

In order to alleviate his supply difficulties, Howe needed to take control of the Delaware as soon as possible. Naval reconnaissances in the spring and summer of 1777 had determined that the river was well defended by a small American flotilla and by two forts located just below the mouth of the Schuylkill. Fort Mercer was situated on the

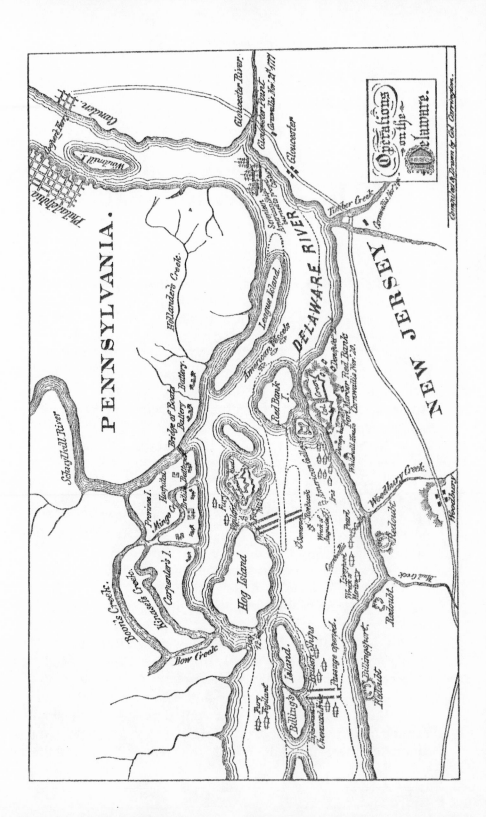

Jersey shore about four miles due south of Philadelphia, and Fort Mifflin had been built nearby on Mud Island in the middle of the river. More significantly, two lines of underwater obstacles had been placed across the river in the stretch between the forts and Billingsport, New Jersey, three miles to the south. Called "chevaux de frise," these obstacles were formed of heavy wooden frameworks about 40 by 60 feet that supported iron tipped spikes that could rip the bottom out of a passing vessel. The concept had originated in Holland around 1600, and the versions used in the Delaware and in the Hudson below West Point were supposedly designed by Benjamin Franklin. The strength of these obstacles and the rest of the American river defenses below Philadelphia had been a major factor in persuading Howe to sail up the Chesapeake instead of the Delaware in late July.

Howe knew that he would have to clear the Delaware's river defenses by himself with little help from his brother's fleet, which had left Elkton around 1 September and would need a few weeks to round Cape Anne and return to the Delaware. Even then, the fleet would be unable to pass the first line of chevaux de frise at Billingsport and could do little more than add artillery support until the American river defenses could be overcome from the land.

The first stage in Howe's river campaign began the instant that Cornwallis occupied Philadelphia with four battalions of grenadiers and other support troops on 26 September. Cornwallis at once sent detachments to secure the town's waterfront and confiscate all the ships and boats they could find. Washington had sent orders to Captain Charles Alexander to gather up and remove all the shipping in the area, but Cornwallis' sudden descent (see Chapter 4) prevented him from completing his assignment. Though a number of boats managed to escape to New Jersey, British agents brought in over 50 vessels that soon would prove quite useful to their cause.

Cornwallis also set to work fortifying the city's waterfront against attack. The *1st British Grenadiers* was garrisoned in the shipyards, and engineers set to work laying out 3 batteries that would contain a total of 12 guns. The powerful lower battery, set up at the foot of present Washington Avenue, was constructed first for fear of a prompt American retaliatory attack. Early on the 27th, platforms were erected for two 12-pounder guns, and three other guns (two 12-pounders and a 5 1/2-inch howitzer) were stationed adjacent on their fixed carriages.

The American naval commanders were not about to allow Cornwallis to turn Philadelphia's waterfront into a fortress without a fight. Early on the 27th Commodore John Hazelwood, commander of the Delaware River fleet, directed Captain Alexander to sail up to the city and threaten to open fire if the British would not cease erecting shore fortifications. At 0830 Alexander set sail from his base at Fort Mifflin with two warships, the *Delaware* (24 guns) and *Montgomery* (10 guns), plus an armed sloop, the *Fly* (8 guns), and five row galleys (each carrying 1 gun).

The American fleet approached Philadelphia's waterfront with the *Delaware* in the lead. She was tacking in order to reach the British lines, but did not yet have a flag of truce flying as Captain Alexander had ordered. The commander of the British battery, Captain-Lieutenant Francis Downman of the Royal Artillery, had been ordered "not to fire till I was fired at," but could not restrain himself. When the *Delaware* was about 400 yards distant, he let loose a blast that instantly demoralized the *Delaware*'s inexperienced crew. Captain Alexander attempted to run his warship upriver past the enemy guns, but the boat ran aground on a small island only 250 yards from Downman's battery.

The experienced British gunners pummeled the *Delaware* for several minutes until she was forced to strike her flag. They then turned their attention with equal success to the rest of the American flotilla. The *Fly* soon lost 10 men and had her main mast shot away, whereupon she drifted out of range until she grounded on the opposite Jersey shore. The rest of the American boats wisely decided to disengage, and returned to Mud Island.

As soon as the fighting stopped, the British sent a squad of

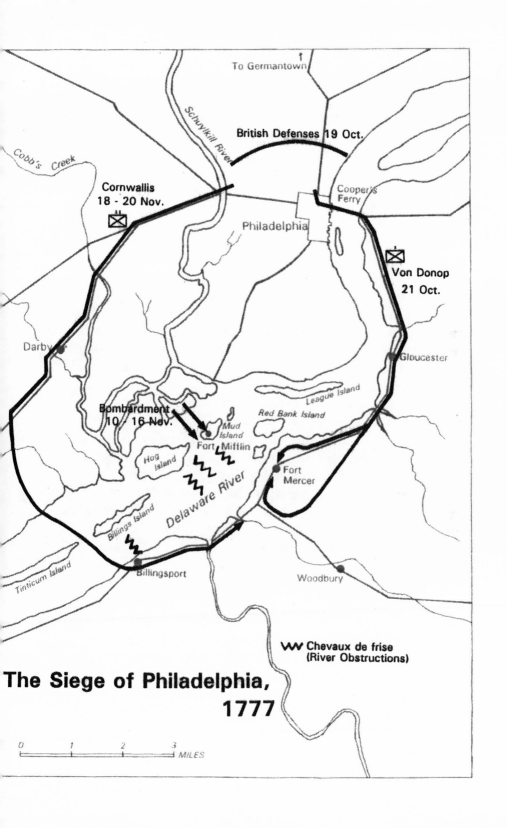

To Germantown

British Defenses 19 Oct.

Cobb's Creek

Cornwallis
18 - 20 Nov.

Schuylkill River

Cooper's
Ferry

Philadelphia

Von Donop
21 Oct.

Darby

Gloucester

Bombardment
10 - 16 Nov.

League Island

Mud
Island

Red Bank Island

Fort Mifflin

Hog
Island

Fort
Mercer

Delaware River

Billings Island

Tinticum Island

Billingsport

Woodbury

WW Chevaux de frise
(River Obstructions)

**The Siege of Philadelphia,
1777**

0   1   2   3
⊢⊢⊢⊢⊢⊢⊢⊣ MILES

10 grenadiers in a rowboat to take possession of the *Delaware*. They found that the ship was not badly damaged, though it had been set afire in three places. The boat's casualties had amounted to only 1 man killed and 6 wounded out of a crew of 152. All the captured, including Captain Alexander, were at once imprisoned, and the ship was moved the next day to the protection of a newly completed battery located at Front Street and Girard Avenue. Her repair work was carried out by a detachment of 50 sailors from the warship *Roebuck*, which had come upriver as far as Chester. The loss of the *Delaware* was a great blow to American morale and gave the British a warship to employ behind the American river defenses.

Howe decided to make his next objective the elimination of the lower line of chevaux de frise that extended from Billings Island to Billingsport. Several supply ships had reached Chester from New York, and the advance elements of his brother's fleet were beginning to arrive, so he was anxious to reduce the American defenses in order to resupply his army, most of which was stationed at Germantown in order to keep an eye on Washington's command. Late on 28 September he detached Lieutenant Colonel Thomas Stirling with the *10th* and *42nd Regiments* for the task of reducing the undermanned American fort at Billingsport. Stirling had orders to march to Chester, where he would cross to Jersey under the protection of several recently arrived British warships. The news of Stirling's departure would be a major factor in influencing Washington to attack Howe's reduced command at Germantown (see Chapter 6).

Stirling reached Chester on the morning of 29 September, and at noon started ferrying his troops across the river in longboats furnished by the warships, which stood by to cover the crossing. The operation was still going on at 1900 when the British were surprised to see three burning fire rafts come drifting down the river with the tide. The fast thinking British captains quickly threw lines from their ships to the long boats, which managed to tow the warships out of danger by 2100. As a result, Stirling had to wait until the next day to complete his crossing.

The local American commander, Brigadier General Silas Newbury, was aware of Stirling's crossing, but grossly underestimated the size of the British column. Nevertheless, he decided to move most of his 300 man militia command from Woodbury to reinforce Billingsport's 112 man garrison, which was commanded by Colonel William Bradford of the Pennsylvania militia. The fort was armed with six cannons, mostly 9-pounders. In addition, nineteen 18-pounders were emplaced on two floating batteries near Billings Island at the eastern end of the chevaux de frise anchored at Billingsport. Ironically, Major General Nathanael Greene had just finished a study of the fort at Billingsport and had recommended that it be evacuated because it was too vulnerable from its landward side. Washington was also anxious to pull back the valuable guns in the floating batteries and remove them to Fort Mifflin. Orders to this effect were in fact issued on 28 September, but they could not be carried out before Stirling attacked.

Stirling held his troops at their landing site all day on 1 October, and did not begin marching on Billingsport until shortly before dawn on the 2nd. At about 0900 he ran into most of Newcomb's command, which had deliberately marched south from Billingsport on the Salem Road in order to engage the enemy. The superior British column easily pushed Newcomb back and drove the Americans past the turnoff to Billingsport. The greatly outnumbered garrison there was alerted to his advance and barely had time to jump aboard a waiting brig, the *Andrea Doria*, after spiking most of the fort's guns and setting its barracks afire. The action shifted to the river when several American row galleys began shelling the British troops that moved into occupy the fort, and four British warships came up to oppose them. The action was as one sided as the earlier land engagement had been. The row galleys took a beating and withdrew past the chevaux de frise; that night two full crews deserted to the British.

After securing Billingsport, the British set about trying to move the nearby chevaux de frise enough to allow their ships to pass through. They succeeded at opening a small passage late on 5 October, but had to stop work because of a reversal of fortune on the Jersey shore. During the 4th, Stirling had assigned a 300 man garrison to the fort and then departed for Pennsylvania with the rest of his command. When General Newcomb heard this, he gathered his militia and marched on Billingsport. The British commander there was so alarmed that he set fire to the fort and evacuated his men to the nearby warships.

The Americans were once again masters of Billingsport, but they chose not to reoccupy the fort for fear of a British counterattack. Instead, they focused their attention on blocking the newly created gap in the chevaux de frise. Their solution was to sink two of their ships (*Vesuvius* and *Strombolo*) in the opening. Their effort did not deter the British, who returned on the morning of the 7th with more warships and simply pushed the sunken hulls aside. It then took them a full week to widen the opening to 100 feet, a width sufficient enough to let their biggest ships through safely.

After the river obstacles at Billingsport were overcome, Howe turned his attention to the remaining chevaux de frise near Hog Island. These were ably guarded on their eastern end by Fort Mercer, located on the Jersey Shore near Red Bank Island. Their western end, however, was less strongly protected by Fort Mifflin, an incomplete line of ramparts constructed on Mud Island. The fort, which was manned by only 200 troops, offered adequate defenses on the two sides facing Jersey, but little attention had been paid to its up river sides because no attack had ever been expected from that direction. Ironically, the British officer who had originally designed Fort Mifflin six years earlier, Captain John Montresor, was present with the English army as Howe's chief engineer. Montresor was well aware of the fort's Achilles heel, and obtained Howe's permission to begin constructing batteries on Carpenter's and Province Islands, less than a mile behind the fort.

The Americans were well aware that Montresor's batteries would batter Fort Mifflin into submission if they were allowed to be completed. For this reason they made several raids to disrupt the British work. The first, made at 0930 on 11 September, was by far the most successful and managed to capture about 60 of the enemy. Other forays by troops and ships were not as fortunate, though they managed to force Montresor's men to do all their work at night.

Work on Montresor's batteries proceeded so slowly that Howe came in person to inspect their progress on 16 October. His troops, which had been in Philadelphia for three weeks, were beginning to run short of critical supplies, despite what could be requisitioned in the city. When Montresor was unable to target a completion date for his batteries, Howe decided he would have to take stronger steps in order to clear the river. He pulled his troops back from Germantown two days later, and began preparations for a three pronged campaign against the American river forts. One column would be sent to New Jersey to assault Fort Mercer and another column would attack Fort Mifflin. The third prong would consist of his fleet at Chester, which would move upstream to engage the American fleet. Operations along the river would occupy Howe's full attention for the next four weeks, and would allow Washington much needed time to rest, resupply and reinforce his battered army in his camps north of Philadelphia.

Washington had already anticipated Howe's plans, and also began channeling his attention and reinforcements to the river forts. On 7 October he directed Brigadier General James Varnum, who was en route from the Hudson Highlands, to send two regiments of his Continentals to reinforce the small detachment of New Jersey militia that was holding Fort Mercer. The troops, commanded by Colonel William Greene, began arriving at the fort on 11 September. Greene took command of the station, and at once set about strengthening its slight earthen ramparts. He also added underground magazines, and set up a strong line of abatis (sharpened tree trunks set in the ground at an angle). On the 19th, Greene was instructed to send 150 of his Continentals to help man Fort Mifflin. Their loss was more than compensated for by the arrival of the 6th Virginia Regiment and a large number of militia from General Newcomb's command. These reinforcements raised Colonel Greene's force at Fort Mercer to about 1,000, of which 400 were Regulars.

The troops selected by Howe to attack Fort Mercer consisted of a reinforced Hessian brigade to be commanded by Colonel Emil Ulrich von Donop. This 1,228 man force was composed of all three Hessian Grenadier battalions, the *Von Mirbach Regiment*, 10 cannons and all the mounted jägers except a small detachment that was left on scouting duty in Philadelphia. Von Donop had been at Trenton and bore part of the blame for the Hessian defeat there on 26 December 1776, so he and his men were eager to avenge themselves. When he asked Cornwallis if the pending attack should be made "at all hazards," he was told "to be guided on his own judgement on the spot, unless he saw good reason to the contrary."

Captain James Lee of the 2nd Continental Artillery, Commander of Varnum's battery, had only one gun in position when the British began moving a squadron of five warships (*Somerset, Roebuck, Iris, Cornwallis* and *Pearl*) north from Billingsport at 0900 on 5 November. Soon after Lee opened fire, 12 American galleys arrived to assist him, and the British advance was brought to a standstill. The large warships (particularly the 70 gun *Augusta*) simply were not able to elevate their guns high enough to hit Lee's battery, a difficulty also encountered at Fort Mercer, and their cumbersome vessels were unable to get a bearing on the fast moving, shallow draught American galleys. The strength of the Colonial resistance soon forced the British vessels to drop back downstream. In the process, the mighty *Somerset* ran aground, and remained a sitting duck until the tide rose and a wind came to aid its withdrawal.

Von Donop's command formed at the Philadelphia docks at sunrise on 21 October and were ferried across to Cooper's Ferry (Camden) in 14 flatboats by 1400. The force met only slight resistance from Colonial militia, and encamped for the night at Haddonfield. They broke camp the next morning (22

October) and marched directly towards Fort Mercer, but had to alter their line of advance when they discovered that the militia had taken up an important bridge over Big Timber Creek, two miles south of Gloucester. A slight detour brought the column to the vicinity of Fort Mercer at noon.

Von Donop let his men break for rest and lunch while he went forward to reconnoiter the fort. All evidence indicated that the Americans were not expecting an attack, and several of the Hessian officers urged him to conduct an immediate assault. Others urged that he wait until the next morning for naval support that had been promised by Howe. Von Donop, however, was determined to take the fort as soon as possible. In an effort to secure its surrender without incurring casualties on his own troops, he sent three officers and a drummer to convey a surrender ultimatum. The party was met by Colonel Jeremiah Olney, who was told to surrender or be given no quarter (meaning that no prisoners would be taken). Olney's reply was prompt and determined, "We shall not ask for nor expect any quarter, and mean to defend the fort to the last extremity." (Another source quotes his words as "We'll see King George dammed first—we want no quarter!", which may be more accurate.)

Upon hearing Olney's defiant response, Von Donop completed his attack plans. The officers who had carried his unsuccessful surrender ultimatum described to him the layout of the fort and its defenses, large sections of which appeared to be unoccupied. He directed the *Minnegerode Battalion* to attack the fort's most eastern face, which was not completely guarded by abatis. The *Mirbach Regiment* would face the fort's strong southeast face, and Von Donop himself would lead the *Linsing Battalion* against the southwest side of the fort, which was guarded by a line of abatis. Each battalion was ordered to prepare 100 fascines (large bundles of sticks) for use in filling ditches or mounting the abatis. Lastly, Von Donop placed the *Lengerke Battalion* near the river to prevent any possible landing of American reinforcements from Fort Mifflin or elsewhere.

Von Donop ordered his cannons to open fire at 1600, and

still hoped he could compel the fort to surrender without a fight. The American commander, Colonel Greene, still had no intention of giving up. He had not been surprised by the Hessian arrival, as Von Donop supposed, but had been informed of the enemy's advance by his active scouts. He had deliberately kept most of his men out of sight in order to disguise his slim numbers—at the time of Von Donop's approach he had only his 400 Regulars in the fort, and none of the militia that was supposed to be supporting him. Greene had also taken successful measures to camouflage most of his 14 cannons from Von Donop's view. In order to steady his troops, Greene bravely mounted his parapet to survey the enemy line, and then advised them, "Fire low, men. They have a broad belt just above the hips. Aim at that."

Von Donop issued another unsuccessful surrender demand, and then ordered his troops forward at 1645. Minnegerode's northern column advanced the quickest because it faced no initial opposition. His men easily overran some unoccupied works and eagerly shouted "Victoria" because they thought that the Americans had fled from that part of the fort. This was far from the truth. Because of the small size of his command, Greene had deliberately abandoned the large northern section of the fort, and had contracted his lines to a newly constructed short traverse that ran from the fort's principal redoubt to the river. When *Minnegerode's Battalion* neared the traverse a concealed battery opened fire and the American infantry let loose a crashing volleys. The Hessians lost several key officers, and were thrown into confusion by continued enemy volleys. Nevertheless they pressed on until they reached the abatis in front of the traverse. While the Hessians waited for their fascines to be brought forward, the American galleys opened fire on their right flank. Canister blasts from Greene's guns tore huge holes in their lines, and Minnegerode himself went down, shot through both legs. The survivors had no choice but to withdraw for safety.

The attack by the *Mirbach Regiment* met the same fate. This column advanced against the main face of the fort's principal redoubt, and used its fascines well to successfully mount the abatis. However, its men were then mowed down by concentrated American fire from Greene's well posted and well protected defenders. The unit's commander, Lieutenant Colonel Von Schieck, was killed early in the action, and the survivors were soon forced to pull back.

Von Linsing's Battalion had an even more difficult time advancing against the fort's southern face. Its advance troops had not been equipped with the axes and saws needed to break up the abatis, and therefore needed additional time to break through the obstacles. At length two openings were made, and the fascine bearers hurled their burdens into the adjoining ditch. The Hessians quickly rushed forward through a severe American cross fire, only to run into yet another ditch. Since all their fascines had already been deployed, the column could advance no farther and had to engage in an unequal fire fight with American troops protected by the fort's parapet. When additional defenders arrived, made available after Minnegerode's men retreated from the other side of the fort, the fate of the attack was sealed.

The turning point of the battle came when Colonel von Donop was mortally wounded while accompanying the *Von Linsing battalion*. The brave commander had advanced to the front lines, trying to get his men to cross the last ditch (15 feet across and 12 feet deep) that blocked their front. He fell at the edge of the ditch, struck by an eventual total of 13 bullets. His loss (he died three days later in an American house) created a severe command problem, as well as a loss of morale. Minnegerode had been wounded, Von Schieck was dead, and Von Linsing was not with his troops because of illness. Command devolved on Lieutenant Colonel von Wurmb of the jägers, an officer who was not familiar to most of the grenadiers.

Von Wurmb readily admitted that the attack was a failure and Trenton had not been avenged. He ordered all the Hessians to disengage and bring back all the wounded they could. Unfortunately, most of the wounded then had to be left behind because Von Donop had been so over confident that he had brought no ambulance wagons on the expedition. The

Monument at Red Bank, site of Fort Mercer. The battle there on 21 October 1777 was the only clear-cut American victory during the Philadelphia campaign.

wounded officers were placed on ammunition wagons, and the dispirited column headed by forced march to Clements Bridge over Big Timber Creek. The command's only relatively intact unit, the *Von Lengerke Battalion*, reached the bridge first and guarded it until the rest of the column passed at midnight. Von Wurmb allowed his men to rest until 0200, when they marched to Haddenfield and then to Cooper's Ferry. Here they were met at noon on the 23rd by the *1st Light Infantry* and the *27th Regiment* which had been sent to aid the column.

The Hessians had suffered almost 500 casualties in their unsuccessful assault on Fort Mercer. One report cited 377 killed and wounded, and at least 120 captured or missing.

Incredibly, the American losses amounted to only 14 killed and 23 wounded. The engagement (also known as the Battle of Red Bank) was one of the most one sided of the war, and was also the only clear cut American success during the entire Philadelphia campaign. The victory was due partly to the Greene's brave defense, but was due more to Howe's failure to send more troops on the expedition, and to Von Donop's haste in ordering the assault before scouting the fort's defenses fully. In addition, the Hessians were not able to mount the fort's main parapet because they had not been supplied with scaling ladders.

In coordination with Von Donop's attack on Fort Mercer, Howe planned a combined arms assault on Fort Mifflin. He felt that a naval attack by several men-at-war, supported by the land batteries of Province and Carpenter's Islands, would weaken Fort Mifflin enough to enable a force of 200 grenadiers to cross to the fort in small boats and capture it. Howe also hoped that this attack would distract the attention of the American river fleet, and so aid Von Donop's assault.

Howe's plan got off to a bad start when his nautical charts were found to give inaccurate depths for the critical channel between Hog Island and the Pennsylvania shore. This meant that his armed galley, the *Vigilant*, would not be able to move north and lend its weight to the bombardment of the fort. Even more problematical was the north wind that blew on the 22nd, the day before the planned attack. The contrary wind made it most difficult for the British warships to head northeast to reach their assigned pre-attack positions. The only way they could proceed was to tack back and forth, a procedure that proved very difficult because of the Delaware's tide and narrow channel. It was not long before the 50 gun warship *Iris* and the galley *Cornwallis* ran aground. In spite of this difficulty, the British fleet continued to press forward when guns were heard from Fort Mercer, a sign that Von Donop had attacked a day early, without waiting for his naval support. As they pushed forward, the 18 gun sloop *Merlin* ran aground. Then the 64 gun *Augusta*, the largest boat in the squadron, got stuck in the mud when the tide went out.

American Commodore Hazelwood was delighted by the British difficulties, and at daybreak on the 23rd sent 12 galleys and two floating batteries against the stranded enemy boats. At about 1100 the Americans succeeded at setting the *Augusta* afire. The British quickly evacuated their warship, but lost over 60 men drowned in the process. The mighty boat blew up at 1400. Meanwhile the British deliberately set the *Merlin* afire for fear that she would be captured. The sloop blew up at 1430. Commander Hazelwood then tried to destroy the remaining British ships by sending fire rafts against them, but the English sailors succeeded at pushing them aside. Howe at last decided to withdraw his fleet below Hog Island before any more boats were lost.

Despite the two defeats at Forts Mercer and Mifflin, Howe had no choice but to continue his operation to clear the river.Washington's army at Whitpain was successfully preventing the British foraging parties from gathering needed foodstuffs and available resources in Philadelphia were rapidly being drained. Heavy guards were needed to bring supplies overland from Chester, and only a fraction of what was needed could be brought upriver by rafts that hugged the Pennsylvania shore. Howe directed his batteries facing Fort Mifflin to pound the enemy for several days straight, and they did so until a heavy rain began on the 26th. The storm did not let up for five days, and by the 28th both Fort Mifflin and British shore batteries were largely under water.

Because of the failure of Von Donop's advance against Fort Mercer from Cooper's Ferry, Howe decided to retake Billingsport for use as a more effective base in New Jersey. A force of 200 marines easily recaptured Billingsport, and were soon joined by a garrison force from the *7th Regiment*. The reoccupied position guaranteed additional security to the British fleet as its boats passed the crippled chevaux de frise nearby.

Washington was concerned by the British occupation of Billingsport and directed Brigadier General James Varnum to proceed to Woodbury with his entire brigade (two of his regiments were at Fort Mercer). Varnum proceeded as ordered and at once began erecting a battery on the river about

The British fleet suffered a heavy loss when the 64-gun warship **Augusta** *ran aground near Fort Mifflin on 22 September 1777 and was burned by the Americans the next day.*

a mile north of Billingsport in order to dispute the passage of any more British warships upstream. Varnum had a 12-pounder in place on 5 November, but had difficulty with his other two pieces. He had little ammunition for his captured British 24-pounder, and his 18-pounder was delayed by an accident on the road.

Howe was by now becoming increasingly frustrated with his inability to drive the Americans away from the river. His troops in Philadelphia were becoming disheartened by a lack of supplies and the psychological pressure of being "besieged" in the city. In addition, the river attacks were draining

137

off a large number of troops from the force that had so successfully beat Washington in every engagement. Indeed, the success of the American river defense to this point was most remarkable, especially in view of the small number of troops involved. In addition, the American effort was greatly hampered by a lack of unified command over forces that included militia in two states (New Jersey and Pennsylvania), detachments from Washington's army north of Philadelphia, and the various forces of the river fleet. Their greatest asset was the aggressiveness of Commander Hazelwood and the capabilities of his war galleys.

At a meeting on 5 November Howe was convinced by his chief engineer, Captain Montresor, to concentrate his efforts on Fort Mifflin instead of frittering away his energy on multiple targets as he had been doing. Montresor's plan called for a combined land and naval bombardment that would soften up the fort for an assault by a force of 300 *Grenadiers of the Guards*. The assaulting troops would be equipped with scaling ladders, fascines, and four 20 foot long bridges. To enable Admiral Howe's warships to join the attack with lessened danger of running aground, the assault would be scheduled soon after 9 November, when there would be higher tides than normal because of a full moon.

Howe's greatest reservation about Montresor's plan was a concern for the safety of his land batteries facing Fort Mifflin. Increased American militia activity "from the direction of Darby" made him fear for an enemy attack from that quarter. As a precaution, he posted the *27th* and *28th Regiments* facing seaward behind the batteries on Province and Carpenter's Islands. Little did he know that Washington was making no plans for such an attack. The American commander had simply ordered his militia to "harass the parties of the enemy on Province Island in such a manner as to produce a Great diversion in favor of Fort Mifflin." Washington did have indications that the British were planning some new operation along the river, and he so warned Varnum. However, his generals on 7 November agreed unanimously that the army should make no attack on the British lines at Philadelphia in the event that the enemy should attack the river forts again.

Montresor's plan went into action on 8 November, when the British naval squadron passed the chevaux de frise at Billingsport and moved cautiously out of range of Captain Lee's nearby battery. The bombardment of Fort Mifflin was scheduled to begin the next day, but Montresor requested that it be delayed until he finished reinforcing the middle battery facing the fort with six 24-pounder guns. Two days of rain delayed the completion of the project until the morning of the 10th, when all 14 heavy guns in Montresor's batteries began a steady pounding of Fort Mifflin, under orders to fire only 80 rounds per gun per day until the fort was sufficiently reduced.

The British artillery bombardment of Fort Mifflin was an uneven contest from the start. The Americans had only four cannons facing the Pennsylvania shore, and the two heaviest were put out of action in the first minutes of the fight. The first British shot broke off the muzzle of one American 18-pounder, and another early shot carried off the trunions of another 18-pounder. This left only two 4-pounders functioning on this side of the fort.The American defenses received a terrible pounding the rest of the day, and by the end of the 11th, most of its ramparts on the Pennsylvania side were smashed beyond repair. In addition, the two senior American officers fell casualty when Captain Treat of the artillery was killed and Lieutenant Colonel Smith was badly wounded in the hip.

Even though the fort was in ruins, its defenders continued to hold on. To their misfortune, the fort had most of its guns uselessly trained on the Delaware, and its poor design left it particularly vulnerable to raking fire from the Pennsylvania shore. By the end of the 10th, only one gun, a 32-pounder, was available and in position to reach the British land batteries. The Americans, however, had no ammunition for it, and had to resort to the dangerous expedient of collecting unexploded British 32-pounder shells to fire back at the enemy. Most of the available short supply of gunpowder was saved for use by the river batteries in case the British attempted an amphibious attack from that quarter.

As the British bombardment entered its third day on 12 November, the fort's defenders were exhorted to hold on "to the last extremity." Bold words, however, were of little consolation to the weary survivors of the 300 man garrison. With some difficulty, Major Simeon Thayer managed to bring 100 fresh replacements into the fort on the night of 12-13 November. These troops set about strengthening what defenses they could; three of the fort's four block houses had been destroyed and most of its ramparts were in ruins. Despite the continuance of the British bombardment, the rest of the fort's original garrison was relieved on the night of 14-15 November by about 400 troops from Varnum's command in New Jersey (4th and 8th Connecticut plus an artillery battery). The new garrison was under the command of Major Simeon Thayer, assisted by Major Fleury, the only holdover from the fort's original garrison.

The struggle for Fort Mifflin was now reaching epic proportions. On the 14th, the British attempted to move two floating batteries closer to the fort, but they were driven back by a repositioned battery of two guns set up by Major Fleury. When the garrison at Fort Mercer attempted to fire one of their 18-pounders in support of their companion fort, it burst and caused nine casualties. (A section of the exploded tube, which had originally been part of the armament of the British ship *Augusta*, is now preserved at the Gloucester County Historical Society Museum in Woodbury. The same museum also has a section of the chevaux de frise from the American river defenses.)

The British played their trump card early on 15 November, when they finally had a 16-gun floating battery, a former troop transport named the *Vigilant*, ready and in position to be moved against Fort Mifflin. Supported by the sloop *Fury*, the *Vigilant* easily advanced to within 40 yards of the American defenses. Its blasts literally blew the remains of the fort to pieces. "The buildings of every kind were hanging in broken fragments... The Blockhouse flew about in splinters." Major

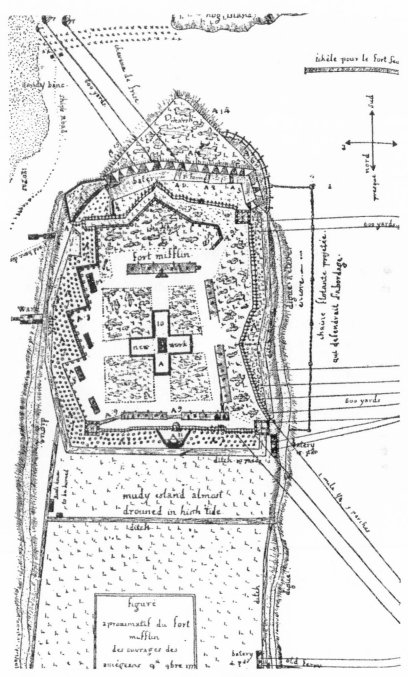

The British bombardment of Fort Mifflin.

141

Fleury was knocked senseless by a flying timber, and Major Varnum fell wounded in the arm and leg by grapeshot. At the same time the British advanced six warships from Billingsport to assist in the attack and suppress any fire from Fort Mercer. They encountered a flotilla of 40 assorted American boats near Billingsport and entered a spirited contest that would involve 350 cannons for over two hours.

At the height of the battle, Commodore Hazelwood sent four of his galleys to face the *Viligant*. They achieved some hits, but only managed to force her to shift to a new position less than 100 yards southwest of the forts. From there two marksmen in her topmasts succeeded at felling a number of the fort's defenders with musket shots and hand grenades. By 1300 only two guns of the battered fort remained in use. Nevertheless, its bold garrison held on until dark, when its flag was still seen flying from "an old ship's mast, having shrouds to the ground, and the round top still remaining."

The fort's defenders paid a terrible price for their heroic fight on the 15th, as they lost 250 casualties and expended almost all their ammunition. The survivors knew well that they would be unable to withstand the British amphibious assault that was certain to follow the next day. For this reason Major Thayer secured permission from General Varnum to evacuate the ruined fort. All but 40 of the surviving garrison were sent to New Jersey at about 1900. The last defenders loaded about ten cannons onto a scow destined for Fort Mercer, only to see it sunk en route by the continuing enemy fire. At about 0200 on 16 November, Major Thayer set fire to what remained of the fort and rowed with his last squadron to New Jersey. He deliberately left the garrison flag still flying, a symbol that the fort never surrendered. It was taken down by a British landing party at 0730, and Union Jack was raised in its stead about 0900.

The capture of Fort Mifflin still did not guarantee Howe control of the Delaware, which was contested by Fort Mercer, the battery above Billingsport, and Hazelwood's small fleet. The Americans promptly began strengthening their defenses, and Washington sent Generals St. Clair, Knox and DeKalb to evaluate the situation. The three generals were conferring at Fort Mercer on 18 November when they received the distressing news that the British had landed a strong column at Billingsport. The force consisted of about 3,000 fresh troops from New York City under the command of Major General Thomas Wilson. The next day they were joined by another 3,000 men from Howe's army, under Cornwallis. On the 18th Howe had also sent another column across the Delaware, dispatching the *42nd Regiment* to Cooper's Ferry.

It was clear to all the generals at the conference that Howe was mounting his most serious threat yet to Fort Mercer. They appealed to Washington for aid, and the general responded at once by sending Huntington's 1,200 man brigade to New Jersey on the 19th, followed by Greene's entire division the next day and Morgan's riflemen on the 21st. These reinforcements, combined with Varnum's Brigade already stationed in New Jersey, would place over 5,000 troops at Fort Mercer, not including militia.

Washington's effort was a classic case of sending too little too late. The British column at Billingsport, commanded by Cornwallis, began moving north on the 19th, and forced the Americans to abandon their river battery near the mouth of Mantua Creek. A false report that the British had crossed the creek in force so alarmed Colonel Greene, the commander at Fort Mercer, that he began preparing to evacuate his post. When General Varnum went to the fort at 1700 to discuss the situation, he was alarmed to find that Greene had ordered gunpowder dumped all over in preparation to blow it up. In spite of the dangerousness of the situation, Varnum persuaded the fort's garrison to hold on for reinforcements. When none appeared, and the approach of Cornwallis' advance parties was confirmed, Greene evacuated his troops and stores on the morning of 21 November. The column marched to Haddonfield, leaving behind a rear guard of about 50 men to see to the destruction of the fort. Fort Mercer, scene of the great American victory exactly a month earlier, was blown to pieces at about 0600 on 21 November.

Commodore Hazelwood knew all too well that abandonment of Fort Mercer meant great danger to his fleet, most of which was stationed between there and the river battery north of Billingsport. When Greene first announced the pending evacuation on the evening of 19 November, Hazelwood summoned his captains and directed them to proceed to Cooper's Ferry as best they could; if they were hindered by the enemy or unfavorable tides or winds, they should burn their boats. The fleet's 13 surviving war galleys, being powered by oars, left for Cooper's Ferry at 0300 on the 20th and had no difficulty reaching their destination. The sailing vessels, on the other hand, experienced great difficulty trying to escape. The wind was so strong on the 20th that none could move. They were able to get underway early the next morning soon after the fort blew up, but by then the British warships and land batteries were waiting for them. The vessels that managed to get by the British guns were becalmed when they tried to pass up the river's western channel near League Island. At least 17 boats were set afire by their crews in a magnificent blaze that alarmed the residents of Philadelphia, two miles distant. The valiant American river defense fleet was no more.

Cornwallis was certainly pleased to achieve his objective without a fight. He had encamped at Woodbury on 20 November, and early on the 21st sent his light infantry to reconnoiter the way to Fort Mercer. They had not gone far when they heard the explosion of the fort being blown up. He next spent two days destroying the American defenses at Red Bank, and then headed north for Cooper's Ferry. General Greene, who was assigned command of the 7,000 man force being assembled near Mount Holly, attempted to cut the British off at Gloucester, where a spirited skirmish was fought on the evening of 24 November. Greene declined to pursue the engagement the next morning because of the roughness of the terrain and the presence of a number of British ships, which guarded Cornwallis' crossing that day to Gloucester Point, Pennsylvania.

The lengthy fight for the Delaware was now a total British victory. On the 23rd a few light boats sailed over the long chain that had been stretched across the river near Fort Mifflin. When the chain was cut three days later, Admiral Howe and 62 ships sailed triumphantly up to the Philadelphia docks, bringing much needed supplies and confidence to the British troops there. The river campaign drew then to a quiet close when Howe withdrew a garrison he had left at Billingsport, and Greene marched his command to Burlington in order to cross over to Bristol. Not long afterwards Howe had his troops level the works they had constructed on Carpenter's and Province Islands, for fear the Americans might use them at some future point.

The Hessians

King George's large scale use of German mercenaries in the Revolution was considered by no means unusual at the time. Mercenaries had regularly been employed in Europe for hundreds of years. German troops were particularly respected because of their training in tactics developed by Frederick the Great. They were also readily available because of the number of small German principates, the financial need of their rulers and the Hanoverian connections of the English royal house. It should be noted that not all the troops obtained from the German states came from Hesse. The first large contingent actually came from Brunswick, and several other principalities also furnished troops (see accompanying chart). These troops were generically called Hessians, a term that has persisted to this day, because that is where about two-thirds of them originated. In addition, all three of the top German mercenary generals were Hessian (Von Heister, Von Knyphausen, and Von Lossberg), while a fourth, Riedesell (who led Burgoyne's German troops in the Saratoga campaign), was originally a Hessian but served in America with the Brunswickers.

The sole reason for contracting mercenary troops to serve in America was King George's lack of troops in 1775. At the outbreak of the Revolution, only about 20,000 soldiers were available to defend the entire British empire. In times of stress, the king had usually recruited extra soldiers from the poor farms of Ireland, but in 1775 times were more prosperous and recruits were difficult to obtain. Poor pay, worse living conditions, and harsh discipline made it quite difficult to obtain recruits in England, especially when the army had to compete with the navy's great needs of manpower. The king's recruiters soon became so desperate that they readily took debtors and prisoners in jail as well as paupers and vagrants. When these lower elements of society were not able to satisfy the army's needs, the king had no choice but to turn to the hiring of mercenaries, the greatest pool for which was Germany. Curiously, Charles Carroll of Maryland and a few other American leaders for a time advocated the hiring of mercenaries from Europe, but the proposal was dropped, primarily because Congress did not have the money needed to purchase them.

Lord North and his cabinet were painfully aware in 1775 that they would need to hire foreign troops to help put down the American rebellion, and they were prepared to pay the necessary costs. Initial hopes were to obtain 20,000 troops from Russia, but necessary arrangements could not be made. Though Catherine the Great had sufficient troops available, she held them back in hope that the conflict in

America might be settled peaceably. At length five battalions with 2,365 men were recruited from Hanoverian lands belonging to George III. These were sent to Gibraltar and Minorca, so freeing the English garrisons there for duty elsewhere.

It was not long before the Prince of Hesse-Cassel (a nephew of King George) offered a regiment to his uncle, as did the Prince of Waldeck. Other negotiations were entered, some successful and some not, with the rulers of Brunswick-Luneburg, Anspach-Bayreuth, Anhalt-Zerbst, Bavaria and Wurtemberg. The first treaty to obtain German mercenaries was made with the Duke of Brunswick on January 1776. Its terms will be explained in detail because they were typical of those arranged with other German states. The Duke was to provide King George with 3,964 infantry and 336 unmounted dragoons, all uniformed and equipped. The troops were to be paid by the king at the same rate as he paid his own troops; pay was not to be routed through the duke for fear he would keep some for himself. Wounded and sick would be cared for in British hospitals at the king's expense. Each year the duke would provide uniformed and trained replacements for any troops who were lost in combat, died of disease or deserted. However, if any unit was totally lost due to epidemic, combat or disaster at sea, the king would bear the cost of recruiting replacements. The duke would appoint officers for his units. As a fee for supplying the troops, the duke would receive 7 pounds, 4 shillings, and 4 1/2 pence per day per man, as well as an annual payment of 11,517 pounds, 17 shillings, 1 1/2 pence, which would be double for two years after the troops returned to Europe. In addition, the duke would be paid a fee for each man killed, wounded or maimed. Some other German princes held out for even more favorable rates of payment. It is necessary to note that the British War Office made payments for the mercenaries "off the books" so as to avoid interference on the issue from Parliament, which was supposed to approve all expenditures.

About 20,000 German troops were in service in America in 1776. This number remained fairly constant through each year of the war, and constituted about half of the British force in the Colonies. Altogether almost 30,000 Germans served here, as shown on the chart below. Of this number, only about 60 percent returned home. About 5,000 deserted and melted into the growing American population. Another 7,754 died in service, including two colonels—Johann Gottliebb Rall, who was mortally wounded at Trenton on 26 December 1776, and Carl von Donop, who was mortally wounded at Fort Mercer during the Philadelphia campaign.

At the beginning of the war, the Hessian troops enjoyed great respect from the British and awe from the Americans because of their discipline and the renown of Frederick the Great. It was not long before they gained a reputation for cruelty, and their extensive plundering during the Philadelphia campaign is noted in the text. After their defeats at Trenton, Bennington, and Red Bank, the Hessians were no longer dreaded as before. Their high rate of desertion also helped decrease their reputation. It should also be noted that the Hessians never won a battle in which they fought alone against the American troops. Nor did they learn any lessons from their tour of duty in America, and most returned to Europe still devoted to the tactics of Frederick the Great.

German Troops in British Service in America

Brunswick	5,723
Hesse-Cassel	16,992
Hesse-Hanau	2,422
Anspach-Beyreuth	2,353
Waldeck	1,225
Anhalt-Zerbst	1,160
Total	**29,875**

The Hessian units regularly carried the name of their commander, or occasionally the name of the prince of their native state; the principal exception was the *Leib* (*"Bodyguard"*) *Regiment*. The Hesse-Cassel foot regiments were organized into four brigades, and their grenadier battalions were formed into a bri-gade. Each Hesse battalion had two light cannons as integral support, an effective structure that impressed General Carleton so much that in 1782 he ordered all British battalions to be similarly supported. There were also three separate companies of Hesse artillery, numbering a total of 588 men. The most effective Hessian troops were the jägers (also known as chasseurs), light troops armed with rifles who were specifically adept at marksmanship and irregular service. They saw extensive service on foraging details and as scouts and flank guards.

All branches of Hessian troops—infantry, grenadiers, artillery, jägers and dragoons—had distinctive uniforms and weapons. All except the jägers (who wore green) had a medium blue coat. The color of the uniforms' facings and trim varied by unit. Infantry had tri-colored hats, the grenadiers wore high mitre-shaped caps, the dragoons wore high rimless hats with feathers, and jägers had cocked hats. The infantry carried muskets or a lighter weapon called a fusil. Dragoons were issued short carbines, and jägers were equipped with long rifles and bayonets. All troops were expected to keep their hair well greased with lard and covered with white powder, as was the custom also with the British troops.

CHAPTER VIII

Whitemarsh

*T*he village of Germantown was indeed a dismal sight the day after the battle of 4 October. The American dead, many stripped of their weapons and clothes, lay where they fell, and many of the town's houses had been turned into hospitals, each with a small pile of amputated limbs near the back door. The British troops carefully buried their own dead, but forced the local citizenry to clear the streets and bury the Colonial dead in unmarked graves. The 400 American prisoners were all transferred to downtown Philadelphia, where the officers were imprisoned in the upper floor of the state house and those of lesser rank were thrown into the dirty Walnut House Gaol. Washington's men held only one British prisoner of note, a small dog that had followed the army during its retreat. When some soldiers noted General Howe's name on the dog's collar, they took the dog to Washington, and he had it returned to Howe with his compliments.

On the day after the battle, Howe transferred his headquarters from Trenton to the David Dreshler House (5442 Germantown Avenue) in order to keep in closer contact with his troops, who were understandably jumpy about another American surprise attack. British patrols were in daily contact with the Colonial militia, and false alarms hurried several brigades to form up early on 6 October and again on the 11th. To prevent further such occurrences, Howe had to order that no troops should be formed without the permission of himself or another general.

When Washington showed no inclination to move his command back towards Philadelphia, Howe turned his primary attention towards opening the Delaware for his fleet (see Chapter 7). Meanwhile, friction began to mount between the British troops and the citizens of Germantown. The bored English and Hessian soldiers readily turned to plundering and even rape and murder. Court-martials were soon held daily to enforce rigid discipline, and punishments of several hundred lashes were not uncommon, not to mention more than a few executions. This deteriorating situation led Howe to order his troops to withdraw to Philadelphia on 18 October, where they could be better housed and hopefully better supplied.

Upon returning to Philadelphia, Howe tended to the completion of a defensive line of works that had been started north of the city in late September. The position, laid out by Captain John Montresor, stretched in a two and one-half mile crescent from the Delaware to the Schuylkill. It began near modern Spring Garden Street at the Delaware and ran northwest to Redoubt No. 1, located east of the intersection of Frankfort Road and Germantown Road. From there the line ran west and slightly south to Redoubt Number 9, located below the southern end of Fairmount Park, before terminating at Redoubt Number 10 on Lemon Hill near the Upper Ferry on the Schuylkill. Specific units were assigned to man each redoubt, and their men began constructing huts near their new posts. For added security, two redoubts were constructed about one-eighth of a mile in advance of the main line to watch the Wissahickon and Germantown Roads.

Quite understandably, Washington's army was in no condition to undertake a new offensive in the days immediately following their defeat at Germantown. After the battle, the Americans had retreated all the way to Pennypacker's Mills on Perkiomen Creek. Washington wisely directed them to cross to the west side of the creek and camp at Pawling's Mill in order to have a better defense should the British press their pursuit. When the enemy failed to appear, patrols were sent towards Germantown to monitor their movements. Additional patrols were sent out for 10 miles in all directions "to stop all soldiers and turn them back to the army" because so many men scattered over the countryside.

On the day after the battle Washington issued an order to thank the troops "for the spirit and bravery shown in driving the enemy." He expressed regret that the fog and other causes had hindered their operation and brought on a yet unexplained general retreat. In spite of their defeat, he trusted that his troops, "inspired by the cause of freedom," would be more successful in their next battle, since they had demonstrated that "the enemy are not proof against a vigorous attack." Washington, as usual, laid no blame on specific generals for their shortcomings, even though he was disappointed with Wayne's unauthorized retreat and called Stephen a "drunken rascal." He did, though, express concern "that the troops may be convinced of the necessity of retreating and rallying briskly, and therefore a particular retreat is not to be considered general, without the order to such."

Most of the troops were not particularly disheartened by their defeat at Germantown which many believed to be a near victory. A significant exception was Forman's recently arrived brigade of New Jersey militia, who openly expressed discontent and so secured permission to go home. Most of the Pennsylvania militia, particularly that from Bucks County, proved to be much more reliable and stayed on to protect their homes. Forman's departure and the casualties at Germantown were largely balanced by the approach of General Varnum's Brigade of 1,200 Continentals, which was ordered to cross the Delaware at Coryell's Ferry on 6 October on its march en route from Putnum's command in the Hudson Highlands.

After resting and regrouping his men for three days, Washington ordered his command to recross Perkiomen Creek at 0800 on 8 October and head east towards Kulpsville. After a march of less than 10 miles, the army stopped to encamp on the farm of Frederick Wampole in Towamencin Township. Washington's purpose in making this march is not clear today; he may have intended to move against Philadelphia from the north, or to be in a better position to defend Allentown and Bethlehem should the enemy move in that direction.

Washington kept his army at the Towamencin camp for a week, gathering supplies and waiting to see if Howe might make a move to the north. When no action occurred in this front, he turned his attention to holding the Delaware river forts in an effort to keep Howe penned up in Philadelphia (see Chapter 7). Washington also had to tend to three important courts-of-inquiry that were held beginning 10 October. Major General John Sullivan was under criticism for his conduct at Long Island and Brandywine, but was honorably acquitted by a unanimous vote. Brigadier General Anthony Wayne was likewise cleared of charges that he "had timely notice of the enemy's attention to attack but neglected making a disposition until it was too late" at Paoli. The third case involved General Maxwell, who was cleared of charges of drinking too much. The army was lucky not to lose any of these three officers, since there was already a shortage of generals, a problem deepened by the death of Brigadier General Francis Nash on 8 October at Towamencin from the wounds he had received at Germantown.

On 16 October Washington decided to begin moving his troops closer to Philadelphia in order to put more pressure on the enemy and to distract their attention from the Delaware River forts. The American army took two days to march a few miles south to Methacton Hill, near Worcester, where it had encamped before beginning its march to battle at Germantown 13 days earlier. At 0400 on the 17th Washington sent Wayne with three regiments (13th Pennsylvania, 2nd and 5th Virginia) in a probing expedition to Whitemarsh, 10 miles from British lines at Germantown. Howe learned of Wayne's advance at 1000 and promptly dispatched two brigades under Grey and Grant on separate routes to intercept the American columns. Howe's troops were gravely disappointed when they reached Whitemarsh and found that Wayne had already withdrawn. Even so, the boldness of Wayne's advance may have encouraged Howe to withdraw his command from

Germantown to Philadelphia two days later. The primary motive for Howe's withdrawal, however, was a need to contract his lines in order to have more troops available to open up the Delaware.

Washington was pleased to learn of Howe's withdrawal, but was wary of a possible trap and chose not to push his command forward immediately. When a reconnaissance by a cavalry troop confirmed the British departure, Washington moved his command another 5 miles closer to Philadelphia and on 20 October encamped near Ambler in Whitpain Township, just 15 miles from the occupied capital. The army remained here for two weeks as the full attention of both sides focused on the fight for the Delaware. The only significant movement was a diversion that Sullivan, Greene and McDougal conducted when they marched past Germantown on the 20th and 21st. The British, however, paid no attention to this probe, and the three American columns returned to their camps at Whitpain.

Howe's continued inactivity north of Philadelphia enabled Washington to detach Varnum's Brigade on 29 October and send it to New Jersey to support the Delaware defenses from that quarter. On the same day, Washington summoned his commanders to a council of war to discuss what course of action the army should pursue. Washington framed nine queries for consideration, and listened carefully to what was said without expressing his own opinions, which might have affected the course of discussion. The council was unanimous in advising against an all-out attack on Philadelphia. Howe was known to have at least 10,000 men behind prepared defenses, while the Colonial army consisted of only 8,313 Continentals and 2,717 militia, with 1,886 of the latter due to go home soon. They recommended the best course of action would be to encamp on some hills east of Whitemarsh, and then send all the troops that could be spared to reinforce the forts along the Delaware. No agreement could be reached on the best way to keep Howe from gathering supplies from the local countryside. Nor did the generals decide when and where the army should go into winter quarters.

Washington's Headquarters at Whitemarsh from 2 November to 11 December 1777.

Washington accepted the recommendation of his council of war and moved the army's camp to Whitemarsh on 2 November. This encampment, located just 13 miles from Philadelphia, was soon strongly defended by redoubts and connecting works erected on three principal hills, Militia Hill on the southwest, Fort Hill in the center, and Camp Hill, the highest of the three eminences, to the northeast. The army's main preoccupation at Whitemarsh was not to be the enemy, who were largely inactive on this front while focusing their attention on the Delaware forts. Instead, Washington was concerned largely with the basic task of securing sufficient food and supplies. About one-quarter of his men were barefoot, and there was a scarcity of blankets and heavy clothing as winter was fast approaching. Morale was so low because of food and equipment shortages that desertion became an even greater problem. Washington already on 24 October had felt the need to offer a pardon to all deserters who would return to their units by 1 January. Washington also had to see to the completion of General Stephen's court of inquiry, which had

Major General Horatio Gates, the victor at Saratoga, was for a time a serious rival to Washington in popularity.

been postponed at Whitemarsh on 26 October. The general was found guilty of drunkenness at Germantown, and elsewhere, and Washington on 20 November approved the court's recommendation to dismiss him from the service.

Washington's inactivity and the loss of the Delaware forts brought increasing criticism from Congress in late November. The exasperated general wrote back that he was amazed that the army "keeps the field at all this season of the year" because of the chronic supply shortage. He also complained that Gates was inordinately slow in forwarding him troops after Burgoyne's surrender at Saratoga on 17 October. Washington had willingly stripped his own army to reinforce Gates earlier in the year, but that general, partly out of jealously, was tardy at sending Washington troops he so badly needed. The only men that reached Washington in November were Colonel Dan Morgan's riflemen, who arrived at Whitemarsh on the 18th. Morgan had pushed to be released from the northern army because of a severe personality conflict with Gates, and his return was greatly appreciated. Three additional brigades from Gate's army (Glover's, Paterson's and Poor's) were en route in New Jersey.

Howe's headquarters in Philadelphia was established in a house belonging to the American general John Cadwalader.

Pressure from Congress nevertheless compelled Washington to convene a council of war on 24 November to consider the feasibility of an attack on Philadelphia. The proposal was not received favorably by the army's generals, who voted against an attack eleven to four. Even so, Washington the next day rode down the west side of the Schuylkill to inspect the British lines for himself. He was dismayed to find "their works much stronger than I had reason to expect from the accounts I received." An attack was clearly unfeasible, though the army was able to reinforce its skirmishers posted in front of Howe's position. They soon annoyed the British so much that the enemy burned at least 20 houses outside their lines that were suspected of harboring American troops.

The onset of colder weather now made it necessary for Washington to determine a location for the army's winter camp. On 31 November he called a council of war to consider three proposals—a movement south to Wilmington, a withdrawal west to Reading and Lancaster, and the maintenance

Lydia Darragh's house was used for meetings by British officers.
On 2 December 1777 Lydia overheard discussion of a march against
Washington's army encamped at Whitemarsh. She bravely walked
many miles through snow to deliver a warning.

of a line close to Philadelphia between the Schuylkill and the Delaware. There was little support for the Philadelphia line and not much more for a camp at Wilmington. There was more support for the Reading-Lancaster line, but Washington did not like it, and adjourned the council before a final decision could be made.

Washington did not reconvene the council of war on 1 December because more pressing matters demanded his attention. General Armstrong, commanding some of the militia near Philadelphia, reported that "every intelligence agrees that General Howe now, no doubt with his whole force, is immediately to take the field in quest of this army." Armstrong's message was confirmed by Washington's chief spy in the city, Major John Clark, Jr., who reported that the enemy was "in readiness to march...either to surprise your army or to prevent an attack on them."

The Saga of Lydia Darragh

One of the lesser known heroines of the war was Lydia Darragh, a Quaker housewife who risked her life to tell General Washington of Howe's plans to conduct a surprise attack on the American camp at Whitemarsh on 5 December 1777. The story that follows was never told by Lydia herself, but was attested by her daughter, Ann, who may have embellished it. Nevertheless, the essentials of the account are authenticated by Elias Boudinot, one of Philadelphia's leading citizens and the president of the Continental Congress at the time.

Lydia was a middle-aged housewife who lived at Second and Dock Streets in Philadelphia (now 177 South 2nd St.). Her house was not far from General John Cadwallader's house, which was occupied by General Howe as his headquarters when he captured the Colonial capital. Soon afterwards Captain John Andre of Howe's staff came to Lydia with an order to move out of the house so that British officers could occupy it. Lydia objected strongly because she had two young children at home and had no place to go (her two youngest children had been sent to relatives in Frankford, and her oldest son was an ensign in the 2nd Pennsylvania Regiment with Washington's army). She boldly went to Howe's headquarters to plead her case. By chance, the officer she met first happened to be a second cousin of hers from Ireland. Because of this connection, General Howe permitted her to remain in her house, provided that she made one room available for officer's meetings.

By chance, Lydia's home was selected for the 2 December meeting at which Howe finalized his plans to march against Washington's camps at Whitemarsh on 4/5 December. The conference ran until late at night, and Lydia, unable to sleep, bravely slipped into a linen closet abutting the meeting room in order to hear what they were talking about. She was astonished to hear plans discussed to send 10,000 British troops against Washington just two days later. Excitedly she sneaked back out of the closet and went back to bed, and pretended to be asleep when Captain Andre knocked on her door to let her know the meeting was over.

Mrs. Darragh was up all night trying to think up a way to get her important news to General Washington. At length she decided to go to her cousin at Howe's headquarters and request a pass to go and get some flour at a mill in Frankford. The cousin, a Captain Bar-

Washington held his troops on the alert for three days, and on 4 December received positive information through Lydia Darragh (see sidebar) that the enemy would march that night. In order to receive the enemy, Washington formed his troops

rington, readily granted her plea, and Lydia set out on her mission early on the morning of 4 December. Carrying an empty flour sack to reinforce her ruse, she used her pass to get through British lines and then trudged through the snow the five miles to Frankford. From Frankford she turned east on Nicetown Road, heading for Rising Sun Tavern on the Germantown Road, over two miles distant. Just before she reached Rising Sun Lane, she happened to run into Lieutenant Colonel Thomas Craig of the Pennsylvania militia, who knew her son Charles. She shared her information with Craig, who promised to carry it personally to General Washington. After getting something to eat from a Quaker woman who lived nearby, Lydia began the long walk back to Philadelphia along the route on which she had come.

Elias Boudinot tells a different version of the last stage of the story. He says that he was dining at a "small post at the Rising Sun" when "a little, poor looking insignificant old woman came in and solicited leave to go to the country to buy some flour." The woman gave him a "dirty old notebook" that had in one of its pockets a rolled up piece of paper with a message that Howe was going to march the next morning with 5,000 men, 13 pieces of can-

non, baggage wagons, and 11 boats on wheels. Boudinot concludes his account, "on comparing this with other information, I found it true and immediately rode post to headquarters." Since Boudinot's account appears in his private journals, it probably should be preferred to Ann Darragh's later and more anecdotal version of the story, which nevertheless agrees in many details with Boudinot's narrative.

It is interesting to note that Ann Darragh's account concludes with an illuminating postscript. General Howe was greatly annoyed that his plans had apparently been leaked to the enemy, and after his return from Whitemarsh had several suspects brought in for questioning. During this investigation, Captain Andre came to Lydia's home on 9 December and asked her if anyone in the house had been awake during the meeting held on the night on 2 December. She nervously replied that everyone had been asleep, and Andre believed her. Before he left he noted that "one thing is certain the enemy had notice of our coming, were prepared for us, and we marched back like a parcel of fools. The walls must have ears."

Lydia and the rest of her family were later "read out" of the Philadelphia Friends Meeting for their active support of the Colonial cause.

into two wings. Greene was assigned the left wing on Camp Hill, and Sullivan was given command of the right wing, stationed on the Fort and Militia Hills. Washington placed the Maryland militia and Morgan's riflemen on Greene's left, and the Pennsylvania militia was stationed on Sullivan's right. Stirling was directed to form a secondary defensive line behind Greene and Sullivan.

The American reports were indeed accurate. Howe had heard through his own spies that Washington was planning to move to a new camp, and he decided to move against the enemy in hope of catching the Americans out in the open away from their defenses at Whitemarsh. His troops left their camps in Philadelphia at midnight on 4/5 December, marching in two columns. Cornwallis led the vanguard (right column) up the Germantown Road, a force that comprised the light infantry, jägers, *Hessian* and *British Grenadiers, 4th British Brigade, 16th Dragoons* and four pieces of artillery. The main body (left column) was commanded by Knyphausen and consisted of Von Donop's and Von Wurmb's Hessians, *British Guards,* two and one-half brigades of British infantry, *17th Dragoons, Queen's Rangers,* and four cannons. Altogether Howe's advancing force consisted of over 10,000 men. General Leslie was left to hold Philadelphia with a reinforced brigade consisting of *Von Woellwarth's Brigade,* the *Mirbach Regiment, 63rd British Regiments* and a few dragoons and other troops.

Cornwallis' advance passed silently through Germantown without being detected, but at about 0300 ran into an American patrol under Captain Allen McLane stationed at the bridge over Three Mile Run in Beggarstown (Mount Airy). McLane sent a messenger to alert the main American camp at Whitemarsh. When the alarm gun was sounded, the troops grabbed their arms and rushed to their assigned positions. The British would achieve no surprise attack this day.

Lieutenant Colonel Robert Abercrombie of the British light infantry, who led Cornwallis' advance, easily pushed aside McLane's small command and marched on to Chestnut Hill, which he reached at dawn. While the troops halted for breakfast, he and Cornwallis rode forward to survey the American position. They were dismayed to see enemy troops swarming into position along the North Wales Road (Bethlehem Pike), and were apprehensive of the large number of campfires blazing on the hillsides. Washington had directed his men to double their campfires in order to deceive the enemy, and was successful. Cornwallis decided to wait for Knyphausen to come up, and the British surrendered their initiative.

Washington was surprised to see Cornwallis halt his advance and at mid-morning decided to send a probe forward to determine the size and intent of the enemy column. The task was assigned to General James Irvine, who led a battalion of about 600 Pennsylvania militia. Irvine advanced from his position on the army's right and soon closed on Abercrombie's light infantry. The Americans got off the first volley, but the better trained British troops responded with fire by platoons. Their blasts scattered Irvine's militia, who broke for cover, only to be outflanked by an advancing Hessian column. Their appearance caused the Americans to run for the rear, ending the brief skirmish that lasted less than 20 minutes. American casualties numbered about 40, including at least 6 dead and 200 captured. Among the latter was General Irvine, who had been knocked from his horse by two musket balls, one that grazed his head and another that tore three fingers off his left hand. The British lost 12 casualties, including a captain who was killed.

Abercrombie pressed his advantage and pushed north to St. Thomas Episcopal Church, located on a hillock near the intersection of Church Road and Bethlehem Pike. A short while later General Howe came up and climbed the church tower to inspect the American lines, less than a half a mile to the north. He did not like what he saw, and decided that their position was too strong to attack with the force he had on hand. For the moment, he directed some artillery to form near the church and began shelling the enemy. When his guns were unable to reach the American lines, he withdrew them during the afternoon and allowed his entire command to go into camp on Chestnut Hill between the Bethlehem Pike and Church Road.

Washington was aware of Howe's dispositions, and late on the 5th shifted his troops to the right to face the main British column. Howe studied the American lines early on the 6th, and "observing they were not to be attacked with advantage on that side, determined upon a movement towards their left." The plan he developed was to take advantage of Chestnut Hill ridge to conceal a march to the right to Abington, where he could flank Washington's left. While the army marched to the east, "No Flint" Grey would take the grenadiers, jägers, and *3rd Brigade* to front the American center and distract the enemy until the flanking column was in place.

After skirmishing with Washington's troops all day on the 6th, Howe began his flanking move sometime after 2700 that night. The column marched south to Germantown and then turned left on Abington Road towards Jenkintown. They arrived there at dawn, and stopped to reprovision from a supply train Howe had ordered to meet him there from Philadelphia. By mid-morning the column was again in motion towards Abington, where it turned left on the Susquehanna Road towards Washington's far left flank.

Washington discovered Howe's move at about 0800 on 7 December and began shifting his troops eastward to meet the threat. Morgan's riflemen and Colonel Gist's Maryland militia, who had held the far left of Washington's line, led the way, and ran into Howe's advance troops in a heavy woods (modern Ardmore) about a mile west of Abington. The *1st Light Infantry* had difficulty dealing with Morgan's riflemen, who fought "Indian style" from tree to tree. The "Battle of Edge Hill" dragged on most of the afternoon until Cornwallis sent in the *33rd Regiment* and Morgan's men decided it would be best to withdraw. Both sides had lost around 40 casualties.

As Cornwallis' men slowly pushed Morgan's men back, Howe began forming his troops on Edge Hill and prepared to assault Washington's lines. In order to test the strength of the enemy's position, Howe sent forward a detachment of *British Grenadiers*. The column approached within pistol shot of the American abatis, but were then held back because of the strength of the American works. Major Baurmeister, who accompanied the Hessian troops, observed "I went in front of the English Grenadiers and found the rebels entrenched as follows. Before and behind heir strongest abatis, which went up the slope of the hill, they had dug trenches with embrasures every two to three hundred paces. There were no batteries behind the abatis, but on the entire flank I counted nine uncovered pieces...The Marylanders, whom I recognized by their grey uniforms with white trim, stood in a dense line between the artillery."

Meanwhile, General Grey was conducting his own operation against Washington's line. Grey had held his troops near Jenkintown all morning in readiness to move against the American center in support of Howe's primary attack on the right. He grew increasingly restless as the day wore on, and was not pleased at 1130 to receive an order not to advance until he saw Howe's lines move forward. When Howe's attack never developed for the reason's just discussed, Grey, "having waited far beyond the hour at which he had expected orders to advance," decided to move forward on his own.

Grey advanced up Church Road with his light infantry on the right and the *Queen's Rangers* on the left. About a mile past the intersection with Limekiln Pike he "ran into musketry fire from a woody ridge on the left." The enemy fire came from a body of Maryland militia that happened to be withdrawing from the skirmish on eastern Edge Hill that was being waged more than a mile to the east. The militiamen were easily routed, with the loss of 15 prisoners and 20 other casualties.

Grey's men continued to push forward, and in the process cut off General John Cadwalader and Colonel Joseph Reed from the American lines. Reed's horse had been shot, and the colonel was injured when it fell to the ground. Cadwalader bravely drew his sword to defend his friend against a body of Hessians who came rushing forward with fixed bayonets. Just in the nick of time Captain Allen McLane rode up with a squadron of calvary and saw Cadwalader's and Reed's predicament. He promptly ordered a charge that scattered the Hessians, and then snatched the two officers to safety.

At this point the 2nd Continental Regiment attacked Grey's troops and brought the British advance to a halt. Grey later claimed that he had been attacked by "very superior numbers," but such was not the case. The Continentals soon withdrew to their main line and were not pursued. Grey was uncertain what was happening to his right, and felt that he had accomplished the purpose of his feint. Towards sunset Sir William Erskine came up with two battalions of Hessians, who filled the gap between Grey's right and Howe's left. All the British troops rested on their arms that night.

Washington had all his troops in line ready to fight at 0500 on the 8th, but Howe was in no mood to make a frontal assault. His maneuver the previous day had not gone far enough around the American flank, and several of his officers urged yet another flank march to the east. However, the British commander did not favor such a move because the men had already exhausted the two days' supply of provisions that they had been issued at Jenkintown early on the 7th. In addition, the nights were getting quite cold, and the troops had left most of their tentage and camp gear in Philadelphia. These considerations persuaded Howe to order a withdrawal to Jenkintown at 1530. Their retreat was contested for only a short distance by a small body of American cavalry. From Jenkintown the army began withdrawing to Philadelphia, which the last British troops reached by 2230. The three day campaign had cost him about 350 casualties, including desertions. The number would have been much greater had he attacked Washington's well defended lines. American losses numbered a little more than 100.

CHAPTER IX

Valley Forge

*D*espite his successful parrying of Howe's thrusts against the strong American lines at Whitemarsh from 5-8 December, Washington had no intention to remain in this position indefinitely. The Whitemarsh camps were too close to the British lines at Philadelphia, and Washington knew from experience that his troops might not be able to meet another determined foray by the enemy. In addition, the position was not well suited for a winter camp, and the increasing severity of the weather made it imperative to seek more permanent winter quarters.

These considerations persuaded Washington that it was necessary to take his command west across the Schuylkill in order to move closer to his supply bases. The army marched out of Whitemarsh on 11 December, led by Sullivan's Division. Sullivan proceeded up the Bethlehem Road, and then turned south on Butler Pike to Matson's Ford (now Conshohocken) where he constructed a wagon bridge across the Schuylkill. The first troops across were astonished to run into a strong force of the enemy occupying a defile known locally as "The Gulph" (in modern West Conshohocken).

The British force Sullivan's vanguard encountered consisted of the advance elements of a 3,500 man foraging column under Cornwallis that had left Philadelphia at 0300 that morning. Cornwallis' raid had been detected as it passed the outskirts of the city by Colonel Howard Heston of the militia, who is reported to have left his bed naked and ridden bareback to alert the American pickets at Black Horse Tavern (on present City Line Avenue). The reinforced picket line contested Cornwallis' advance all the way to Merion Meeting House, and then fell back along the Gulph Road. Cornwallis pushed the pesky militia back from Harriton (present Bryn Mawr) after a heavy skirmish. His progress was aided by a local guide from Gulph who had been pressed into service, a miller named John Roberts. Roberts later claimed that he was forced to aid Cornwallis on threat of death, but his neighbors did not accept his argument and he was hanged for treason after the British evacuated Philadelphia.

With Roberts' aid, Cornwallis pressed on to the heights at Gulph (now known as Rebel Hill), which had to be wrested from the persistent American militia. He then went into camp as planned, prepared to continue his foraging in the morning. Cornwallis was astounded as Sullivan's men were to see American Regulars approaching from the Schuylkill. Sullivan, unaware of the size of the enemy column, was the first to react. He withdrew across the Schuylkill and hastily destroyed his wagon bridge. Washington was equally anxious about the enemy force, which he feared might be Howe's entire army. As a precaution, he marched four miles west to Swede's Ford (Norristown) in order to block any enemy move in that direction. He spent 12 December constructing a bridge at Swede's Ford and scouting for the enemy. He was much surprised to learn that the British force had withdrawn to Harriton. The fact of the matter was that Cornwallis had achieved the objective of his mission, and was returning to Philadelphia with a herd of 2,000 sheep and cattle foraged from the unfortunate farmers of Lower Merion Township.

Washington led his army across the Schuylkill at 1800 on 12 December, and proceeded on towards Gulph the next morning. Later in the day a sleet storm came up and the Continentals could do little more than struggle forward to the abandoned British campsite at Gulph. The continuing bad weather and an uncertainty about Howe's intentions led Washington to hold his troops at Gulph for several days. At last some tentage arrived on the 16th to provide minimal shelter against the wind and snow flurries. Some of the men thought that Gulph would be their permanent winter camp, and expressed disappointment that "There seemed very few families to steal from."

Washington, however, did not intend to spend the winter at Gulph. The problem of determining a suitable winter campsite had been on his mind for some time, since he openly disagreed with those who recommended that the army be disbanded for the winter. Some officials suggested that a line of camps be set up from Lancaster to Reading, but Washington feared that the splitting up of his command might lead to its disintegration. He tended to favor a plan supported by Greene, Lafayette and a number of his generals, that called for a winter camp to be set up near Wilmington. This locale offered a milder climate and a base from which to harass British shipping on the Delaware.

A committee from Congress visited Washington's camp at Gulph and concurred that the army was in no shape to conduct any offensive campaigns that winter. Instead, the committee recommended to Congress on 16 December that the army should go into winter quarters at a place near a supply of provisions from which it could protect the countryside and "be most likely to overawe the enemy." The committee's report was underscored by a letter the Pennsylvania Executive Council sent to Congress when they learned of Washington's possible plans to abandon the state for the winter. The Council was gravely disturbed at the possible loss of property to British patrols near Philadelphia, and argued strongly for the army to stay and protect eastern Pennsylvania and nearby New Jersey.

This pressure from the Pennsylvania and national governments forced Washington to reshape his thinking. He certainly did not wish to encamp too close to the British lines and so be vulnerable to sudden enemy movements like the recent affair at Whitemarsh. On the other hand, a camp at Wilmington or some other point at a totally secure distance from Philadelphia would be unable to protect the considerable American interests in that area. At length a compromise campsite was worked out, perhaps suggested by General

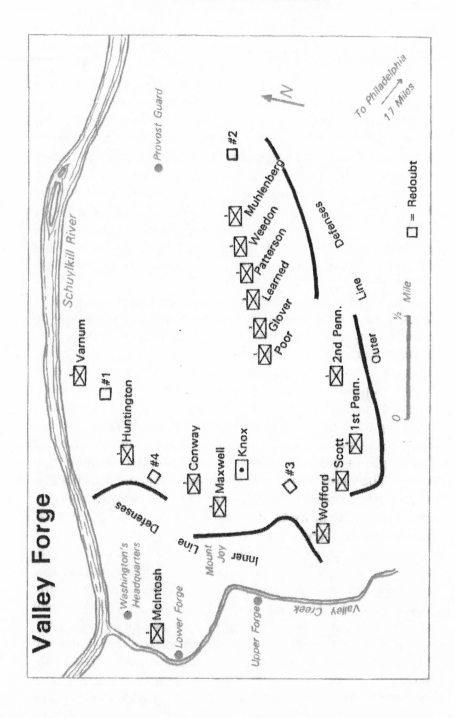

Wayne—a place called Valley Forge, located on the south bank of the Schuylkill just six miles west of the Gulph camp.

The weary and cold Continental army left Gulph at 1000 on Friday, 19 December, and trudged westward in a column that required eight hours to reach Valley Forge. The army's route was literally traced by bloody footprints in the snow. Years later Washington told historian William Gordon that "you must have traced the army from Whitemarsh to Valley Forge by the blood of their feet."

The men were exhausted when they arrived and Private Joseph Martin noted that "he was suffering excessively of thirst" because "there was no water to be found" in the darkness. Since campsites had not yet been prepared, the men had to seek what natural shelter and warmth they could find as they arrived.

The Valley Forge campsite was not exceptionally strong, but was good enough to hold off any attack by a force the size of Howe's. It was located some 18 miles from Philadelphia, a distance great enough to guard against enemy surprise attacks but still close enough to keep a watchful eye on the city. It also had the advantage of being situated between the enemy and the key towns of Reading, where the army's supply base was located, and York, the temporary national capital.

Baron de Kalb was totally unimpressed by the Valley Forge campsite, and at the time wrote that it must have been selected "at the instance of a speculator or on the advice of a traitor, or by a council of ignoramuses." The site, however, was not nearly as weak as de Kalb insisted. It was located on a broad plateau of about 2,000 acres adjacent to the Schuylkill, and had plenty of fresh water as well as timber for huts and defenses. The Schuylkill ably guarded the north side of the camp, and the hills along Valley Creek protected the site's western side. Washington soon set his troops to work constructing several redoubts and lesser works along two lines of defense. The outer line ran along the southwestern side of the camp and included two earthworks. The stronger inner line, placed on the lower slopes of Mount Joy, included two redoubts and artillery replacements. Its earthworks (long sections of which are still preserved) ran behind a dry moat (six feet wide and four feet deep) that was in turn fronted by abatis. A large star shaped fort was built to protect a wooden bridge over the Schuylkill. It must be noted that these defenses were built gradually over the length of the encampment, and were not effectively completed until after 27 March 1778.

Washington soon assigned his troops to campsites according to their brigades, as shown on the accompanying map on page 168. The eastern stretch of the outer line defenses (between Redoubt Number 2 and today's National Memorial Arch) was held by six brigades—two in Greene's veteran division and four newly arrived from Gate's army; two of the recently arrived brigades were organized into a new division led by Baron de Kalb and two (Glover's and Poor's) were still unattached. The western end of the outer line (between the National Memorial Arch and the southern slope of Mount Joy) was assigned to three brigades, the two in Wayne's Division and Scott's of Stephen's old division, now commanded by Lafayette since Stephen had just been court-martialled for drunkenness at Germantown. The inner line defenses were held by four brigades, Woodford's of Lafayette's Division, the two of Stirling's Division and Huntington's of McDougal's former division (which was not functioning at the moment because McDougal had been sent to the Hudson Highlands and had not been replaced). The river line was held by McIntosh's unattached brigade, encamped near the mouth of Valley Creek, and Varnum's brigade of McDougal's old division, stationed at Redoubt Number 1 about a mile east of Valley Creek. Other units at the encampment included Knox's artillery (parked at the eastern base of Mount Joy), Pulaski's Light Dragoons, Morgan's riflemen and some Pennsylvania militia under Brigadier General James Potter. Most of the Maryland troops of Sullivan's Division were detached and sent along with Hazen's regiment to occupy Wilmington, Delaware.

Washington was particularly concerned for his troops to

have warm quarters for the winter. He directed that the men be formed into 12-man squads, and that each squad was to build a log hut 14 feet wide, 16 feet long and 6 1/2 feet high. The huts, which were to be set up along orderly company streets were to be chinked with clay and roofed with whatever material was at hand. There was plenty of green timber available, but few boards, so Washington offered a $100 reward to whomever could suggest the best roofing material. Most troops used evergreen branches or saplings, since tent canvas was deemed too valuable for this purpose. It is not recorded if anyone received Washington's prize money. Bedding was to be made of straw appropriated from local farmers; Washington directed that if any farmers objected "the Straw will be taken with the Grain in it and paid for as Straw only." Bunks were the only furniture in each hut besides a crude plank table and perhaps a few makeshift chairs.

Washington was anxious for his troops to be housed as quickly as possible, and offered a $12 reward for the first well-constructed hut to be completed in each regiment. The men worked quickly in spite of a shortage of tools and draft animals to pull the logs. The first hut was reportedly finished late on 21 December, and over 800 were under construction by the end of the month. Recent archaeological digs have shown that the soldiers cut corners in building their huts, usually by making them smaller than the prescribed size (one measured only 8 by 10 feet). In order to save time and shield themselves from the cutting winds, many squads dug their floors some two feet into the ground, an unsound measure that kept the huts damp all winter. Nor was close care paid to the construction of chimneys, which were built into any wall or corner each squad wished. The huts were always filled with unhealthful smoke due to poor ventilation and the use of green fuel. It wasn't until 14 May 1778 that orders were given to make sure each hut had two windows for draft and ventilation. Another major problem was cleanliness. Archaeological work has shown that many men simply left their garbage in the corners of their huts. The stench of animal and human

General George Washington's daily life at Valley Forge was much easier after his wife Martha arrived on 10 February 1778 for a four month stay.

filth was so great that officers of the day were directed beginning 7 January 1778 to inspect the huts daily for cleanliness. The problem got so bad that on 27 May an order was given to remove the chinking of the log huts in order "to render them as airy as possible." Lafayette wrote that the men's huts—a number of which have been reconstructed at the park—were "little shanties that are scarcely gayer than dungeon cells." Even so, most of the men felt that their quarters were "bearable good." One soldier wrote, "We have got our Hutts to be very comfortable, and feel ourselves happy in them."

Shortage of food was probably a more severe problem than the lack of shelter when the troops first reached Valley Forge. There was no meat available, and only 25 barrels of flour. Affairs were so dire that Washington was genuinely concerned that "this Army must inevitably....starve, dissolve or disperse." Repeated appeals to the national and state legislatures brought in only sporadic supplies of provisions, barely

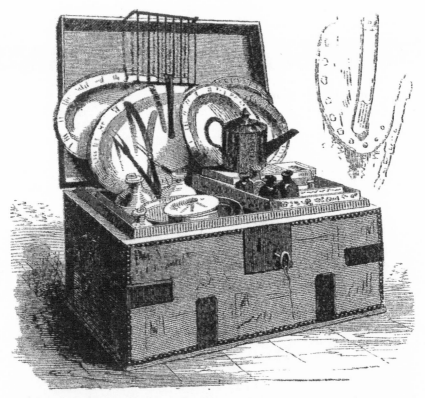

Washington had to improvise when he did not have his camp chest during the first month at Valley Forge.

enough to keep the 10,000 man army alive. The troops were supposed to receive a daily allowance of a pound of meat or fish, but were sometimes lucky to get that much in a week. Many resorted to hunting local small game such as squirrels, rabbits and raccoons. The meat shortage did not begin to ease up until spring, and was not eliminated until the local shad run on the Schuylkill came as a godsend in April. Bread was in equally short supply. Each soldier was supposed to receive a pound per day, but flour was scarce, and at times even rice and Indian meal were unavailable as substitutes. Forage was in such short supply that General Knox feared his cannons would be lost if the British ever attacked simply because his draft animals were too weak to pull them. Over 1,500 horses

Valley Forge Vignettes

Washington at first promised his men "to share in the Hardships and partake of every inconvenience" at their encampment. For the first week he kept his pledge and slept in his "marquee," warmed only by a nearby campfire (the tent is now preserved by the Valley Forge National Park Museum). The tent, however, soon proved totally inadequate for a headquarters, and he was forced to seek shelter at a local dwelling. He chose the Isaac Potts house, conveniently located near the mouth of Valley Creek, and rented it for $100 from its occupant, Mrs. Deborah Hewes. Here he spent the entire winter. He was inconvenienced by the fact that his personal equipment did not reach camp until late January, but his daily life was made much easier after Martha arrived for a four month stay beginning 10 February 1778. Most other generals also rented nearby farmhouses, and some even had their families with them for extended periods—Catherine Greene was with her husband from January to 25 May; Lucy Knox arrived on 20 May; and Lord Stirling's wife and daughter spent considerable time in the camp.

Christmas Day 1777 was far from cheery for Washington's cold and hungry army. Records show that 2,898 of the men were unfit for duty. It snowed four inches that night, and Washington had no rum to issue to the troops as was his custom on special days. Washington invited Lafayette and some of his other generals for a Christmas dinner that consisted of limited amounts of veal, mutton, potatoes and cabbage; and water had to be served in the absence of wine.

It is estimated that over 3,000 troops died because of poor supplies and bad conditions at Valley Forge. Strangely, only about 30 soldier graves have been found at the campsite. Most of the deaths occurred at the hospitals set up in towns to the north and west (Bethlehem, Reading, etc.), where the bodies were interred or sent home. The 9th Virginia sent 40 sick members to one hospital in Bethlehem, and only one recovered to return to duty.

Because of unhealthy conditions and a continuing clothing shortage, most of the troops suffered from scabies and other afflictions of the skin. On 8 January Washington was "informed many men rendered unfit for duty by the itch" and ordered his doctors "to look attentively into this matter as soon as men who are affected with this disorder are promptly disposed in Hutts to have them anointed for it."

The camp apparently smelled quite bad because of the dirtiness of the men, the number of dead horses, and the overflowing "necessaries" (latrines). On 13 March

Washington complained "that much filth and nastiness is spread amongst ye Hutts, which will soon be reduced to a state of Putrefaction." Observing "the smell of some places intolerable" a month later, the commander directed that "any Soldier who shall attempt to ease himself anywhere but at a proper necessary" should receive five lashes immediately. Nevertheless the camp was so unhealthy that it had to be moved on 10 June to a new site a mile away.

Records show that there were 161 court-martials at Valley Forge for the following charges: desertion, 42; disobedience or insubordination, 18; neglect of duty, 16; conduct unbecoming a gentleman, 14; fraud, extortion or embezzlement, 13; assault, 11; abuse of authority, 10; absence without leave, 7; theft, 7; gaming, cowardice, and misc. causes, 5 each; perjury and issuing challenges to duels, 2 each; sodomy, plundering and manslaughter, 1 each. These cases resulted in 86 convictions. In addition, 29 civilians were tried for aiding the enemy, of whom 21 were convicted. Punishment usually consisted of reductions in rank or whippings of up to 100 lashes. The death sentence was ordered 14 times for offenses such as desertion, cowardice, mutiny and sleeping while on guard duty. However, the punishment was carried out only in four cases—two soldiers were hanged for desertion in January, a civilian was hanged for

being a guide for the enemy, and Thomas Shanks, an ensign with the 10th Pennsylvania, was hung on 4 June for being a British spy.

The 12,000 troops at Valley Forge included a handful of Indian and black troops. There was a detachment of 60 Oneida Indians, under the command of Louis Tussard, and the death of one Indian member of the 1st Connecticut was reported. It has been estimated that about 2 percent of the army was composed of black troops (there were 378 blacks in seven specified brigades on 24 August 1778). The most famous black soldier at Valley Forge was Salem Poor, of Massachusetts, who also fought at Bunker Hill.

A number of women were in the camps all winter, some legitimately and more not so. Washington permitted nurses and laundresses to remain in camp, especially when they had a husband or son in the ranks. Two women known to have spent the entire winter were Mrs. Mary Geyers, whose husband and son were in the 13th Pennsylvania, and a Mrs. Milliner, whose son was a drummer boy. Other records show that more soldiers may have had their families in camp than is generally realized. Nor did the army lack "women of bad reputation" who lurked about the troops for their own gain or to try to entice the men to desert. The army's general orders and court martials contain frequent references to such camp followers.

The Potts House, Washington's headquarters at Valley Forge during the winter of 1777-1778.

and mules starved to death, and it was 24 May 1778 before an effective cavalry force could be mounted.

The winter at Valley Forge is noted for its suffering, as over 3,000 of the 12,000 troops quartered there perished during the six month long encampment. Most losses were not due, however, to the severity of the weather. The winter of 1777-78 was actually milder than usual, and was not nearly as severe as the bitter weather encountered the next winter at Morristown. What afflicted the troops most was shortages of all kinds, particularly of food, blankets, clothing and shoes. The sad point is that most of these shortages—and the ensuing suffering by the troops—were unnecessary. Plenty of supplies were available, but the Congress at York was unable to deliver them in a timely manner. While the principal supply base at Reading was only 40 miles away, poor roads, a lack of transport and frozen waterways combined to reduce deliveries at Valley Forge to a trickle. What was most distressing was the fact that many of the farmers in the area chose to sell their produce to the British in Philadelphia, who offered much better prices than the Continental agents. In addition, the Congress chose not to advertise the plight of the army for fear of encouraging the enemy and discouraging their own cause.

Baron von Steuben, drill-master and Inspector General at Valley Forge, greatly increased the American army's battle-field efficiency.

Had the Colonists been made aware of the true conditions at Valley Forge, they might have been more energetic in their efforts to supply the army.

The clothing shortage was also a severe problem. Many of the men had little more than the clothes on their backs when they entered camp, and their damp huts usually ruined what few extra belongings they had. Some of the men were authorized to trade the hides of slaughtered cattle for shoes, but the irregular supply of cattle and large number of destitute soldiers (over 2,000 needed shoes) made this only a limited expedient. Affairs got so bad that tentage was cut up to provide coats, and clothing was confiscated from civilians, a necessity that particularly distressed Washington. On 5 February some 3,989 were unfit for duty because of a lack of clothes or shoes. Von Steuben, of whom more will be heard in the accompanying sidebar, noted soon after his arrival that: "The men were literally naked....The officers who had coats had them of every color and make. I saw officers at a grand parade at Valley Forge mounting guard in a sort of dressing gown made of old blanket·or woolen bed cover."

The lack of clothing and food made the troops extremely vulnerable to disease as they remained encamped in their unhealthful huts. Washington had sent all his sick troops to Reading before the army marched to Valley Forge, but it was not very long before the sick roles were again filled. Everyone developed colds, which often turned into pneumonia. The stale air and general unsanitary condition in the crude huts led to dysentery, typhus and typhoid. The threat of a smallpox epidemic was faced by an inoculation program that began on 6 January 1778, but proceeded slowly because of the lack of supplies and a number of men became sick from the inoculations, only adding to the overcrowding of the hospitals. The bed space at Valley Forge itself was extremely limited, and it was deemed best for a number of reasons to transfer the sick to hospital sites at Reading, Ephrata, Bethlehem, Easton, Lititz and Yellow Springs (now Chester Springs). Soon even these hospitals became overcrowded, and death rates rose above 33 percent. Over 4,000 men were on the sick roles in May, and 18 percent of the army's strength (2,300 men) were reported to be sick in camp as late as 17 June.

Despite the terrible conditions at Valley Forge, the army managed to endure—much to the wonderment of its officers. Supplies began to arrive more regularly when Major General Nathanael Greene was persuaded to take over the quartermaster department on 2 March, replacing the inefficient Thomas Mifflin. A large amount of clothing was captured aboard the British ship *Symetry*, which grounded near Wilmington on 1 January, and large shipments began to arrive from France in the spring. Even so, the major reason for the army's survival that awful winter was Washington's stubborn refusal to give in, and the allegiance of so many of the men to their general and cause. Washington knew that all he had to do was hold on until spring came along with the opportunity to fight.

The poor living conditions contributed to a high desertion rate that was increased by the fact that the troops had not been paid in months. In early February most soldiers were due from three to five months pay. A bonus of an extra month's pay voted by Congress on 3 January was not paid until 11 March. Washington was well aware of the importance of paying the men on time and wrote "Besides feeding and clothing a soldier well, nothing is of greater importance than paying him with punctuality." When the men were not paid, he observed, they were more likely to complain of the poor food and lack of other supplies.

The poor conditions of camp led soldiers to frequently leave camp without authorization for short periods or permanently. Those caught could receive harsh punishment. Some 49 soldiers were court-martialed for desertion or improper leave, of whom 2 were executed and 23 were given a flogging of 100 lashes. Interestingly, the Americans were not the only army to suffer from desertions that winter. Small numbers of Howe's troops, particularly Hessians, sneaked off whenever they could; 11 English and Germans wandered into the Valley Forge camp on one day, 30 December 1777.

As previously noted, Howe constructed 10 redoubts in a line across the northern edge of Philadelphia to protect the city from Washington's army. Each redoubt was assigned to a specific command, and was to be held by a garrison of 53 men that were to be relieved every 12 hours. Redoubts One, Two and Three, at the eastern end of the line, were held by the *British Guards* and *Queen's Rangers*. Redoubts Four through Eight were assigned respectively to the *1st, 2nd, 4th, 3rd* and *5th British Brigades*. Redoubt Number Nine was held by Stirn's Hessians, and Number Ten by the *Walworth Regiment* and jägers. This arrangement was maintained until the end of February, when Howe ordered that the redoubt garrisons be furnished by the grenadiers and light battalion companies. Access to all points north of town was restricted by five manned barriers set up on principal roads (Ridge Road, and Seventh, Fifth, Third and Second Streets). On 7 January all the barriers were closed except those on Ridge Road and Second Street.

Howe clearly had no intention of evacuating his hard won prize, even though his position was made awkward by Burgoyne's disaster at Saratoga and the subsequent Franco-

American alliance. Lord Germain had strongly urged him not to conduct a winter offensive, and Howe strongly agreed that there was little potential benefit to be gained from such a campaign. After Whitemarsh the only troops he sent afield were foraging expeditions, large and small. His troops were particularly active in Salem County, New Jersey, where they foraged in competition with a detachment of several hundred Continentals under Wayne. In late February they set a trap for Wayne at Salem, but the wily American managed to slip by to Burlington and successfully recross the Delaware to Bristol. Howe's men had more success against Wayne on 18 March when a combined force of Regulars under Colonel Charles Mawhood and some Tory militia, managed to ambush an American column at Quonton's Bridge. Three days later Mawhood failed to carry out a surprise attack on a militia camp at nearby Hancock's Bridge.

The principal reason for Howe's inactivity during the Valley Forge winter, though, was the fact that he did not expect to continue as commander-in-chief for another campaign season. He did not feel he had received proper support from his government before the campaign began, when he did not receive the level of reinforcements he desired and all the attention seemed to be focused on Burgoyne. When Burgoyne was captured, the failure of Howe's own Philadelphia campaign to achieve a significant change in the course of the war became more glaring. Rumors were already beginning to fly about whether Howe should have supported Burgoyne more. Be that as it may, the fact of the matter remained that Howe's capture of Philadelphia, however well conducted militarily, was a strategic failure. Tories failed to flow into British arms, as Howe predicted, the Continental Congress simply adjourned to another town, and Washington's army, though defeated on several occasions, was still in the field. All Howe had to show for his campaign was a half empty conquered city, a prize that would be difficult to hold now that France was about to enter the war on America's side.

In view of these facts, Howe felt a change in command was called for and offered his resignation in a letter Lord Germain

A ticket for the "Mis-chianza" held on 18 May 1778. It was the fanciest party ever held in Phila-delphia.

received in early December 1777. Howe spent five months awaiting a reply, and on 14 April 1778, at last received authorization from Germain, dated 4 February, to turn over his command to Clinton and return home. Clinton arrived in Philadelphia on 8 May, and Howe turned over command three days later. Before he left America, the popular general was given a spectacular party on 18 May. The Mischianza, as it was called, was planned by Captains John Andre and Oliver de Lancey, and allowed the British officers and staff to let loose all their frustrations over the long winter and the uncertain future of the campaign. The 12 hour party began at 1600 when Generals Howe and Clinton, and their guests were rowed in barges down the Delaware past the British fleet. Upon landing, the procession made its way to the Wharton mansion, south of town, where pavilions had been set up on the lawn. Here a mock tournament was held for the benefit of the ladies by appropriately costumed "Knights of the Blended Rose" and "Knights of the Burning Mountain." The party then went inside for dinner, after which a fireworks display was given. Dancing continued on almost until dawn.

Due to the elaborateness of the preparations for the Mischianza, Captain McLane's American scouts were aware of the British party long before it happened. McLane correctly surmised that a large number of enemy officers would be absent from their troops in order to attend the festival, and planned a quick raid against the defenses north of Philadelphia. At the height of the Mischianza, a number of McLane's men sneaked up to the British works and set fire to a long stretch of abatis. The raid, however, did not cause any substantial damage; one historian has observed that the "attack was more of a prank than anything serious."

Another much more serious operation also began on the night of the Mischianza. General Washington had heard reports that the British were planning to leave Philadelphia, and that they had already begun loading ordnance on to their ships. In order to investigate more closely, Washington, on the 18th, ordered Lafayette to take about 2,200 men and five guns and march towards the enemy's lines between the Delaware and the Schuylkill. His precise orders were to "obstruct the incursions of the enemy's parties and obtain intelligence" of the enemy's "notions and designs." If the enemy were indeed embarking his troops, Lafayette was to fall upon their rear if he could.

Lafayette's command left Valley Forge soon after midnight on 18/19 May and crossed the Schuylkill at Swede's Ford (Norristown). From there the column headed down Ridge Road towards Barren Hill, where the men went into bivouac. Lafayette held his men back all day on the 19th while he attempted to learn the enemy's intentions and the meaning of the fireworks that were set off the night before during the Mischianza.

Lafayette's inaction on the 19th almost proved fatal. His advance was reported to the British soon after it began, and Howe at once determined to try to capture the American column by sending three converging forces against it on the night of 19/20 May. Howe himself would lead one large column up the Ridge Road directly towards Barren Hill, Grey would advance with 2,000 grenadiers up the Germantown Pike towards the enemy's left, and Grant would take 5,000

The Marquis de Lafayette was one of the best foreign officers to aid the American cause during the Revolution. He was only 20 years old in 1777 and adored Washington like the father he never knew.

men to Whitemarsh and then move into Lafayette's rear. The plan was an ambitious one involving most of the Philadelphia garrison on a lengthy night march, but promised a fine "catch" if successful. Howe, in fact, was so confident that he planned a dinner for the next night so that the generals could meet the "Marquis de La Fayette."

Grant's column started first at 2230, since it had the farthest distance to cover. It reached Whitemarsh without being detected by the Americans, even though Lafayette had specifically ordered a militia detachment and a band of scouts to keep a close eye on the area. Fortunately for the Colonists, a local militiaman saw the column and reported it to Lafayette just before dawn on the 20th. When a message arrived a short while later from Captain McLane that another enemy force was advancing up the Ridge Road, Lafayette at once understood his predicament. He roused his troops and placed a few companies in a defensive posture on Barren Hill. The rest were ordered to begin withdrawing to the east, where they ran into Grant's vanguard. Once again the Americans were

St. Peter's Church at Barren Hill, where Lafayette narrowly escaped being captured on 20 May 1778.

lucky—Grant had stopped his men for breakfast at Plymouth Meeting House and so came up later than he otherwise would have. Lafayette shrewdly ordered the head of his column to fan out, a move that forced Grant to deploy his troops into battle line. While the British were forming, Lafayette turned his men back to Barren Hill, and then turned down the Barren Hill Road to Matson's Ford (Conshohocken) where they successfully crossed at noontime in water up to their armpits.

Grant was still moving his line slowly away to safety. Howe and Grey approached Barren Hill more quickly, but to their disappointment found only a few American irregular units. One of these was a recently arrived squad of Oneida Indians, who were hiding in the woods to ambush the first British unit that came up. However, when some dragoons rode by, the Indians were so amazed by the redcoats' unfamiliar uniforms

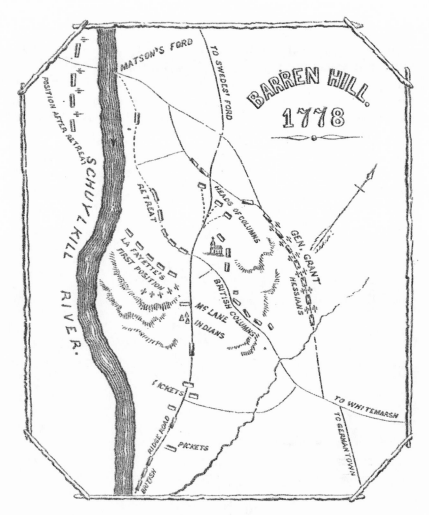

Map of the action at Barren Hill, 20 May 1778.

that they let out a whoop and fled. Most of the dragoons, startled by the noise, also took off. A few continued on to Matson's Ford, where they ran into Lafayette's rear guard, composed of two platoons of the select Commander-in-Chief's Guard. The two parties exchanged shots, causing a few casualties on each side, the only losses in the "Battle of Barren Hill."

Lafayette formed his troops facing Matson's Ford and invited the enemy to attack. Howe, who had heard a false rumor that all of Washington's army was on the move from Valley Forge, decided to return to Philadelphia at 1400. Lafayette encamped at Gulph that night, and crossed the Schuylkill at Matson's Ford the next morning. He then returned to Barren Hill, where he remained, unmolested, for three days before returning to Valley Forge on 23 May. Washington received his protege with great gladness, and was indeed fortunate that the expedition had returned in tact. This was Lafayette's first attempt at independent command, an assignment he received largely because of the significance of the French alliance ratified by Congress on 4 May 1778.

Baron von Steuben

Of all the foreign officers who served with the American forces during the Revolution, it was probably Baron von Steuben who had the greatest impact on the war through his role as the army's drillmaster at Valley Forge and then inspector general. He was born at Magdeburg, Germany, in 1730 with the name Friedreich William Ludolf Gerhard Augustin von Steuben but was known in America as Friedreich Wilhelm Augustus von Steuben. His father was a lieutenant of engineers, and he grew up as what today is called an "army brat." Quite naturally, he took up the military as a career, and entered the Prussian army at the age of 17. He served as an infantry officer during the Seven Years War and later became staff officer at the headquarters of Frederick the Great.

What looked like a promising military career ended in 1763. For reasons not totally understood today, Von Steuben was discharged from the Prussian army and had to seek employment elsewhere. He ended up obtaining the post of chamberlain for the prince of Hohenzollern-Hechingen, who also made him a Baron. His court life ended in 1771 when the prince went bankrupt. Von Steuben then spent several years living in France while he attempted to gain military employment.

The American Revolution came as a godsend to Von Steuben. In 1777 he was introduced to Ben Franklin by a friend, and luckily obtained a strong letter of recommendation from the French war minister. Franklin, who was seeking to secure experienced foreign officers for American service, was so impressed with Von Steuben's credentials that he purposefully stretched the truth and wrote a letter to Washington introducing him as "a Lieutenant General in the King of Prussia's service." Franklin's recommendation won Von Steuben instant attention, and he became a minor celebrity when he landed at Portsmouth, New Hampshire, on 1 December 1777. Congress did not hesitate to accept his offer to serve as an unpaid volunteer, and he was gladly accepted in the American army in early 1778, with orders to report to General Washington at Valley Forge.

Von Steuben arrived in Valley Forge on 23 February, and his first interview with Washington went exceptionally well, even though he spoke no English and Washington knew no German or French (Washington's aide Colonel John Laurens handled the translating chores). Baron Steuben, as Washington called him, was honored to have his name chosen as the army's password that night, and at once set about inspecting the army and its camp. He was not at all impressed with what he found. There was no uniformity of dress, or equipment, and some of the men were "literally naked." In addition, the troops did not know how to march or maneuver in close order; they were poorly drilled and their officers and non-coms were generally unschooled as to their responsibilities. The troops, on the other hand, were greatly impressed by Von Steuben's appearance and military bearing. Washington himself wrote that he was "an impression of the ancient fabled god of war...a perfect personification of Mars."

The thoroughness of Von Steuben's inspection of the army's camp quickly persuaded Washington to accept him as a staff officer, particularly since the German was not pushing for a field command like so many other knights errant who were seeking positions with the army. Before long Von Steuben's position was defined as head of the "division of inspection," and Washington selected him to be inspector general 30 April. The appointment, carrying the rank of major general, was confirmed by Congress on 5 May.

Von Steuben strongly felt that the army's greatest fault was a lack of organization and drill at the most basic levels. Low ranking officers and the non-coms, who were supposed to be the backbone of any army, did not know military duty and procedures, and the troops did not know how to move or march in the field. The men did not lack courage; they simply could not match the maneuvers and formations of their well-drilled opponents.

To remedy this situation, Von Steuben set about creating a simplified drill system that he would teach to the army. The system, which defined the role of non-coms and officers as well as the proper way to fire weapons and move in formation on the field, was written up under the title "Regulations for the Order and Discipline of the Troops of the United States." It was formulated with the advice of General Greene and Colonels Laurens and Hamilton of Washington's staff, who also reviewed the English translation. The final version was approved by Washington, who ordered that copies be made for every general and field officer. At the same time, Von Steuben prepared a set of proposals to expand the office of inspector general (ineffectively run by Thomas Conway since 13 December 1777) and improve the administration of the Commissary Department.

Washington wholeheartedly endorsed Von Steuben's drill manual and other suggestions. To implement the drill system, Von Steuben proposed the novel approach of teaching it first to a select body of men to make sure that it would work; these trainers would then go out and become drill masters for the rest of the army. The first members of the "military school" were to be the commander in chief's personal guard and a body of 120 "men from the line" selected for their aptitude. Since all the men of Washington's guard were from Virginia, it was decided to draw the additional recruits from other state regiments, in order to avoid any possible charges of favoritism.

Von Steuben's drill lessons, held twice a day, must have been a sight to behold. The general often took up a musket himself to show the men the proper way of performing required motions, and he would yell and swear in various languages because he knew so little English. Fortunately, Captain Benjamin Walker of the 2nd New York volunteered to be translator for the general so that his commands could be understood by the recruits. Von Steuben was well aware of the amusing spectacle he often made when berating his men, and purposely played the part to the hilt. The recruits, at first bemused, soon took their lessons seriously, and made rapid progress learning how to maneuver and perform the manual of arms.

Within two weeks Von Steuben's students "knew perfectly how to bear arms, had a military air, knew how to march, to form columns, deploy and execute some little maneuvers with excellent precision." He then gave a demonstration drill for the army's officers, where the troops "formed in column, deployed, attacked with a bayonet, changed front," and carried out other new maneuvers. The demonstration made quite an impression, and Von Steuben's "apostles" were then sent out to train companies on their own. When sufficient companies were trained, Von Steuben began drills by battalions, and then by brigades, until the entire army was covered. The troops, strangely enough, did not seem to have objected to this regimen during the long and hungry winter; the training sessions probably gave a routine to their day and instilled in them a greater confidence as soldiers. The strongest objections to Von Steuben's drilling came from many officers of all ranks, who had no desire to be out in the cold with their troops. Steuben and Washington, though, forced them to do so for their own good.

The importance of Von Steuben's drill system to the American army cannot be underestimated. Up until 1777 the troops were fighting in a disorderly and often unpredictable manner—they did not know how to form and hold formations, and they had particular difficulty maneuvering, especially when under fire. In addition, they could not march in formation and took excessive time to move anywhere in their only marching order, best described as "Indian file." This condition often caused dangerous awkwardness on the field, most recently at Brandywine, where the Colonial troops experienced great difficulty moving to Birmingham Hill and forming lines there. The immediate benefits of Von Steuben's training can be seen at Barren Hill, where Lafayette was able to extricate his men quickly from a perilous entrapment. Similarly, Lee at the opening of the battle of Monmouth was able to move his units rapidly forward in orderly ranks and then pull them back without totally disintegrating, as often happened in previous battles. The afternoon's fighting at Monmouth was also the first time in the war that the Americans were able to face British regulars on even terms in open combat.

Von Steuben rendered valuable field service at Monmouth by rallying portions of Lee's command at Englishtown and then helping to steady the front line during the battle's final stages. He remained on Washington's staff until the fall of 1780, when he went south with Nathanael Greene. He did not fare well there because of personal conflicts and an unfortunate field command in the contest between Lafayette and Cornwallis. After a brief absence due to illness, he rejoined Washington for the siege of Yorktown, where he commanded one of the army's three American divisions. He remained with the army until after the close of the war and was not discharged until March 1784.

Von Steuben decided to remain in America after the war, and gratefully accepted the citizenship offered to him by Pennsylvania (1783) and New York (1786). He set up residence in New York City, but his social activity soon brought on heavy debt. His situation improved somewhat with the help of Alexander Hamilton and other friends, and the receipt in 1790 of an annual pension of $2,500 from the Federal government. For the remainder of his life he spent his summers near Utica and the rest of the year in the city. He died in 1794, ever a bachelor, and left his property to two former members of his staff.

The Conway Cabal

As much as George Washington is idolized and idealized today, it is difficult for us to appreciate the fact that he was not popular with everyone during the Revolution. Several of his generals criticized him openly, and a few conspired to take over his position as general in chief. During the Philadelphia campaign a fierce rivalry developed between Washington and Horatio Gates, the victor of Saratoga, and, in addition, Charles Lee, who was only slightly junior to Washington in rank, coveted command of the army after he was exchanged by the British in the spring of 1778. To make matters worse, there was ongoing tension in the army between the Virginia generals, headed by Washington, and the New England officers, who were stirred up by the army's inspector general, Major General Thomas Conway.

Conway, who was born in Ireland in 1733, was raised in France and became a professional soldier in the French army. He rose to the rank of major by 1776, but was unhappy with his situation and was one of the first foreign officers recruited by Silas Deane for service in the American army. He met with Washington at Morristown in May of 1777 and received such a favor-. able recommendation that he was appointed a brigadier general. As such he commanded a brigade in Sullivan's Division from Brandywine to Germantown.

Somehow Conway developed an inflated opinion of himself and began lobbying for a promotion to major general ahead of a large number of senior brigadiers. In the course of promoting himself he began to criticize Washington, calling him a gentleman with miserable talents for the command of an army. At the end of October he wrote to Gates saying, "Heaven has determined to save your country; or a weak General (i.e., Washington) and bad councilors would have ruined it." His goal was probably to gain a promotion and transfer to Gates' command, but the uncircumspect letter had quite other results. One of Gates' officers leaked the contents of Conway's letter to an officer of Stirling's staff, who told Stirling and Stirling in turn told Washington. Washington chose to confront Conway with the letter, and Conway unsuccessfully tried to talk his way out of the corner he had painted himself into. The matter seemed to end on 14 November, when Conway resigned, not so much because of the letter but because of his anger over Baron de Kalb's promotion to major general (Conway had held superior rank to de Kalb in the French army).

Things then took a very strange turn. Congress did not accept Conway's resignation but instead referred it to the Board of War, whose most powerful member was Thomas Mifflin. Mifflin was no great fan of Washington, and had close connections with several other northerners, including Samuel Adams and Benjamin Rush, who felt the same. The War Board took its time to consider Conway's resignation, and before it reached any conclusion several members of Congress decided to promote him to inspector general, with the rank of major general! Conway was clearly being sent to serve on Washington's staff by powers who would not have been upset to see the commander replaced by Gates or anyone else.

Needless to say, Conway received quite a cold reception from Washington when he arrived at Valley Forge on 29 December 1777. The two proceeded to exchange strained notes in which Washington pledged to respect the appointments made by Congress, no matter what his personal feelings were. Conway, on the other hand, compared Washington to Frederick the Great, and then proclaimed, "I can expect no support in fulfilling the laborious duty of Inspector General." Washington, who had previously pledged cooperation with Conway, laid the situation before Congress (which was already buzzing with a complaint from Gates that one of Washington's officers had "stealingly copied" Conway's correspondence critical of Washington). Gates also supported Conway's contention that his comments concerning Washington were not as harsh as Stirling claimed.

Washington was greatly of-fended personally by the entire situation, but was gratified by the support he received from his loyal officers, particularly Lafayette. In addition, nine brigadiers wrote to Congress to protest Conway's promotion and other officers objected to a promotion given to Brigadier General James Wilkinson, a close ally of Conway. When Gates' case about the purloined letter began to fall apart because neither he nor Conway would publicly release a true copy of the missive, the movement to unsettle Washington began to lose all its steam.

The party favorable to Washington triumphed when Mifflin resigned from the Board of War, which would no longer interfere with the army's operations and Wilkinson, who was secretary of the Board of War, resigned in late March 1778 after unsuccessfully seeking duels with Stirling and Gates. He was later involved in Aaron Burr's conspiracy to take over Louisiana. Conway was transferred to a subordinate command in the Hudson Highlands in late March, whereupon he again protested by tendering his resignation. This time Congress acted promptly to accept his offer. Before returning to France, Conway fought a duel with John Cadwalader (a strong Washington supporter) on 4 July and received a bullet wound in the mouth. He became a general in the French army but had to go into exile during the Revolution. He died about 1800, never having returned home.

The defeat of the Conway Cabal, as it is known to history, is significant for unifying the support of Washington during the critical winter at Valley Forge. It must be noted, however, that some historians question whether an actual alliance to unseat Washington really existed. This is difficult to determine today, though it cannot be denied that there were a number of important figures openly critical of Washington to the point that he felt there actually was a conspiracy against him.

The Marquis de Lafayette

Lafayette is perhaps the best remembered of the many foreign adventurers who risked their lives to help the Colonists win the Revolution. He was born to a family of minor French nobility in 1757 and bore the lengthy sobriquet Marie Joseph Paul Yves Roch Gilbert du Motier, Marquis de La Fayette. His father, a colonel in the grenadiers, was killed at the battle of Minden in 1759, and young Lafayette became a wealthy orphan after his mother died when he was 12. At the age of 14 he was engaged to Marie Adrienne Francoise de Noailles, who was only 12, and the couple married two years later.

Lafayette was by nature shy and awkward, and did not enjoy drinking or carousing, the two primary staples of French court life. He would have been destined for a banal existence on his estates had he not developed a passion for the army, where he dreamed of earning distinction. He joined the Noailles regiment of dragoons as an officer in 1771, and was promoted to captain after his marriage two years later. However, he saw little real action because France was at peace at the time.

The cause of young Lafayette's life was changed on 8 Aug. 1775 when he was inspired by remarks made by the Duke of Gloucester in favor of the rebellion in America. Here, the Marquis felt, was a perfect opportunity to win glory and take revenge on the hated English. Through his connections he met Baron DeKalb, who had just himself received a commission as a major general in the American army, and DeKalb introduced him to Silas Deane, who had arrived in Paris in mid-1776 for the express purpose of recruiting foreign officers. Lafayette, who was only 19, rashly asked Deane for a commission as a major general—mostly in order to impress his father-in-law into giving him permission to go to America. Deane was much more impressed by Lafayette's offer to serve without salary, as long as expenses were covered, and granted the Marquis' request on 7 December 1776.

Lafayette, DeKalb, and a party of 13 other adventurers who were seeking American commissions experienced some difficulty securing permission to leave France. At length Lafayette managed to hire a ship, and the group slipped out of the country on 29 April 1777. They arrived in South Carolina seven weeks later and headed to Philadelphia, where DeKalb and Lafayette petitioned for the commissions that Deane had promised. When Lafayette volunteered to serve without pay, Congress felt that there was little to be lost by commissioning him major general "at large," with no command. Lafayette accepted, and made application for staff duty with Washington. Washington liked the charming young officer very much, even though the Marquis spoke almost no English. The two would eventually develop a strong and close relationship that may best be described as that of a father and son—Washington regarded Lafayette as the son he never had, and Lafayette respected and admired Washington like the father he never knew.

Lafayette's first field service with the American army came during the Philadelphia campaign of 1777-1778. At the height of the battle of Brandywine—the first battle he ever experienced—he bravely rode forward to try to rally Conway's Brigade during its retreat from Birmingham Hill. During the fighting he received a slight wound in his left leg and had to withdraw to get a field dressing from Washington's personal physician. He then rejoined the army in its retreat and helped reassemble the troops.

Lafayette's wound proved to be a fortunate one, for it increased his stature in the eyes of both Washington and the army. After convalescing for two months in Bethlehem, he rejoined the army at its camp at Whitemarsh, and led a successful reconnaissance in New Jersey on 25 November. Washington praised him highly for his "bravery and military arder," and Congress rewarded him by giving him command of the division formerly led by Adam Stephen, who had been court-martialed on 20 November for drunkenness.

Lafayette spent much of the winter at Valley Forge, and was perhaps Washington's staunchest supporter during the Conway cabal. At the end of January 1778 he was selected by Congress to lead a planned invasion of Canada, and proceeded to Albany to gather his troops, but returned in March when the project was called off. His adroit handling of his troops during the Barren Hill operation of 18-23 May is described in the text. Washington's continued high regard for his protege can be seen in Lafayette's appointment on 25 June to lead the army's vanguard against Clinton, a post he held for only one day until Charles Lee invoked his seniority to take over the post.

Lafayette served in a number of various capacities after the close of the Philadelphia campaign. In the summer of 1778 he led two brigades in the unsuccessful campaign against Newport, Rhode Island. Early in 1779 he returned to France to lobby for American interests and hopefully win greater commands for himself. Disappointed in the latter hope—he won only a promotion to colonel of dragoons—he returned to America in April 1780. At first he held no significant command, but he did serve as an important intermediary between Washington and Rochambeau, commander of the large newly arrived French force. His greatest military successes came when Washington appointed him to command the detachment facing Cornwallis in Virginia. Here he showed such good tactical and strategic skill that

Washington gave him command of an infantry division at Yorktown.

Lafayette returned to France after the war and remained to the end a loyal friend of America. He visited Washington in 1784, and was of great assistance to Jefferson when the latter was U.S. minister to France. As "the most popular man in France," he could not avoid being caught up in the chaos of the French Revolution. In 1789 he was commander of the National Guard, and as such helped save the King's family from a mob. However, the radicalization of the Revolution forced him to flee to Belgium. Soon he was captured by the Austrians, who turned him over to Prussia. He was held in various prisons for five years, until he was set free by Napoleon in 1800.

Lafayette returned to France only to find his fortune lost. He declined a number of honors offered by both Napoleon and President Jefferson (including the governorship of Louisiana), and chose to remain on his estate at Lagrange, safely distant from the turmoil of politics.

Lafayette's isolation ended in 1824, when he accepted an invitation from President Monroe to visit America. The 67-year-old hero toured his foster country for 13 months from 15 August 1824 to 8 September 1825, receiving frenzied accolades from a new generation of Americans for whom the Revolution was already a distant memory. One biographer wrote that this was perhaps the happiest year of Lafayette's life, since the general was once again on center stage by himself. He died nine years later, and is buried at Picpus with his beloved wife Adrienne.

Another historian has noted that it is a shame how Lafayette's contribution to the Revolution has not been fully recognized; too much attention has been paid to his failures in France in 1789 and again during the French Revolution of 1830. He spent over $200,000 of his own money to support the American cause, and aided it even more by his spirit and his connections with France. Yet another historian has noted how the "Lafayette Myth" was started and grew. Lafayette originally came to America for his own glory and to get revenge on the British, not solely for the purpose of promoting American liberty. Yet, when he became a symbol of the French love of liberty, he "lived the role to such an extent that the symbol became a reality."

CHAPTER X

Monmouth

The American alliance with France and the likelihood of French military intervention in America greatly altered the nature of the Revolution and forced a major revision of British strategy. Instead of trying to crush the Colonists' principal armies and occupy their major cities, the policy advocated by Howe, Lord Germain had to consider a revival of the Seven Years War and the necessity of defending the entire Empire. Since large numbers of fresh men were not available, the best source for troops to defend Canada, Florida and the entire West Indies was the armies already in the field—specifically, Howe's large command at Philadelphia. After lengthy discussions in London, Clinton was ordered on 8 March 1778 (the day after he was appointed Howe's successor as commander-in-chief in America) to withdraw from Philadelphia and send about one-third of his men to the West Indies. British strategy for the year would be to harass the Americans along the coast, and then conduct an invasion of Florida and South Carolina in the fall.

After the publication of the French alliance with the Colonists on 13 March, King George decided, in a secret letter sent to Clinton on 21 March, to concentrate his efforts on taking the French island of St. Lucia in the Caribbean. Most of the troops for the expedition would have to be taken from Clinton's new command. Since Clinton would certainly not have enough strength left to hold Philadelphia, he would have to withdraw to New York. Hopefully New York could be held long enough for a new peace commission under Lord

Carlisle to complete its work. However, if Clinton found himself pressured at New York, he was authorized to abandon that post and Providence and withdraw to Halifax, Nova Scotia. Curiously, neither Germain's orders of 8 March nor the king's letter of the 21st directed Clinton to be on the alert for the French fleet, which was strong enough to challenge British naval superiority. Any French success at sea might isolate Clinton's new command at Philadelphia or New York, or could seriously interrupt all the planned British troop transfers at sea.

Clinton, who had been commanding the British forces in New York City during the entire Philadelphia campaign, received his appointment and orders in April. He was not enthused about the honor since he saw the dangers of imminent French intervention, and replied to the king that he had been hoping to be recalled to London. Nevertheless, he accepted the honor thrust upon him, and on 2 May left Sandy Hook for Philadelphia. He arrived there on 8 May, and at once took command, although Howe seems to have remained in charge until he left for England on 24 May.

Howe's departure was but one indication that the British were preparing to evacuate Philadelphia. Late on the 24th, the very day that Howe left, Clinton ordered the troops to send all their surplus baggage to the docks for immediate shipment to New York. In the ensuing days he also began evacuating his sick and many of the soldier's families. The army's planned departure caused great consternation among the town's loyalists, who feared to lose their protectors and knew that an uncertain fate awaited them once Washington's forces regained control of the capital.

Clinton's preparations to depart consumed three full weeks. By then everyone was aware the British were going to leave, and the only question was when. Washington knew the day was fast approaching when he heard that English engineers were breaking the trunions of the heavy artillery pieces they had to leave behind. In addition, spies reported that the enemy was loading up all the spare horses and lumber they could find, and that British officers were collecting their

Sir Henry Clinton was given the unenviable task of withdrawing from Philadelphia. He conducted a successful withdrawal across New Jersey despite Washington's sharp attack at Monmouth.

laundry whether it was finished or not. Then on 15 June the British released some 900 prisoners they were holding in various temporary prisons around the town.

In view of these preparations, Washington called a council of 16 of his generals on the 17th. After explaining that he had about 11,000 men able to take the field against Clinton's 14,000 to 15,000, he invited opinions on three possible strategies: to attack the enemy's rear as he withdrew; to wait to take the field until the enemy was gone; or to move at once towards the Delaware. The generals discussed these propositions for a long time but came to no consensus. Several argued strongly that there was nothing much to gain by engaging the enemy's rear guard as they left town, and an unsuccessful attack might persuade the enemy to stay. Nor was there any unified support for marching directly towards New York, or attacking the enemy on the march should he withdraw overland across New Jersey. Washington dismissed the council without coming to any conclusion, and invited each general to submit his opinions in writing.

Unknown to Washington, Clinton's departure plans had been made awkward because of the expected arrival of a peace commission from London. This commission, led by

Lord Carlisle, had left Portsmouth on 16 April, and Clinton felt obliged to await its coming, particularly because he himself had been appointed a member. He was also anxious for the boat to arrive because it was carrying his newly appointed second-in-command, Lord Cornwallis. The commissioners' ship finally arrived in Philadelphia on 6 June, and Clinton set about helping to make contact with the American Congress. Carlisle was authorized through the Conciliatory Acts of 2 March 1778 to negotiate the suspension of the laws and taxes England had passed since 1763 to control the colonies. By then, however, it was too late for a reconciliation, as Clinton understood well. Congress replied on 17 June that they would only negotiate for a British withdrawal and recognition of independence. Carlisle and his commission would remain in America five months, but would make no more progress even through the employment of secret diplomacy and bribery.

Lord Carlisle attempted to persuade Clinton to remain longer in Philadelphia, but Clinton had no faith in the negotiations that seemed to be headed nowhere. Instead, he finalized arrangements for his withdrawal, a move that had become much more complicated because he had decided to withdraw by land rather than by sea, contrary to the orders he had received from London. His change in plans was necessitated, he felt, by both political and military considerations. Soon after arriving in Philadelphia, he had been approached by Joseph Galloway, the town's leading Tory, who convincingly argued that Clinton should take with him all the Tories who wanted to come in the event that Philadelphia had to be abandoned. If the Tories who had cooperated with Howe were left behind, they would be treated most cruelly by the American government, and this would set a poor precedent for the faithful Tories in New York, Providence and elsewhere. Galloway's arguments made sense to Clinton, and he invited Galloway and his followers to join his army on its pending withdrawal by sea. However, so many Tories (about 3,000) accepted the offer that Clinton found himself lacking enough transports to carry them as well as all his troops, horses, supplies and provisions. Another major consideration was the fact that the French fleet might appear at any time to intercept his convoy to New York. These factors led Clinton to decide to march most of his men across New Jersey with what supplies they needed. The navy's transports, which were already partly loaded with the army's heavy gear, would be filled with sick soldiers and the Tories with their baggage. Only two regiments of line troops, the Hessian Anspachers, were sent with this fleet, as Clinton wisely decided to take almost entire command by land in order to protect his trains.

Clinton began his withdrawal on 16 June by pulling his artillery out of line and sending some British and Hessian troops across the Delaware to Cooper's Ferry and Gloucester. The movement continued in earnest all day on the 17th, when most of the army's supplies and the remainder of the German troops were transferred to New Jersey. The artillery was sent to Cooper's Ferry at 2100, guarded by the *Queen's Rangers*. The withdrawal was covered by most of the *British Guards*, grenadiers and light infantry, who held the fortifications north of town until they were withdrawn at dawn on the 18th. They then crossed the river quickly and safely in open boats, whereupon the remainder of the British fleet began heading south down the Delaware. Most of Philadelphia's inhabitants were surprised to find their streets eerily quiet when they ventured out that morning. The last British soldier to leave town was reportedly Lord Cosmo Gordon, who somehow overslept (perhaps because of a hangover from a party the night before). He hurriedly dressed and rushed to the docks, where he found a Tory boatman to take him across the river. The only German and Hessian troops who remained behind were deserters, some of whom decided to stay behind with local girls they had married.

When most of the army was safely across the Delaware at about noon on the 18th, Knyphausen took the *Hessian Grena-diers* about six miles inland to secure Haddonfield, which was marked to be the army's base for the night. He was joined later in the afternoon by the wagon train and the *15th Regiment*, which came up from Billingsport. Clinton arrived

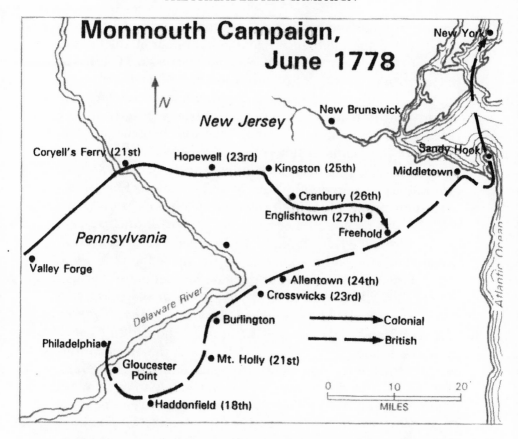

Monmouth Campaign, June 1778

with the rest of the army by evening. He had entertained thoughts of converting his withdrawal from Philadelphia to an offensive by moving directly against the American force holding the Hudson Highlands, but the size of his wagon train (about 1,500 vehicles) made him change his mind. Because of the poor condition of New Jersey's roads and anticipated opposition from local militia, Clinton felt he would be lucky to get safely across New Jersey to the security of New York City without being attacked by Washington's army. In order to keep his supply train intact and his command secure, the general felt it would be best to send half of his troops in advance of his wagons and half behind them. This meant that his column could proceed only as fast as the wagons, and the commanders of the advance and rear guards would have to be extra alert to remain in mutual supporting distance—no mean feat in view of the fact the entire column would cover 12 miles when strung out on the road; sometimes the vanguard would be making camp before the rear guard left the previous night's camp.

The army's march continued on the morning of 19 June when Clinton led the *3rd, 4th* and *5th British Brigades* north out of Haddonfield. The column had covered only six miles when a rainstorm arose in the afternoon, so it encamped at Evesboro. A smaller force proceeded over a different route to Evesboro, where it encountered a few militia, and then encamped at Moorestown in Burlington County. Knyphausen remained behind at Haddonfield with the trains, *Hessian Grenadiers*, and the *1st* and *2nd British Brigades*. More rain on the morning of the 20th allowed Clinton to proceed only about seven miles to Mount Holly. Here he rested all day on the 21st while Knyphausen brought up troops and the trains from Haddonfield via Chester Meeting House.

The reunited British army left Mount Holly on the 22nd and marched seven miles in the rain to Black Horse (now Columbus). On the 23rd, Clinton divided his force into two columns in order to try to make better time. The left column, led by Cornwallis, departed at 0300 and marched to Bordentown. It then headed towards Crosswicks, which was reached after a skirmish with some militia at Watson's Ford. The right column, under Knyphausen, left Mount Holly at 0400 and joined Cornwallis at Crosswicks that evening, though its rear stretched as far as Gibbstown (now Ellisdale).

The British column crossed Crosswicks Creek at Walnford early on the 27th, and proceeded on as before in two columns. Because of the day's excessive heat, Cornwallis covered only four miles before going into camp at Eglinton mansion in Allentown, while Knyphausen's column proceeded only as far as Imlaystown. Clinton was aware that two alternate routes were available for the remainder of the journey from Allentown—to march north to Brunswick and Amboy and then cross over to Staten Island, or to head northeast through Freehold to Raritan Bay near Sandy Hook, where sloops could be boarded for the remainder of the trip to New York. Clinton decided to choose the latter course because it was about 40 miles shorter than the route through New Brunswick and because he wished to avoid contact with Washington's army, which was reported to be crossing the Delaware north of Trenton.

On the 25th Clinton directed Knyphausen to take the advance and Cornwallis to form the rear guard. Knyphausen's column, which included the trains, embraced the following commands—"Brigadier General Leslie's Corps, consisting of the 5th Brigade and the Hovendon's dragoons, pontoons and Baggage, cattle, 4th Brigade, 3rd Brigade, Guards, Artillery, Hessian Grenadiers, British Grenadiers, light infantry, Corps of Jagers, Allen's Corps to flank the Baggage on the left." Knyphausen broke camp at 0500 and proceeded toward Monmouth Court House, encamping about four miles short of his goals. Clinton traveled with Cornwallis' command and stopped for the night at Rising Sun Tavern (Clarksburg), six miles south of Knyphausen.

Clinton was concerned with the heat and increasing enemy activity throughout the day's march on the 25th. Major John Andre recounted other problems the troops encountered: "The roads were in general very sandy, and the land, except in the neighborhood of Allentown, deemed poor. The weather, which after the first two or three days' march, which were rainy, was very sultry, and as we approached Freehold water was very scarce. The Rebels have added to this by stopping up the wells."

Because of the hot weather, the British command was exhausted when it reached Freehold on the afternoon of 26 June. Knyphausen's command, which arrived first, encamped one-half mile east of Monmouth Court House along the road to Middletown, and Cornwallis' command halted on high ground along the Allentown Road west of the Court House. Detachments were posted to guard the roads to Englishtown and Amboy. Clinton set up his headquarters at the house of Mrs. Elizabeth Covenhoven (still preserved), located on the western edge of Monmouth Court House. The town, now called Freehold, contained only about 10 buildings and had a population of less than 100. The locals had plenty of advance warning about Clinton's coming, and many had fled or at least concealed their valuables and foodstuffs. Nevertheless, the British troops conducted considerable foraging on the 27th while they remained in the area to rest and prepare for the last leg of their journey.

While Clinton was marching across New Jersey, Washington had moved his troops out of Valley Forge and was attempting to intercept the British column. At the council of war held on 17 June, his generals had been divided as to whether to try to attack the enemy or just "annoy" him if Clinton withdrew by land across New Jersey. Washington could do neither until he caught up with the British column, which he hastened to reach as quickly as he could. The decision to conduct a summer campaign rather than remain in Pennsylvania was a momentous one, as historian Douglas Southall Freeman has pointed out. A decisive victory over Clinton's command, coupled with Gates' victory at Saratoga, might possibly have brought the war to an end, but another defeat at British hands might have ruined the American cause.

Washington had been anticipating Clinton's withdrawal from Philadelphia since early June, and had ordered Maxwell's Brigade of about 1,300 men at Mount Holly to be vigilant. His first indication of the actual British evacuation came at 1130 on 18 June when a militia scout named George Roberts rode excitedly into the camp at Valley Forge with the news of Clinton's departure. Washington at once ordered Major General Charles Lee's newly formed division (composed of Poor's, Varnum's and Huntington's brigades) to march for the Delaware above Trenton, and Wayne's Division was sent across the Schuylkill and encamped three miles from the river. Both units continued their march on the 19th followed by the rest of the army—Lafayette's Division, De Kalb's Division (composed of Glover's, Patterson's, and Lained's Brigades), Knox's artillery, and Stirling's Division. Philadelphia was to be occupied by Jackson's Massachusetts regiment and other local troops, all under the command of

Benedict Arnold, who was still recovering from a leg wound suffered at Saratoga. The 2nd New York Regiment was directed to remain at Valley Forge to guard the numerous hospitals nearby.

The bulk of Washington's army began leaving Valley Forge for the last time at 0500 on 19 June. The troops proceeded across the Schuylkill and up the Ridge Road towards Buckingham in the same rain that hindered Clinton's progress that day. They encamped near Doylestown, where they remained all day on the 20th. Meanwhile Lee's and Wayne's Divisions reached the Delaware at Coryell's Ferry on the 19th, and crossed to New Jersey the next evening. They then marched three miles inland and encamped at the village of Amwell in Hunterdon County. The remainder of the army crossed at Coryell's on the afternoon of the 21st and morning of the 22nd. Washington concentrated his army at Hopewell on 23 June, and held his men there on the 24th while he waited to determine whether the British were headed towards New Brunswick or Sandy Hook. While they rested, the troops were ordered to clean their muskets and prepare for action.

Washington was interested in pushing on to engage the enemy if possible, but, as was his custom, he first called his generals to a council in order to hear their opinions. The meeting occurred near Hopewell at 0900 on 24 June, just when an eclipse of the sun was underway. The results of the conference were far from decisive. Major General Charles Lee, who had only recently joined the army, argued strongly for a push on to the Hudson Valley and suggested that only a small force should be sent to harass the enemy, who should be encouraged to hurry to New York as quickly as possible. Lafayette, on the other hand, thought that it "would be disgraceful and humiliating to allow the enemy to cross the Jerseys in tranquillity." He was supported by Greene and Wayne in his suggestion to send a strong detachment to intercept the enemy, who would be engaged by the whole army if favorable circumstances developed. The compromise result of the meeting was that Washington sent 600 riflemen under Colonel Daniel Morgan to help Maxwell's command operate against Clinton's right and rear. Later on the 24th he sent Brigadier General Charles Scott with a 1,440 man force of four select regiments (1st New Hampshire, 9th Pennsylvania, 1st Virginia and 4th Maryland) to harass the British left and rear. Major General Philemon Dickenson's New Jersey militia was also encouraged to continue to annoy the British column with constant pressure that included destroying bridges and stopping up wells. Reportedly there was a militia detachment of 25 men who were doing nothing but felling trees along Clinton's line of advance.

The morning of 25 June found the American army proceeding eastward to Kingston and Rocky Hill. From Rocky Hill Washington sent a third detachment forward to harass the British column, 1,000 selected troops under General Anthony Wayne. At the same time, Lafayette was sent forward with orders to take command of all the troops (now numbering well over 5,000 men) that had been advanced towards the enemy. Lafayette was delighted to accept the assignment, which more rightly belonged by seniority to Charles Lee or any of the other division commanders. Not long after Lafayette went forward, Lee went to Washington and complained that he was "disgraced" that command of the army's advanced wing had been given to a junior officer.

Washington considered Lee's request as the army began marching to Cranbury that evening (the 25th). He decided to hold most of his men at Cranbury on the 26th because of rainy weather, conditions which did not deter Clinton from continuing his own advance. In order to placate Lee, Washington decided to grant his request, and sent him forward with a makeshift brigade of 600 men under Colonel William Grayson of Scott's brigade with orders to take command of all the troops under Lafayette's direction. This awkward command structure, plus the irregular organization of the various detachments sent to the vanguard, would have a significant effect on the force's efficiency. Lee began concentrating his new command of about 5,000 men at Englishtown on 27 June, and established his headquarters at the Village Inn. The

Major General Charles Cornwallis held tactical command of the British troops engaged at Monmouth. He is better known for his surrender at Yorktown in 1781.

British army was less than five miles away at Monmouth Court House.

While Lee was forming the army's advance guard at Englishtown, Washington moved the main body of his army from Cranbury to Ponolopon Bridge, located in Manalapan Township less than five miles from Lee's camp. Washington hoped to engage Clinton's troops as soon as they began marching out of Monmouth Court House, and rode to Englishtown late that afternoon to present his plans. He was gravely disappointed that Lee had not yet investigated the terrain in front of him or the enemy troop positions around Freehold, but still felt that an attack should be pressed before the enemy had a chance to escape unscathed. Lee was ordered to be ready to attack Clinton's rear guard in the morning (the 28th), but no specific plans were drawn up. Curiously, Lee appears to have retired for the evening without making many further preparations. It was Washington who had second thoughts about the meeting. On his way back to Ponolopon Bridge, he sent orders for Lee to take precautions lest the enemy attack Englishtown during the night. He also directed Lee to send Dickenson's militia towards the enemy camp. In addition, Lee was told to order Morgan to attack the British

Colonel Dan Morgan and his riflemen were not engaged at Monmouth because of the confusing orders they received.

right "on the next day." Morgan, however, was confused by the heading of Lee's orders, which was dated "one o'clock in the evening," and believed that the attack was to be made on the 29th.

Ironically, Clinton had waited all day on the 27th for Washington to attack his force, which was carefully massed near Monmouth Court House. When the Americans did not rise to the bait, he felt it was necessary to continue his march on the 28th. He directed Knyphausen to lead the way towards Middletown at 0300, followed by the army's trains. Cornwallis' Division would form the rear guard and remain near Monmouth Court House until Knyphausen and the wagons were safely on their way.

Knyphausen got underway at 0400, an hour later than ordered. The American troops were also up early. Dickenson's militia began skirmishing with the Queen's Rangers before dawn, which came at 0430. Clinton did not take their probes seriously because they were easily driven back and because various militia detachments had been constantly harassing his column. Nevertheless, Dickenson's men successfully carried out their mission when they detached Knyphausen's departure and reported it to Lee and Washington.

Flag of Morgan's elite "Rifle Corps," the 11th Virginia Regiment.

Dickenson's news excited Washington, who was eager to engage the enemy, but did not excite Lee, who distrusted his "amateur" soldiers and was not interested in opening an engagement unless he was certain he could win. Because of a breakdown in intelligence gathering the previous day, Lee was not certain of the British positions or withdrawal routes. Consequently he had informed his officers at the 1700 meeting that he had no preset plan of action other than to move against the enemy's rear guard as soon as they began to move out.

Upon receipt of Dickenson's report that the enemy was on the march, Lee sent orders for Colonel William Grayson to advance towards Monmouth Court House with his detachment of 600 men and 4 cannons. Grayson, who had been previously directed to be ready to march at dawn, had difficulty securing guides and did not get underway until 0600. Lee's main force did not begin to leave camp until an hour later and was not entirely on the road until 0800. Wayne's detachment (1,000 men and 2 guns) led the way, followed by Scott's detachment (1,440 men and 4 guns), Maxwell's New Jersey brigade (900 men and 2 guns) and Jackson's command of two small regiments (200 men). Including Dickenson's militia, Lee had close to 5,000 men to lead into battle. He left another 700 behind in camp to guard the baggage.

Lee did not leave Englishtown until about 0815, after all his troops had moved out. He had not advanced far when he received information from Dickenson that there was still a large force of the enemy in Monmouth Court House. As a precaution, Lee decided to reinforce his advance guard, but for some reason chose Jackson's command for the task. Since Jackson was at the rear of the column, Lee's entire force had to stop and wait for him to move to the front. For some reason Lee also asked Wayne to take command of the reinforced advanced guard. Wayne was a well known and energetic commander well suited to the post, but he was unfamiliar with the troops he was asked to lead. His reassignment further confused an already jumbled American command structure, a handicap that would severely affect the course of the approaching battle. Few of Lee's units were serving with their original brigades under familiar officers, and it is difficult even today to reconstruct the exact organization of his command.

After he reached his new command, Wayne pushed Grayson's small detachment past Tennent Church. Grayson linked up with most of Dickenson's militia near the West Morass, and the officers, joined by Wayne and Lee, conferred to discuss the situation. Their greatest concern was Dickenson's insistence that there was still a large enemy force at the Court House. After a somewhat lengthy discussion, Lee decided "to march on and ascertain with my own eyes the number, order and disposition of the enemy, and conduct myself accordingly."

It was after 1100 by the time Lee's command resumed its advance. It seems that his lead troops (Jackson's command) were suffering from thirst and the day's heat (it was already close to 90 degrees) and requested to be relieved. Lee assented, and delayed his column long enough for the 9th Pennsylvania of Scott's command to take the lead. Once in motion, the column did not advance far before it was again halted. After crossing Weamaconk Creek, a report came in that the British were advancing on the left. Lee promptly sent part of Grayson's command to meet the threat, which turned out to be one of Dickenson's militia regiments.

By the time the 9th Pennsylvania reached Monmouth Court House at 1130, the British had already left. Clinton had been concerned about the American force coming up from Englishtown, but Lee's tardy advance persuaded him that the enemy was not about to make a serious effort. Since he had seen only about 1,000 enemy troops in the area (Dickenson's militia and Wayne's command), he thought it was safe to start Cornwallis on his way up the Middletown Road. Appropriate orders were sent at about 1000, with instructions to form a strong rear guard of 3,000 men (*16th Dragoons, Queen's Rangers, 1st Light Infantry,* and *British* and *Hessian Grenadiers*) in case the enemy pursued too closely.

After occupying Monmouth Court House, Lee allowed his men to eat lunch and get some rest from the heat that was now well over 90 degrees. Meanwhile he and General Wayne rode out the Middletown Road to reconnoiter. He was pleased to see a force of 600 enemy cavalry and infantry not too far distant, which he judged to be the entire British rear guard. He felt he would have no difficulty overwhelming this command by sending Wayne directly against it and moving two other columns against its flanks. He at once sent Wayne to take the 9th Pennsylvania and Jackson's command straight up the Middletown Road. Colonel John Durkee was then ordered to take three regiments (2nd Rhode Island, 4th and 8th Connecticut) against the northern flank of the British rear guard, and Morgan was directed to move his riflemen against the southern flank.

Lee's plan never had the chance to develop as planned. Because of the confusing orders he had received during the night, Morgan did not have his men ready to move. Durkee found that he could not advance against the enemy's northern flank without first making a detour to his own left around a nearby creek called the East Morass. His march north towards Forman's Mill and Lake Topanemus would delay him until well after the battle began along the Middletown Road.

Wayne also was experiencing some difficulty getting his advance started. He was surprised to learn that the men of Colonel Jackson's regiment, which had just been put under his command that morning, had only about 14 rounds of ammunition each because they had previously been on garrison duty in Philadelphia. Wayne felt he had no choice but to halt this unit until additional rounds could be borrowed from Lee's other troops resting in Monmouth Court House.

While Jackson's men were awaiting their ammunition, Wayne advanced Colonel Butler's 9th Pennsylvania past the East Morass. They had only proceeded about one quarter mile when they were attacked by the *16th Dragoons* at about noon. The dragoons were easily repulsed, and during their retreat caused considerable confusion among their own light infantry. Butler attempted to follow up his success, but was stopped by the fire of two British 3-pounder cannons and withdrew to the edge of the East Morass.

Wayne now brought up two guns under Lieutenant Colonel Eleazar Oswald, who with some difficulty moved across the East Morass to Butler's support. Soon, however, he fell under fire of superior enemy artillery, and Wayne had to bring Jackson's regiment to his aid. During this movement he was disturbed to see a large body of enemy advancing towards his right. He was definitely facing many more British troops than a few hundred cavalry and light infantry.

The troops Wayne observed were the *British* and *Hessian Grenadiers*, which Clinton had sent to aid his light infantry and cavalry when the fighting began northeast of the courthouse at noon. He had been hoping that Washington might pursue too closely, and was not reluctant to strike back. Besides sending the grenadiers to help his rear guard, he directed Cornwallis to countermarch the rest of his division, which had not progressed far towards Middletown. If Washington had sent only a few troops into Monmouth Court House, Cornwallis would surely destroy them; if additional Colonials were coming up, Cornwallis would delay them long enough for the British wagons to travel to safety.

It should be noted that Clinton was concerned with other American units than Lee's at Monmouth Court House. Local militia activity and the location of Washington's camps beyond Englishtown seemed to indicate that Washington might also try to intercept the British line of march by advancing past Scot's Meeting House, located six miles north of Monmouth Court House, about halfway between Freehold and Middletown Point (now Matawan). To guard against this possibility, Clinton directed Knyphausen to detach Grant's *2nd Brigade* and the *17th Dragoons* to a position near Scot's Meeting House. For some reason, this order was not carried out and the British northern flank was totally unprotected all day. Unfortunately for the Colonials, they were unaware of the fact; the only American troops in the area were some militiamen who were too tired to accomplish anything of significance. Nor was Washington able to take advantage of the unprotected British southern flank. Morgan, as we have seen, was supposed to be operating in that sector, but he had received no clear orders to do anything on the 28th. As a result he held his troops inactive at Richmond Mills, located on Squan Brook about three miles southeast of Freehold.

Strange to say, Lee was not alarmed when he saw the heavy column of enemy grenadiers moving against Wayne's right flank. Instead, he sent Wayne a few reinforcements (Grayson's command) and directed him to "halt the enemy" while he himself marched the rest of his command (Maxwell's Brigade, Lafayette's command and most of Scott's) north towards Lake Topanemus in an effort to get into the British rear. Apparently Lee hoped to crush the reinforced enemy rear guard between his force and Wayne's, and felt that his 5,000 man strength was sufficient to ensure success.

Wayne, however, did not understand the thrust of Lee's strategy, if it ever had been clearly explained to him. He had a fire fight on his hands east of the East Morass, and was delighted to receive Grayson's much needed reinforcements. Soon after he received Lee's orders, he saw the *Queen's Rangers* move forward against Jackson's regiment. When the Rangers were driven back by an infantry volley and several rounds from Oswald's guns, Wayne ordered Patton's regiment to make a counterattack. Patton pushed forward until he ran into heavy British artillery fire, whereupon he withdrew to join the 9th Pennsylvania in the cover of the woods along the edge of the East Morass.

While the fighting was raging on Wayne's front, Durkee's three regiments came up on Wayne's left after their circuitous march around the northern side of the East Morass. Durkee's men faced the weakest part of the British line but still suffered a number of casualties, particularly among their officers. Colonel Durkee was badly injured in his right arm and had to leave the field, while Major Steven Thayer of the 2nd Rhode Island lost an eye when he was grazed by a cannon ball.

Wayne's action lasted about 45 minutes while Lee marched most of his command around the northern side of the East Morass following the same route Durkee's regiment had taken. By 1300 he had his units formed south of Lake Topanemus, ready to pounce on the right flank of the British rear guard. By then, though, the situation on the American front had changed dramatically. Lee was dismayed to see most of Cornwallis' Division—the *British Guards, 3rd Brigade* and *4th Brigade*—marching south over Briar Hill, about a mile to the east.

Control of the battle now shifted to the British side. Clinton had set up an observation post on Briar Hill and had seen the dust of Lee's column proceeding against his right. He was not concerned with Lee's maneuver since Cornwallis would soon have over 8,000 men on the field, more than enough to deal with whatever force the Americans had. Rather that engage Lee head on, Clinton felt it would be easier to march around Wayne's right and head straight for Monmouth Court House, which was apparently unguarded and stood squarely in the American rear. Clinton knew the local road net well from his stay in Freehold the previous day, and was certain he could easily get into Lee's rear.

Lee realized the peril he was in, and at once sent Lafayette with three nearby regiments (13th Pennsylvania, 4th New York and 9th Massachusetts) to attack Clinton's right flank. Lee directed Scott to guard the left of the line while he followed Lafayette and all the other units he could commandeer.

At this critical juncture the American line spontaneously collapsed. This disaster was sparked by the withdrawal of Oswald's battery from Wayne's front. As already related, most of Wayne's and Durkee's infantry had withdrawn to the shelter of the woods along the East Morass in order to obtain cover from the increasingly superior force in their front. Their withdrawal left Oswald's guns alone and unsupported east of the Morass. He held on as long as he could, losing two horses and two men killed in the process, but soon ran out of round shot and had one gun disabled. This left him no choice but to withdraw beyond the Morass. General Scott saw Oswald pull back, and became alarmed when he could not see any of Wayne's infantry, which he feared had also withdrawn. He was also disturbed by the large number of enemy troops he saw moving past his far right towards the Court House, and by another large column (the *British Guards*) that seemed to be headed from Briar Hill directly against his position. Since the situation seemed to be critical and his superior, General Lee, could not be located at once, Scott took it upon himself to put his men into column and begin withdrawing to the west. Before leaving he rode up to Maxwell and said that "we must get out of this place" because the troops to their right had retreated. Maxwell, whose left was uncovered by Scott's withdrawal, had no choice but to follow; "I ordered my brigade to face to the right about, and march back."

Lee was flabbergasted to see his left flank retreat without orders. Before he could act to recall Scott and Maxwell, Grayson's and Jackson's detachments were also falling back, as was Butler's 9th Pennsylvania. Lee felt he had no choice but to order the withdrawal of the rest of his force. His

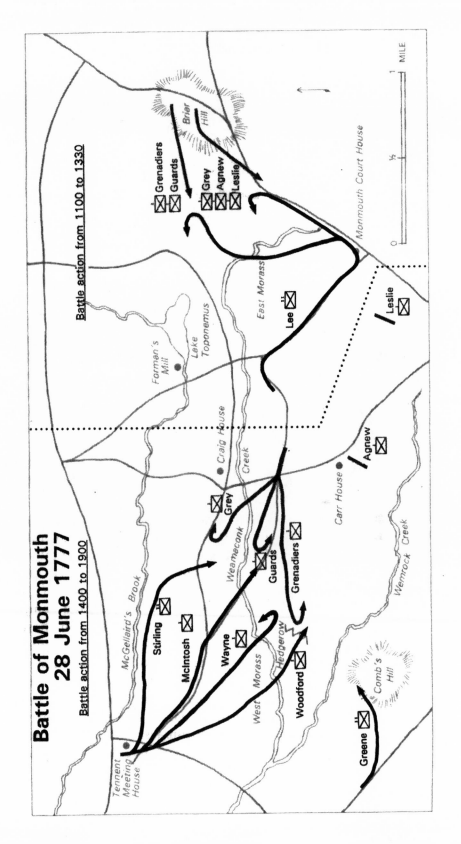

Battle of Monmouth
28 June 1777

Battle action from 1400 to 1900

Battle action from 1100 to 1330

Tennent Meeting House

McGellaird's Brook

Stirling ⊠

McIntosh ⊠

Wayne ⊠

West Morass

Hedgerow

Woodford ⊠

Weamecank

Grey ⊠

Craig House

Creek

Guards ⊠

Grenadiers ⊠

Greene ⊠

Comb's Hill

Carr House

Agnew ⊠

Wemrock Creek

Forman's Mill

Lake Toponemus

East Morass

Lee ⊠

Leslie ⊠

Grenadiers ⊠ Guards ⊠

Grey ⊠ Agnew ⊠ Leslie ⊠

Brier Hill

Monmouth Court House

MILE

½

0

This flag of the British 7th Regiment was captured at Yorktown. The 7th served in the 5th Brigade during the Monmouth campaign.

greatest concern was for Lafayette's three regiments, which were then approaching the Middletown Road amid the mass of Clinton's command. Lafayette fortunately managed to avoid being overwhelmed. He stalled the enemy briefly by unlimbering his two pieces of artillery and ordering them to fire as fast as they could. He then had the good sense to begin a withdrawal even before orders arrived from Lee. His brief action east of the East Morass had managed to give Wayne's men and the rest of Lee's command the time they needed to withdraw to the west. The time was about 1330, only 30 minutes after Lee had formed east of Lake Topanemus.

Lee somehow managed to form most of his troops on some high ground west of the East Morass, about one-half mile northwest of the Court House. Many of his units, though, were disorganized, and his command structure, already confused to begin with, had totally broken down. A number of his men were already retreating towards their morning camp near Englishtown, and the 9th Pennsylvania had somehow reached Forman's Mill on the north side of Lake Topanemus.

Wayne and Scott held the eastern end of Lee's position, a line that was not particularly well shielded by woods or other cover. When Wayne attempted to suggest strategy to Lee, Lee would not listen; the two officers would not speak to each other for the rest of the day. Their impasse had a significant effect when a messenger from Morgan reached Wayne requesting instructions; Morgan had heard all the firing and was wondering what he should do. Instead of referring the messenger to Lee, Wayne told him that the army's advance guard had been driven back and that Morgan should "govern himself accordingly." Because of this advice Morgan decided it was best to stay clear of the enemy all afternoon.

Lee's position began to deteriorate again as Cornwallis' troops reached the Court House and turned toward the shaky American line. Scott, who was not having a good day, did not like his position and, in the absence of clear orders from Lee, began withdrawing towards Tennent Church. His departure left Lee with only 2,000 men in line, only 40 percent of his original force. Lee realized he was no match for the large body of the enemy that was approaching, and ordered a withdrawal to a hill near the Carr House, about a mile to the west. His force was further weakened when Colonel Jackson, who heard only the orders "march on, march on," continued withdrawing all the way to Englishtown.

While forming the remains of his command near the Carr House, Lee noticed a hill to his front that gave too much strength to the enemy, thereby rendering his position untenable. After making inquiries of a local farmer named Wikoff, he thought it would be best to withdraw another mile and a half to Tennent Church, where there was a good sized hill and support could be secured from the rest of the army. He ordered the movement at 1400; Wayne followed rather than be left alone to face the enemy.

It was now the crisis of the battle. Clinton was determined to attack the enemy with his entire command, but could not engage because Lee's units kept melting to the rear. At 1430 he finally met some of Lee's troops between the Carr House and the West Morass, and the battle was renewed in earnest.

Lee's men would surely have been overwhelmed had General Washington not arrived to stabilize the situation with reinforcements. Washington had breakfasted that morning with a local doctor in Englishtown, to whom he stated, "he did not like fighting on the Sabbath, but he must yield for the good of his country." At noon he wrote a letter to the president of Congress stating that Lee had been sent forward with "orders to attack their rear if possible." Shortly afterwards he began heading towards Tennent Church to see how Lee was progressing. Since he had received no news from Lee, he assumed all was going well. However, he had not proceeded far when he was presented with one of Lee's fifers who reported that the advance guard was in full retreat. Washington refused to believe the story and put the fifer under guard to prevent him from alarming the rest of the army.

Washington rode on barely another 50 yards when he ran into more soldiers. These he assumed to be the normal stragglers from combat, but the real situation became more apparent when he saw entire regiments coming up—the 2nd North Carolina, Grayson's regiment, Jackson's regiment, then most of the New Jersey brigade, all exhausted and unable to explain the reason for their retreat. One of his officers noted that the commander became "exceedingly alarmed at what he saw when he came up." Nevertheless, he kept his cool and directed the troops he met to reform in a nearby wood. Fortunately for the Americans, one of the officers Washington spoke to was Lieutenant Colonel David Rhea of the 2nd New Jersey. Rhea was a native of the area and told Washington that there was a ridge suitable for defense not far away on the east side of the West Morass. Washington directed Rhea to take his regiment there, and sent some of Grayson's men with four cannons to follow him.

After sending orders for the rest of the army to come up from Englishtown, Washington rode across the West Morass to Rhea's ridge. By chance he ran into Lee, who was looking for him, and one of the most interesting confrontations of the war ensued (the site, two miles west of Freehold on Tennent Road, is commemorated by a bronze tablet). Lee was well aware that his movement had not gone well, and was doing his best to form the remaining half of his force (largely Lafayette's command) near the same position where Rhea was forming. Before he could say anything, Washington sternly demanded, "What is all this?" When Lee stumbled to

Major General Charles Lee may have wanted to take over command of the American army from George Washington. He was court-martialed for his conduct at the battle of Monmouth.

make a reply, Washington repeated, "What is all this confusion for and what is the cause for this retreat?" Lee replied, defensively, "I see no confusion but what has arose from my orders not being properly obeyed." Then he began to ramble, offering the explanation that he had ordered no attack, and that he did not have enough cavalry to match the enemy's mounted troops. Washington interjected that he had been told there was "a small covering force of the enemy" in Lee's front, to which Lee replied, "It might be so but they were rather stronger than I was and I did not think it proper to risk so much." By now Washington's legendary temper was boiling over, and he retorted that he should not have requested command of the advance guard over Lafayette "unless he meant to fight the enemy." He then angrily rode away towards the front.

Reports vary as to whether or not Washington employed foul language in his tirade against Lee. Scott, who was not present, insisted that Washington swore a blue streak, and Lafayette later asserted that Lee freely deserved such language. One witness declared that Washington called Lee "a dammed poltroon," while another witness who saw, but could not hear, the exchange observed that Washington was waving his hand angrily above his head. It would seem normal and understandable for Washington to have spoken profanity to Lee, yet none of the testimony at Lee's court-martial quotes him as using any expletives. An explanation might be the desire to avoid swear words at the court, or that the transcript of the trial was cleansed for publication.

After Washington rode forward, Lee attempted to give orders to the 3rd New Jersey, only to be told by one of Washington's staff that he was no longer in command and Washington would see to the posting of the troops. He then rode to find the commander and came upon him as he was ascending Rhea's ridge east of the morass. When the two generals reached the top of the ridge Washington was so alarmed that he set aside his earlier anger towards Lee and asked him to take command of that sector "in order to give me time to make a disposition of my army." Lee promptly accepted the task and assured Washington that he would be "one of the last to leave the field." Washington then turned back toward the causeway to help rally the troops and bring up the rest of the army.

The situation was indeed critical for the Americans. The largest formed force facing the enemy was three regiments under Wayne (3rd Maryland, 13th Pennsylvania, 5th Virginia) that occupied a woods on the north side of the Tennent Road. The 1st New Jersey was drawn up about one quarter mile to the rear under orders from Maxwell to cover Wayne's retreat. As already noted, the 2nd New Jersey, followed by Jackson's and Grayson's commands, were forming on the ridge behind the 1st New Jersey. Lee also rallied what troops he could in this sector, and posted four cannons under Oswald on the right of the line. The 4th New York moved to a hedgerow still farther to the right, either on Lee's orders or by the direction of its commander, Colonel Henry Livingston.

The British by now were less than 400 yards from Wayne's exposed position and were preparing to attack. Clinton knew he had the Americans on the run and was determined to press his advantage to the fullest. After forming his artillery at the center of his line, he sent his *British Guards* against Wayne and the *British Grenadiers* against Lee's line. The fighting on

Wayne's front was particularly severe, as Colonel Stewart of the 13th Pennsylvania was wounded and Lieutenant Colonel Ramsay of the 3rd Maryland was wounded and captured. Soon the superior British strength began forcing Wayne's line back towards the causeway over the West Morass. Meanwhile the *16th Dragoons* had advanced against Oswald's right flank, and forced him to withdraw his cannons before they had time to fire 15 rounds. The advancing *British Grenadiers* were engaged for only three minutes before Lee's improvised line began to pull back.

Oswald managed to unlimber two of his guns in the hedgerow occupied by the 4th New York, and was joined by the 2nd Rhode Island and the 4th and 8th Connecticut Regiments, all now led by Lieutenant Colonel Jeremiah Olney. Two of Wayne's regiments continued the line near the causeway. These brave commands had a heavy fight on their hands as they covered the withdrawal of the rest of Lee's worn out units. During the fighting Lieutenant Colonel Alexander Hamilton (a member of Washington's staff and later first Secretary of the Treasury) had his horse shot from under him and was hurt in the fall. At 1530 Lee directed this covering force to withdraw across the West Morass, and he was the last man to cross, as he had promised Washington.

Lee's stand at the hedgerow gave Washington time to bring up the rest of his army to Tennent Church. From there he advanced his left wing under Stirling to the ridge north of the West Morass. Stirling's line was strengthened by several well placed batteries, and was well protected from the enemy by the morass. In addition, the height of the ridge and its wooded cover concealed the strength and location of the American reserves from the British eyes. Greene, commanding the army's right wing, had earlier been directed "to file off by the new church (Tennent) two miles from Englishtown and fall onto Monmouth Road (leading from Allentown to Freehold)." His goal had been to make a flank march against the enemy and strike their rear at or near Monmouth Court House while Stirling and Lee engaged their front. However, Lee's retreat changed the strategic situation, and Washington

Major General Nathanael Greene served ably as Washington's acting quartermaster during the latter part of the Valley Forge encampment, but much preferred to lead his troops in battle.

directed Greene to form his troops behind the West Morass on the right of Stirling's line.

As Lee's weary troops pulled back, most were directed to withdraw to Englishtown to reform. Varnum's brigade (now led by Olney) went first, followed by most of Jackson's detachment and Maxwell's Brigade. The regiments of Scott's command, who had not been as actively engaged, were not ordered to the rear but were instead sent to Lafayette, who had been given command of a reserve line being established between the front line and Tennent Church. Oswald's cannoneers, as exhausted as they were, were also retained for more service. Wayne, anxious to stay near the action, asked and received permission to remain at the front.

Lee was ordered to accompany the troops sent to Englishtown to reform, and followed them willingly. After sending Lee to the rear, however, Washington had second thoughts about his capacity to command and sent Von Steuben to take charge of Lee's detachments, as well as the additional troops (Paterson's and Smallwood's brigades) being held in reserve at Englishtown. After Lee's troops reformed, Von Steuben turned his command over to Maxwell and returned to the front. Lee, surprisingly, was not upset by this arrangement and actually said that he was glad to be relieved because he was so tired. Perhaps he would have been wise to retire to his tent. Instead, he chose to return to the field and seek out Washington for the purpose of continuing their earlier discussion. Washington was too busy directing the battle to deal with him, and simply rode away.

Clinton was probably unaware that Washington had his entire army on or near the field, and pushed his men over the West Morass at several points in pursuit of Lee's retreating command. He sent the *British Guards* towards Greene's line on the right, and advanced the *British Grenadiers* towards the American center. His principal effort was made against the left of Stirling's line, which he hoped to outflank with a strong column composed of the *3rd Brigade, Queen's Rangers*, and *1st Light Infantry*.

The fighting was quite heavy on Stirling's left, where the famous *Black Watch (42nd Regiment)* led the British assault. Here the American regiments held on, stiffened by some well placed artillery and the discipline instilled by Von Steuben at Valley Forge. A counterattack by three of Poor's regiments (1st and 3rd New Hampshire and 1st Virginia) against the British far right along McGaillard's Brook brought the British advance to a halt, and the fighting on this flank began to die down by 1700.

The attack on Washington's right flank was even less successful. Here Clinton advanced some of his best troops— the *British Guards, Hessian Grenadiers*, and *37th* and *44th Regiments*, all under Cornwallis' personal direction. The column ran into heavy infantry fire in the front from Greene's line and was particularly distressed by raking artillery fire from the left. It seems that Greene had become aware of a position (Comb's Hill) that dominated this portion of the field while he was making his aborted march towards Monmouth Court House. When he was recalled by Washington because of Lee's difficulties, he decided to post a battery of four guns on Comb's Hill, supported by his lead brigade (Woodford's); the rest of his command was brought up on Stirling's right, about one half mile to the north. Comb's Hill turned out to be a perfect position, since it was ably defended by the thicket along Wemrock Creek on its northern face, and its height and location enabled the cannons posted there to enfilade the entire British left wing. Cornwallis and several of his officers later complained of the destruction caused by the fire of Greene's guns, which were directed by Lieutenant Colonel DuPlessis and General Knox. Supposedly one American shot carried away the muskets of an entire British platoon. Since Cornwallis did not yet have his own cannons available to face Greene's, he had no choice but to recall the *British Guards* and their supporting battalions. Among the British casualties in this attack were Colonel Henry Trelawney of the *Coldstream Guards* and Lieutenant Colonel Robert Abercromby of the *37th Regiment*, who were both severely wounded.

Meanwhile the *British Grenadiers* were meeting more than they could handle in their assault on Washington's center. When they were recalled to the east side of the morass, they were followed by an American counterattack led by Lieutenant Colonel Aaron Burr (later Jefferson's vice president and rival to Alexander Hamilton). Burr led his own command (Malcolm's Pennsylvania regiment) plus the 2nd and 11th Pennsylvania Regiments across the morass and formed on a small hill, where the small command was greeted by intense fire that felled Burr's horse, Lieutenant Colonel Brunner of the 3rd Pennsylvania and a number of men. It was not long before Burr received orders countermanding his advance and directing him to withdraw. The foray cost Burr's regiment almost one-third of its strength.

By late afternoon most of the infantry firing died down because of the day's intense heat (which reached a high of 96 degrees at Monmouth Court House) and mutual exhaustion by the troops. For a considerable time (from one to two hours depending on the source) the opposing armies settled into an artillery duel between Greene's and Stirling's guns on one side and a massive battery of sixteen pieces (twelve 6-pounders, two 12-pounders and two howitzers) that Clinton set up on a height south of Weamaconk Creek at the center of his line. The British had the advantage of a central position, while the Americans, who had approximately an equal number of

A very imaginative sketch of Molly Pitcher and George Washington at the Battle of Monmouth. The two probably never met each other.

guns, benefitted from a converging fire originating from their positions on Comb's Hill and Carr House Ridge. As a result neither side was able to obtain a distinct advantage. It was probably during this stage of the battle that the famous Molly Pitcher incident occurred (see sidebar).

By 1730 it was clear to Clinton that the battle had degenerated into a stalemate that he could not win because of the strength of the enemy position and the number of troops that Washington had on the field. For this reason he directed his troops to disengage and fall back to the Court House. Since he was particularly concerned about the difficulty of pulling back some light infantry which had not withdrawn from the brush along the West Morass because of a heavy American cross fire, he ordered the *1st Grenadiers* and *33rd Regiment* to make a covering attack on Washington's center. Their assault succeeded at extricating the pinned light infantry, which then withdrew with the *33rd Regiment*. The *1st Grenadiers* remained behind, either through a misunderstanding of orders (as Clinton later claimed) or as a covering force.

Molly Pitcher

One of the most noted participants of the battle of Monmouth was "Molly Pitcher," the legendary heroine who served in her husband's place after he fell in the fighting. Her story was told as follows by Private Joseph P. Martin of the 8th Connecticut: "One little incident happened during the heat of the cannonade, and which I think would be unpardonable not to mention. A woman whose husband belonged to the artillery and who was then attached to a piece in the engagement, attended with her husband at the piece the whole time. While in the act of reaching for a cartridge and having one of her feet as far before the other as she could step, a cannon shot from the enemy passed directly between her legs without doing any other damage than carrying away all the lower part of her petticoat."

Dr. Albigence Waldo gave a slightly different version of this incident in a journal entry made at New Brunswick on 3 July 1778, just five days after the battle; "One of the camp women I must give a little praise to. Her gallant [boyfriend or husband], whom she attended in battle, being shot down, she immediately took up his gun and cartridges and like a Spartan heroine fought with astonishing bravery, discharging the piece with as much regularity as any soldier present. This a wounded officer, whom I dressed, told me he did see himself, she being in his platoon, and assured me I might depend on its truth."

Private John Clendenen of the 3rd Pennsylvania gave a clue to the identity of the heroine when he later told his wife that he "greatly suffered from the heat and thirst, that a woman who was called by the troops Captain Molly was busily engaged in carrying canteens of water to the famished soldiers."

The identity of "Captain Molly" ("Molly Pitcher") has been reasonably established by a number of different researchers. She was probably Mary Ludwig, who was born on 13 October 1744. In 1769 she married John C. Hayes, a barber from Carlisle. Her husband served in the 1st Pennsylvania artillery from 1775-76 and enlisted in the 7th

When Washington saw the British center withdraw, he directed Wayne to bring forward three brigades from Stirling's line and pursue the enemy. Due to the confused command structure that day, only three Pennsylvania regiments (1st, 3rd, and 7th) were able to respond. Wayne advanced these units directly across the causeway over the West Morass and ran squarely into the *1st British Grenadiers*. The quickness of his attack caused quite a number of British

Pennsylvania in January 1777. Apparently Molly followed her husband to war, as did so many other unsung "camp followers," and helped with the cooking, laundry and nursing. Hayes was present at the battle of Monmouth, and was probably detailed to the artillery in Stirling's line because of his experience in the 1st Artillery. When he was wounded, Molly performed some act of heroism which was noted by several soldiers. When her husband died after the war, Molly married a "worthless fellow" named John McCauley, and lived at the corner of North and Bedford Streets in Carlisle. She was known to all her townsmen as "Molly Pitcher" and was granted an annuity by the state of Pennsylvania in 1822. An acquaintance described her as "a rough, common woman who swore like a trooper. She smoked and chewed tobacco, and had no education whatever. She was hired to do the most menial work, such as scrubbing, etc." She died in Carlisle on 22 January 1833 and is buried there.

It should also be noted that Molly Pitcher never met General Washington at the field of Monmouth, as several later embellishments of the saga claim and several famous paintings depict. Nor should Molly Pitcher be confused with "Captain Molly" Corbin, who took her husband's place working a cannon when he was mortally wounded at Fort Washington, New Jersey, on 16 November 1776. This "Captain Molly" was severely wounded in the arm and breast by some grapeshot and was hospitalized in Philadelphia. She was voted a military pension at half pay on 6 July 1779 and lived in West Chester, New York, after the war. There she lived as a "hard-driving, impoverished veteran" until her death in 1800. She was reburied at West Point in 1926.

The location of Molly Pitcher's "well" has long been debated. For many years a spring near the intersection of Wemrock and Tennent Roads was labeled as "Molly Pitcher's Well," but this location was not held by American troops for any length of time, nor were any Colonial cannons posted nearby. Recent scholarship has suggested that Molly's well instead was located on a farm near Stirling's artillery line, one-half mile northwest of the traditional well. A historic marker to that effect was erected in 1992.

casualties and forced Clinton to recall several of his front line units to come to the battalion's rescue. These troops readily drove Wayne's command back to the hedgerow that had been such a important American position earlier in the afternoon. It was perhaps during this stage of action that Clinton, who did not hesitate to ride along the front lines, was almost killed by an American officer, who was in turn slain by one of Clinton's staff officers.

Probably at the same time, Lieutenant Colonel Henry Monckton, commander of the *2nd British Grenadiers,* fell in action. Monckton advanced his men to within 30 rods of the American line and ordered them to charge with the words, "Forward to the charge, my brave Grenadiers." Wayne calmly directed his men to hold their fire until ordered and then "pick out the king birds." At the height of the attack Monckton, who was then about 40 yards northeast of the old Tennent Parsonage, was killed. According to an American private, he was, "sitting on his horse with his back toward the enemy when a cannon ball struck his neck and took off his head." Some other American troops who saw him fall rushed forward from the hedgerow to claim his body, and a vicious fight ensued. At length some men of the 1st Pennsylvania won the contest and managed to carry the corpse off before being forced to retreat back across the morass. Monckton was buried after the battle at Tennent Church burial ground, where he still remains today, only two miles from where he fell in action. His sword and flag, which were also captured, may be seen at the museum of the Monmouth County Historical Society in Freehold. During this same action the Americans also lost their highest ranking officer killed in the battle, Lieutenant Colonel Rudolph Brenner of the 3rd Pennsylvania.

When Wayne's troops retreated across the West Morass, Greene's artillery opened fire again and forced Clinton to pull his troops back on the left for a second time. While this action was occurring on the left, Clinton was experiencing an equally difficult time disengaging on his right. Here Washington sent about 300 men from the 1st and 3rd New Hampshire Regiments to pressure the British *3rd Brigade* as it retired. Some of the English formed on the edge of Weamaconk Creek to face their pursuers, who came on in formations recently learned from Von Steuben: "We wheeled to the right and advanced toward them, they began a heavy fire on us as we were descending toward them in open field, with shouldered arms until we had got within 4 rods of them, when our men dressed very coolly and we gave them a very heavy fire from

Original grave marker of Lieutenant Colonel Henry Monckton of the 2nd British Grenadiers, the highest ranking British officer killed at the battle of Monmouth.

the whole Battalion." Despite the strength of this attack, the British troops managed to cross the creek and withdraw successfully.

Washington was not about to let the battle cease now that he had the upper hand. He understood that Clinton's rear guard had withdrawn to the Middle Morass, about a mile east of the hedgerow, and decided to strike at both flanks of the enemy position. Colonel Thomas Clark was directed to take his North Carolina brigade (formerly McIntosh's) from its reserve position near Englishtown and go to the support of Brigadier General Enoch Poor's 1st and 3rd New Hampshire Regiments, which was already headed for the northern flank of the new British line. At the same time Brigadier General William Woodford was ordered to take his Virginia brigade from its position on Comb's Hill and advance against the British southern flank. A battery of artillery, "with proper support," was to be formed on the Tennent Road east of the hedgerow to support the counterattack.

Thomas and Woodford were unable to move forward as fast as Washington wished. Thomas' men were "beat out with heat and fatigue" and required considerable time to come forward and catch up with Poor's regiments. Woodford, who had been supporting the cannons posted on Comb's Hill, had great deal of difficulty passing through the underbrush and soft ground along Wemrock Creek. One account relates that most of the American troops were able to advance only a few hundred yards before they had to stop from utter exhaustion. They then lay on their arms until sunset, which came less than an hour later at about 1930. More gracious sources claim that this advance was slowed by woods and rough ground so much that it could not reach the enemy position before darkness began to fall. Whichever was the case, it is clear that the fighting stopped a considerable time before sunset, and that darkness found the last American advance at least one-half mile short of the British line. Washington directed all his troops to sleep on their arms and be ready to attack the enemy at dawn.

Clinton, however, had no intention of continuing the battle for a second day. He withdrew his rear guard to a new line a half mile east of the Middle Morass at sunset, and allowed the rest of his command to rest in supporting distance near the Court House. At midnight he directed everyone to move out, and Cornwallis' troops withdrew without being detected by Washington's men.

Monmouth was one of the few battles during the war at which the British had to leave their dead and badly wounded behind on the field. The total number of losses the British suffered is difficult to determine. In his official battle report, dated 5 July, Clinton admits 358 casualties—124 dead (including 59 from fatigue), 170 wounded and 64 missing. This number, however, is clearly too low. Washington reported around 240 enemy dead were buried on the field, and the wounded figure given by Clinton is nowhere near the usual killed-to-wounded ratio for battles during the war; perhaps he reported only the more serious cases. One detailed study at the Monmouth County Historical Society estimates Clinton's losses to be 1,134—304 dead, 770 wounded, and 60 prisoners. Clinton's force probably suffered at least 900 casualties. None of these figures include over 600 deserters (of whom 440 were German) who arrived in Philadelphia by 6 July.

The number of American casualties is also difficult to determine. Washington, in his official battle report, dated 1 July, gave a figure of 362 battle losses—69 dead, 161 wounded, and 132 missing. A number of the missing later returned to their units, but 37 of them were found to have died of sunstroke. Washington, like Clinton, seems to have under reported his number of wounded; the killed-to-wounded ratio in contemporary battles was usually 1-to-3 or 1-to-4. The American army's total losses in the battle were more—probably at least 500.

It cannot be underestimated how exhausted and thirsty the men of both armies must have been at the close of the battle. It was the longest action of the war, fought for 15 hours from 0430 to 1930, and the weather was unusually hot and sultry. Temperatures were recorded to reach from 92 degrees to 96 degrees, and it may well have been over 100 degrees at the height of the fighting. Such conditions would have been particularly oppressive on the British and Hessian foot troops, who wore heavy uniforms and were carrying all their gear. One account tells how one British regiment dropped in its tracks after charging up a hill, and other accounts on both sides relate how troops were exhausted by routine maneuvers. At the height of the battle Washington's mount, a fine white horse presented to him by Governor Livingston at Kingston just three days earlier, collapsed and died from the heat. Conditions were not, however, as bad as Clinton intimated when he wrote that "people fell dead in the streets, and even in their houses."

It is also difficult to determine who won the battle. If Washington's purpose was to destroy Clinton's army, or at least Cornwallis' rear guard, he failed, even though he held sole possession of the battlefield the next day and inflicted more casualties than he suffered. From the British viewpoint, the battle was simply a successful rear guard action as Clinton prevented Washington from overwhelming Cornwallis' command and allowed his trains to proceed safely to Middletown. When all factors are considered, however, the battle is perhaps best called a draw. Even so, the Americans gained an immense psychological advantage from the battle, even more than they took from their close defeat at Germantown. Washington successfully reasserted his aggressiveness at Monmouth and for the first time the American troops successfully faced the British in open combat. They had learned their drill and linear tactics well from Von Steuben at Valley Forge, and were at least able to march and redeploy in much the same manner as their enemy. Because of the army's increased efficiency at Monmouth, the British were reluctant to take on Washington again in the field. Thus Monmouth was the last major battle of the war in the northern theater.

*   *   *

After leaving Monmouth battlefield at midnight on 28/29 June, Cornwallis led his weary command northeast towards Middletown. His column crossed Hop Brook at Polhemus Ford, about a mile north of Colt's Neck, and reached Knyphausen's command at Nut Creek at dawn; Knyphausen had halted there at 2100 the previous night in order to be able to send help to Cornwallis if needed. The combined forces reached Middletown, three miles to the north, at 1000, and rested there the remainder of the day.

Washington's troops were surprised to wake up and find the enemy gone from their front on the morning of the 29th. Washington conferred with several officers from Monmouth County and became convinced that he would not be able to catch the enemy before they reached their destination at Sandy Hook, where they would surely be protected by the guns of the British fleet. Nevertheless, Washington decided to send out a few troops (Maxwell's brigade and Morgan's riflemen) to follow the British rear, gather in deserters, and prevent the enemy from foraging. Most of the rest of the army rested at Tennent Church, while fatigue parties, guarded by two brigades posted at Monmouth Court House, performed the grisly task of burying the dead under another sultry sun. Their grim task was completed by 1700, when all the troops in the area retired to Englishtown.

Clinton must have been relieved not to be pressured further by the American army while his men obtained some much needed rest at Middletown. On the evening of 30 June he marched his army to the Highlands of the Navesink, where contact was made with Admiral Howe's fleet, which had arrived at Sandy Hook at 1000 that day as prearranged. The British and Hessian troops were indeed happy to see the sails and masts of their ships as they neared the shore. Their journey across the Jerseys was at last over, and they slept that night under the protective guns of the fleet.

Clinton, however, still needed several more days to bring his campaign to a conclusion. The weather and tides had created an inlet across the base of Sandy Hook, which the troops had to reach in order to board their transports to New York. Captain John Montresor (the army's chief engineer who later wrote an excellent journal about the entire campaign) needed several days to construct a bridge of boats over the inlet. At length the troops were able to cross over, and on 5 July the men were conveyed to New York, which most of them had last seen when they optimistically departed for Philadelphia almost a full year earlier. Washington did not contest the last stage of Clinton's withdrawal, and sent only Morgan's and Maxwell's commands to keep an eye on the enemy. The rest of the army moved slowly north from Englishtown to Brunswick, and then began proceeding towards Paramus.

*   *   *

Thus the Philadelphia campaign of 1777-1778 came quietly to an end with the two armies occupying virtually the same positions they had held before the campaign began a year earlier. Though it was not a decisive operation, the Philadelphia campaign marked a turning point in the war in several regards. The British had clearly held the upper hand in 1776 and had great plans to gain mastery of the northern and middle colonies in 1777. However, due to a shortage of troops, faulty strategy and bad communications, they managed to lose Burgoyne's army at Saratoga and propel the French into a dreaded alliance with the Americans. Howe's campaign against Philadelphia was a brilliant military success, but his failure to enlist more loyalist support and destroy the American will to fight showed all too clearly the enormity of the task that the British faced in trying to reduce the colonies. French intervention forced England to rethink her entire war strategy, and Philadelphia became a hollow prize that had to be abandoned nine months after its capture.

The campaign was also significant for the way Washington once again managed to keep his army together in spite of continued adversity and defeats in the field. He played a significant role simply by occupying Howe's attention while Gates dealt with Burgoyne. Even so, the spirit of his troops was never broken, and his army survived the defeat at Brandywine to fight a close battle at Germantown and then match the British in the draw at Monmouth. The value of the change in the army's efficiency over the course of the Philadelphia campaign cannot be underestimated. In 1777 the American troops could only march Indian file and had difficulty maneuvering in the field. Thanks to Baron von Steuben and his drillmasters at Valley Forge, Washington's army in 1778 was able to march, deploy and fight on a par with the British, as it showed so well at Monmouth. As a result, the British preferred to remain in the safety of their coastal enclaves and refused to risk their troops in pitched battle. There would be no more major engagements in the North, and the focus of the war would instead be shifted to the South.

American Generals and Generalship

Considering the weakness of the American army and the divisiveness and ineptitude of many of its officers, it is amazing that the Continental Army was not totally destroyed during the Philadelphia campaign. What saved the army was the inspiration of a number of its commanders, several of whom will be mentioned shortly. But the glue that held the American army and the Colonial cause together was the indomitable spirit of its commander, George Washington. Washington certainly had his faults as a commander—he played favorites and made tactical mistakes on the field, as happened when he failed to reconnoiter all the fords of the Brandywine and then permitted Howe to march around his right flank. Yet his greatest assets were his ability to work with a variety of officers, his patience at dealing with the balky Continental Congress, and his ability to grasp the basic strategic situation— that the fall of Philadelphia would not end the war, which would continue as long as he kept his army in the field. More basically, he simply refused to give up; he reformed the army after Brandywine and Germantown and endured the awful winter at Valley Forge to see it emerge stronger and better than ever at the close of the campaign.

The most effective of Washington's several division commanders was Major General Nathanael Greene (1742-1786) of Rhode Island. He was a total team player, and rose rapidly in Washington's estimation because of his organizational skills; his only weakness was a certain lack of charisma and aggressiveness on the field. Greene led his men well at Trenton in December 1776, but was not above making mistakes in the field, as his role in the loss of Fort Washington the previous month reveals. He led a division at Brandywine and helped save the army by making a forced march from Chadd's Ford to Dilsworth. At Germantown he led the left wing, composed of his own, Stephen's, and McDougal's Divisions. Because of his administrative abilities, Washington asked him to become the army's quartermaster general when Mifflin was forced to resign in February 1778. He accepted the post only on condition that he could return to field command when battle approached, a proviso he invoked in order to lay claim to the army's right wing at Monmouth. After serving for awhile in Rhode Island, he returned to the quartermaster department and helped ease conditions at Morristown during the terrible winter of 1778-79. Greene's greatest accomplishments came as commander of the Department of the South in 1780-81, where he successfully thwarted Cornwallis. He experienced great financial difficulty after the war and had to sell his property. In 1785 he moved to Savannah to accept a plantation awarded to him by the State of Georgia. He died there of sunstroke in 1786, at the age of 44.

Washington's most aggressive lieutenant was Anthony Wayne, who was just coming into prominence during the Philadelphia Campaign, despite his disaster at Paoli. His career is discussed in another sidebar.

The wartime contributions of General Henry Knox (1750-1806), Washington's chief of artillery, are too extensive to list here. In 1775 he was an overweight bookseller in Boston. He served as a volunteer aide to Washington and impressed the general so much that he was appointed colonel of artillery. He responded by overseeing the transfer of about 50 cannons over 300 miles of rough terrain from Fort Ticonderoga to Boston, where they were used to force the British to withdraw. Knox proved to be an able administrator and help to his post until the end of the war. He had a personal role at Germantown, where he persuaded Washington to deal with Musgrave's command at the Chew House rather than bypass it, and at Monmouth, where he personally supervised Greene's battery on Comb's Hill. He certainly lived a full life—by the end of the war he weighed 300 pounds and had a family of 12 children. He died in 1806 at the age of 56 from a chicken bone that got stuck in his intestines. Fort Knox, Tennessee, is named after him.

William Alexander and John Sullivan were competent division commanders during the campaigns. Alexander (1776-1783) was the son of a New York lawyer who defended the newspaper Peter Zenger in a famous trial in 1735. He took on the title "Lord Stirling" in 1735 while in England attempting to lay claim to the earldom of Stirling. Personally wealthy, he was married to the sister of Governor William Livingston of New Jersey. Alexander was named the colonel of 1st New Jersey in 1775, and soon was promoted to brigadier General. His greatest battle performance was at Long Island, where he was captured. He was promoted to major general after being exchanged, and led a division at Brandywine and Germantown. He then led the army's left wing at Monmouth, and afterwards was presiding officer at Charles Lee's court-martial. In 1781 he was named commander of the Northern Department. He died of gout in 1783. Lafayette succinctly described Alexander as "braver than wise."

Major General John Sullivan (1740-1795) was an "able, if somewhat litigious" lawyer before the war. In 1775 he won an appointment as brigadier general and fought actively at Bunker Hill and in the Canadian invasion. He was promoted to major general in August 1776, and then was captured less than three weeks later at the battle of Long Island. After being exchanged a month later, he commanded a division at New York, and gave significant service at Trenton and Princeton. He led a division at Brandywine, after which he was wrongly charged with misconduct by his enemies. Washington valued his abilities too highly to relieve him, and he fought in his usual capacity at Germantown. Early in 1778, however, he was sent to Rhode Island. Later in 1779 he led a large scale expedition against the Iroquois Indians of New York and Pennsylvania. Sullivan was always ambitious (some historians believe he was involved in the Conway Cabal), and decided to leave the army in 1779 in order to pursue politics. He later became governor of New Hampshire, and then served as a Federal judge in his last years.

The weakest of Washington's division commanders during the campaign was probably Brigadier General Adam Stephen (1718-1791). He was a political opponent of Washington in Virginia and had a knack for doing the wrong thing at the wrong time. For example, he jeopardized Washington's 1776 attack on Trenton by sending an unauthorized patrol across the Delaware only hours before Washington crossed. Stephen commanded a division at Brandywine, and then lost control of his troops at Germantown when they strayed out of position and collided with the rear of Wayne's line near Cliveden. As a result he was court-martialed for drunkenness and "unofficerlike behavior."

The contribution of foreign officers to the campaign cannot be underestimated. Baron von Steuben revitalized the army with his drill manual written at Valley Forge, and the Marquis de Lafayette was coming into his own as a field commander (see separate sidebar on both). Baron Johann de Kalb (1721-1780) commanded a division at Valley Forge, but was ill in early 1778 and was unable to take the field during the Monmouth campaign. He was born in Bavaria, and served in the European wars of 1740-48 and 1756-63. The year 1776 found him a brigadier general at the Metz garrison, but he decided to go to America to seek greater glory. He made contact with Silas Deane and sailed to America with Lafayette. However, he lacked Lafayette's charm and wealth, and so experienced difficulty in securing what he thought to be a suitable command. His most significant contribution came in the South Carolina campaign of 1780. He became a national hero of sorts when he was mortally wounded at the battle of Camden on 16 August. (Another soldier of fortune, Poland's Count Casimir Pulaski, was mortally wounded at Savannah in 1779).

Not all the foreign born generals with the army however, gave beneficial service during the Philadelphia campaign. The controversial careers of Englishmen Charles Lee and Thomas Conway are described in separate sidebars. Frenchman Philippe Hubert, Chevalier de Preudhomme de Borre (born 1717) came to America in late 1776 and won an appointment as a brigadier general. His first major engagement was at Brandywine, where he insisted on being posted on the right of Sullivan's line at Birmingham Hill and so delayed the deployment of the entire division. When he learned that he was under investigation for incompetence, he resigned his commission, all the time insisting that he deserved a promotion to major general! He returned to France in January 1779 and retired from the French army in 1780 for physical disability.

Philippe Charles Jean Baptiste Tronson de Coudray (1738-1777) was yet another weak officer over zealously recruited by Silas Deane in 1776. Because of his experience with artillery, Deane promised him an appointment as a major general of artillery, ordnance, and engineers. De Coudray came to America in May 1777 accompanied by de Borre and about 30 other knights errant. The arrival of this shipload of officers placed Congress in quite a quandary—most were not suited to the high command Deane had promised, yet Congress did not wish to dismiss them and so endanger negotiations for French financial and material aid. De Coudray posed a special problem because of a rivalry with the capable French engineer Louis le Begue de Presk Duportail (1743-1802), who worked on the Delaware River forts during the Philadelphia campaign, and violent objections from Greene, Knox, and Sullivan, who threatened to resign if Coudray was made senior to them. Congress temporarily resolved the problem (as it also did with Conway) by making Coudray a major general "of the Staff" with no authority over generals "of the line." Coudray was assuaged by a fancy title as "Inspector General of Ordnance and Military Manufactories." What he would have done with the position was never learned because he drowned on 15 September 1777 while crossing the Schuylkill Ferry near Philadelphia. He refused to dismount his horse while riding the ferry, and the nervous animal jumped into the water; no one except one staff officer tried to save him and he was drowned "like a schoolboy."

The Court-Martial of Charles Lee

The most controversial character at the battle of Monmouth was Washington's second-in-command, Major General Charles Lee. Lee, who was no direct relation of General "Lighthorse Harry Lee" and his more illustrious son, Robert E. Lee, was a professional British soldier who was born in England in 1731. His first service came at the age of 16 and by the time he was 20 he became a lieutenant in the *44th Regiment*. Soon afterwards he purchased a commission as captain, and then was appointed major of the *103rd Regiment* in 1761. His military career to that point included participation in Braddock's unsuccessful 1755 campaign in Pennsylvania, and in the 1758 attack on Ticonderoga, where he was badly wounded. Lee won attention while fighting in Portugal in 1762, but had to retire when his regiment was discontinued in 1763.

Lee was always an adventurer as is shown by the fact that he married the daughter of a Seneca chief while stationed in upstate New York. After the conclusion of the Seven Years War he sought service in Poland and rose to the rank of major general. Disaffection with the English government, which had failed to promote him beyond the rank of lieutenant colonel, brought Lee to America in 1773. He bought an estate in western Virginia (Berkeley County) and let it be known that he was available for military command should Colonial tensions lead to war.

When war did break out, Lee's experience and personal lobbying won him an appointment as major general. The commission was dated 17 June 1775, making him third in seniority behind Washington and Artemas Ward. Unfortunately, he never lived up to his reputation. His overbearing manner and "dirty habits" made him difficult to work with, and it appears that he was more concerned with advancing his own career than he was with the success of the Colonial cause.

Lee's first service was at the siege of Boston in late 1775. When he became abrasive, he was sent to New York and soon thereafter was named commander of the Southern Department. His greatest success came in the summer of 1776 when he successfully defended Charleston, South Carolina, from an attack by Clinton. In gratitude he was voted the Thanks of Congress and was given the sum of $30,000 to pay off the mortgage on his farm in Virginia.

Late in 1776 Washington recalled Lee to help defend New Jersey after the fall of New York City (the town of Fort Lee is named after him). Lee, however, showed little respect for his commander because of his disdain for volunteer troops and "amateur" officers. He even went so far as to write several letters critical of Washington (one called him

241

"damnably deficient"), and some of his fellow officers believed he was trying to get command of the army for himself.

Such was the state of affairs when Lee encamped his troops near Morristown on 12 December 1776. For entertainment Lee chose to spend the night about three miles away at the home of "Widow White" near Basking Ridge. His decision proved to be a poor one when a British patrol happened by the next morning and learned of his whereabouts from some local Tories. The British easily overwhelmed Lee's small guard of 15 men, and the general was literally captured with his pants down.

The capture of so high ranking an American officer, oddly enough, caused a great amount of embarrassment to the British. There was considerable question whether he had ever properly resigned from His Majesty's Army, and Lord Germain ordered him to be tried in England for desertion and treason themselves. General Howe, though, decided to hold Lee in New York. During his imprisonment Lee engaged in several discussions about strategy with his captors, and claimed he knew how to win the war if he were given command of the British army.

The British, however, would have little to do with his plans, and Lee was exchanged in April of 1778. Had American authorities known of the full extent of his discussions with the enemy, they probably would have tried him for treason.

As it was, his return caused some strain among the army's officer corps until he was given command of a division of troops that had formerly been in Gates' army. The date of his commission made him Washington's second-in-command, and he pressed his seniority to take command of the army's advance wing on 25 June from Lafayette, even though he did not endorse the strategy of conducting an aggressive pursuit of Clinton's army. By the time the battle of Monmouth started four days later, Lee had about one-third of the army under his command. His poor performance at the battle and spirited encounters with Washington are described in the text.

Washington might have let Lee's conduct at the battle pass had Lee not sent him a letter on 30 June complaining of a "cruel injustice" at Washington's hands and demanding "reparation for the injury committed." Washington promised a hearing on the matter, but became annoyed when Lee sent him two more heated letters. The end result was that Lee demanded a court-martial to clear his reputation, and Washington readily agreed. Lord Stirling was appointed chairman of the court, which was convened at New Brunswick on 4 July and followed the army as it moved slowly northward to Paramus over the next six weeks. Most of the army's principal officers were called to testify, and their evidence adds greatly to our understanding of the confused battle.

Lee was formally charged on three counts: 1) disobedience of orders for not attacking as instructed on 28 June; 2) misbehavior before the enemy by "making an unnecessary, disorderly and shameful retreat; and 3) disrespect to Washington in letters written after the battle. Most modern scholars agree that Lee was not guilty on the first two counts, even though the court convicted him on all three charges on 12 August. Apparently the court members felt that Lee had been so disrespectful to Washington after the battle that they felt it necessary to find him guilty of the first two charges also. If he had been found grossly negligent, he would surely have been dismissed from the army. Instead, he was simply suspended from command for 12 months. The sentence was confirmed by Congress on 5 December.

Lee offended a number of his fellow officers with some of his statements at the trial and by his subsequent haughty behavior in Philadelphia while he was lobbying Congress to overthrow the court's decision. Von Steuben almost challenged him to a duel, and Colonel John Laurens wounded him badly enough that he had to decline a challenge from Wayne. After spending the next year at leisure at his estate in the Shenandoah Valley, he wrote angrily to Congress to demand a command commensurate to his rank. When he was instead dismissed from the army, he moved to Philadelphia to work for reinstatement, and died there two years later at the age of 51.

Lee remains today one of the most enigmatic figures of the war. Had he not been so arrogant and had he had more tolerance for the amateur American troops, he might have made a much more significant contribution to the war effort. As it was, he is best remembered as one of the numerous "mercenary" officers of the era, one who temporarily attained more rank and status than the rest.

Guide for the Interested Reader

There is no comprehensive monograph on the Philadelphia campaign on the same scope as presented in this study. A good but much briefer account can be found in the classic study of the entire war, Christopher Ward's *The War of the Revolution* (New York, 1952). Henry Carrington's *Battles of the American Revolution* (1877) is less analytical but contains much good primary source material. *Campaign to Valley Forge* by John F. Reed (1980) is a detailed recent study of the campaign from July to December 1777. John Pancake gives an excellent analysis of the campaign and its relationship to the Saratoga operation in 1777 *The Year of the Hangman* (1977). The best single source on all aspects of the war may well be Mark Boatman's *Encyclopedia of the American Revolution* (New York, 1976). Unfortunately, there are few good readily available monographs on the major battles of the campaign. Samuel S. Smith's *The Battle of Brandywine* (1976) is an excellent short account with a superb order of battle study. Much good local topographical information on Germantown can be found in the booklet *Washington at Germantown* (1971) by Ray Thompson. Thompson also wrote the informative booklet *Washington at Whitemarsh, Prelude to Valley Forge* (Fort Washington, Pa., Md.) Much good information on Fort Mifflin, Fort Mercer, and Red Bank is available in *The Fight for the Delaware, 1777*, by Samuel Smith (1970), and *The Pennsylvania Navy, 1775-1781, The Defense of the Delaware*, by John W. Jackson (New Brunswick, 1974). The best accounts on Monmouth are

The Battle of Monmouth by William Stryker (Princeton, 1927) and *The Battle of Monmouth* by Samuel Smith (1964). Both contain detailed casualty lists, and Smith's study contains an excellent order of battle.

There are a number of good accounts available on the encampment at Valley Forge. Among them are *Valley Forge, Crucible of Victory* (1969) by John F. Reed, *Winter Quarters* (1974) by Noel F. Busch and *Birthplace of our Army, A Study of the Valley Forge Encampment* (Harrisburg, 1990) by John B. B. Trussell, Jr. The activity of the British army that winter is well presented in John W. Jackson's *With the British Army in Philadelphia, 1777-78* (1979).

The study of the Revolution is severely hampered by the fact that detailed battle reports from both sides (like those available for the Civil War) are unavailable. George Washington's letters and reports are available in a number of editions, but they are not very analytical and were often restrained for political reasons. Much good tactical information can be gleaned from the court-martial records of a number of key participants, particularly Charles Lee (Monmouth). Others include Sullivan (Brandywine), Wayne (Paoli), and Stephen and Preudhomme de Borre (Germantown). The letters and reports of General Howe and his associates have been preserved in London, and many of Clinton's important papers concerning the campaign are in the collections of the Clements Library at the University of Michigan.

A great deal of important primary source material is available in three journals by officers on the British side. Major John Andre, who was later executed as a spy for his association with Benedict Arnold, was a member of "No Flint" Grey's staff during the campaign and planned Howe's farewell party, the famous "Mischianza." Major Andre's journal *Operations of the British Army, June 1777 to November 1778* was published in 1904. Major Carl Baurmeister, whose journal was published under the title *Revolution in America* (New Brunswick, 1957) was Von Knyphausen's adjutant and led *Minnegerode's Battalion* in action at Edge Hill. Captain John Montresor was Howe's chief engineer and laid out the defenses of Mud Island as well as the British lines at Philadelphia. His journal was published by the New York Historical Society in 1882. Unfortunately there are no American journals as thorough and important as those from British sources. The war from a private's viewpoint can be seen in *Diary of a Common Soldier in the American Revolution* by Jeremiah Greenman (1978).

Three good collections have been made of various eyewitness accounts of this campaign and the entire war. They are: *Rebels and Redcoats* (1957), compiled by George F. Scheer and Hugh F. Rankin; *Voices of 1776* (1972) by Richard Wheeler; and *The Fate of a Nation, the American Revolution Through Contemporary Eyes* (1975) by William P. Cumming and Hugh Rankin.

There are several important biographies of important figures in the campaign that should be studied by serious students of the war. William Howe's controversial career is provokingly analyzed in Troyer Steele Anderson's significant study *The Command of the Howe Brothers During the American Revolution* (New York, 1936). William B. Wilcox discusses Henry Clinton's equally controversial career in *Portrait of a General, Sir Henry Clinton in the War of Independence* (New York, 1962). No biography on the American side comes near to approaching the thoroughness of Douglas Southhall Freeman's classic multi-volume study *George Washington, A Biography* (New York, 1951), which also serves as a fine analysis of the campaign (volumes 4 and 5).

Biographies of the principal supporting commanders on both sides can be found in *Discipline and Bayonets, The Armies and Leaders in the War of the American Revolution* (1967) by Joseph B. Mitchell, and two books edited by George A. Billias, *George Washington's Generals* (New York, 1964) and *George Washington's Opponents* (New York, 1969). For more information on specific generals, the following biographies are recommended: *Nathanael Greene* (New York, 1960), by Theodore Thayer; *Wayne and the Pennsylvania Line* (1893) by C.J. Stille; *Henry Knox, General Washington's General* (New York , 1958) by North Callahan; *General von Steuben* (New Haven, 1937) by John Palmer; and *Lafayette* (New York, 1977) by Peter Buckman. The strange career of Charles Lee has been reevaluated by John Alden in *General Charles Lee, Traitor or Patriot?* (1951).

Edward E. Curtis has written two fine studies of the British army in the war—*The British Army in the Revolution* (1926) and *The Organization of the British Army in the Revolution* (1926). The history and uniforms of the various British and Hessian units in the war can be found in Philip Katcher's *Encyclopedia of British, Provincial and German Army Units 1775-1783* (1973). For more on the role of the German mercenaries in the war, see *The Hessians and Other German Auxiliaries of Great Britain in the Revolutionary War* (1884) by Edward J. Howell and *German Allied Troops in the North American War of Independence* (1893) by Max von Elting.

The composition of the American army during the war is well presented in Robert K. Wright's *The Continental Army* (1983), which also gives a summary history of the principal regiments and battalions. Data of the strengths of the colonial army can be found in *The Sinews of Independence, Monthly Strength Papers on the Continental Army* (Chicago, 1976), edited by Charles H. Lesser. A companion volume listing the engagements and battle casualties of the war is *The Toll of Independence* (Chicago, 1974), edited by Howard H. Peckman. More information on the American forces can be found in *The Pennsylvania Line* (Harrisburg, 1977) by John Trussell and *The North Carolina Volunteers* (1971) by Hugh Rankin.

There are a number of good reference books on arms and equipment of the Revolution. Three of the more readily available titles are *The History of Weapons of the American Revolution* (1977) by George Neumann, *Round Shot and Rammers* (1969) by Harold Patterson and *Armies of the American Revolution* (1975) by Ian Hogg and John H. Batchelor. An excellent reference book on the uniforms of the American, British and German troops is *Military Uniforms in America: The Era of the American Revolution, 1755-1795* (1974) by John Elting.

The Revolution has not been a particularly popular topic with wargamers. Nevertheless there are a few significant games that portray the aspects of the Philadelphia campaign. *1776, The Game of the Revolutionary War* (Avalon Hill, 1974) gives a good feeling for the strategic problems both sides faced in the entire war. The best tactical game on any of the war's principal battles may well be *The Battle of Monmouth* published in issue 90 of *Strategy and Tactics Magazine* (Simulations Publications, 1982). Also of interest is *The Battle of Brandywine* (Oldenburg Grenadiers, 1976).

The Battlefields Today

Valley Forge National Historical Park is one of the most beautiful military parks in the country. Its 3,000 acres of fields and woods embrace almost all of the famous winter encampment. Several forts and some long sections of the original entrenchments are still extant, as is General Washington's headquarters at the Potts House. The headquarters of several other generals are also within the park's boundaries but are not open to the public. A number of soldier huts have been reconstructed, and numerous cannons, markers and memorials have been set up along the five mile long auto tour. The park, which was for a long time under state supervision, now sports an excellent new museum and visitor complex. Be sure to visit the privately run museum of the Valley Forge Historical Society, located on Route 23 within the park boundaries. It contains an extensive collection of Washington relics.

The second largest park associated with the campaign is Monmouth Battlefield State Park, just west of Freehold, New Jersey. The park comprises over 1,500 acres on which the heaviest fighting occurred during the second half of the battle; most of the ground on which the early portion of the battle was fought is now occupied by the spread of the town of Freehold. There is a nice new visitor center, but the park, which was established in 1978, is largely undeveloped and as yet has only a few markers and no formal auto tour. Nearby Tennent Church, the rallying point for many of the American troops, still stands, and its large cemetery contains the graves of several casualties of the battle. The museum of the Monmouth County Historical Association on Court Street in Freehold contains several artifacts and paintings of the battle.

Brandywine Battlefield Park contains only 50 of the 30,000 acres on which the battle was fought. It is located near Chadd's Ford on ground occupied by Washington's left wing during the battle. The principal features of the park, which is administrated by the Pennsylvania Historical and Museum Commission along with the Brandywine Battlefield Commission, are Washington's headquarters (restored after a fire in 1930), Lafayette's headquarters and a nice museum. Other key points of the battle, particularly the Birmingham Meeting House, survive but are in private lands, though they are well marked with historical plaques.

Red Bank Battlefield in New Jersey contains only about 20 acres at the site of Fort Mercer. It is located near the town of "National Park," but is actually a town park administered by the Gloucester County Board of Freeholders. The site is very well maintained and includes much of the fort's original earthworks as well as the grove of Colonel von Donop, the Hessian commander who fell in the attack of 21 October 1777. Also on display are period cannons and a section of the original chevaux-de-frise (found in 1936) that was used to block traffic in the Delaware.

Pennsylvania's Fort Mifflin, the sister of Fort Mercer, is still preserved on the opposite side of the Delaware. Its condition, though, is dramatically altered from its wartime appearance. It once stood on an island in the Delaware, but a slight change in the river's course has reunited it with the Pennsylvania shore. Unfortunately, little remains from the 1777 fort that so valiantly resisted numerous British attacks and bombardments. The fort, which was actually incomplete at the time of the battle, was almost completely rebuilt in 1789 and was enlarged during the Civil War and World War I. It was still in use through the Korean War and was not decommissioned until 1962. The fort is interesting to visit but can be difficult to find, situated on a back road next to the Philadelphia airport.

There is no battlefield park at all at Germantown, where the town has spread to cover almost all the areas where the fighting occurred. Several key buildings from the time of the battle survive, including Howe's headquarters at Stenton (on 18th Street). By far the most significant of these is the Chew House at Cliveden (6401 Germantown Avenue). The mansion, which still bears scars of the fighting, was the scene of critical action during the battle, part of which was waged on the estate's large and well preserved grounds. It is administered by the National Trust for Historic Preservation.

The site of the Paoli "massacre" is preserved at the Paoli Memorial Grounds in Malvern. The park contains several cannons and markers; adjacent is the Malvern Memorial Park, which contains the mass grave of 53 of Wayne's soldiers who fell in the battle. Anthony Wayne's mansion on Waynesborough Avenue in Paoli is impressive to see but is privately owned and so not open to the public.

Orders of Battle

Unit strengths in parenthesis are estimated.

BATTLE OF BRANDYWINE

British Army, General William Howe, 15,006

Left Division, Major General Charles Cornwallis, 8,214

3rd Brigade, Major General Charles Grey, 1,509
- 15th Regt., 367
- 17th Regt., 233
- 42nd Regt., 597
- 44th Regt., 312

4th Brigade, Brigadier General James Agnew, 1,383
- 33rd Regt., 368
- 37th Regt., 308
- 46th Regt., 312
- 64th Regt., 395

Guards, Brigadier General Edward Matthew, 887
- 1st Battalion, (440)
- 2nd Battalion, (440)

Light Infantry, 1,130
- 1st Battalion, (565)
- 2nd Battalion, (565)

British Grenadiers, 1,080
- 1st Battalion, (540)
- 2nd Battalion, (540)

Hessian Grenadiers, 1,307
- Linsing Battalion, 437
- Minnigerode Battalion, 430
- Lengerke Battalion, 430

Hessian Jägers, 511
- 16th Dragoons (2 squadrons), 234

Artillery, (200)

Right Division, Lieutenant General Wilhelm, 6,825, von Knyphausen

1st Brigade, 1,330
- 4th Regt., 356
- 23rd Regt., 353
- 28th Regt., 286
- 49th Regt., 335

2nd Brigade, Major James Grant, 1,494
- 5th Regt., 307
- 10th Regt., 312
- 27th Regt., 324
- 40th Regt., 300
- 55th Regt., 251

71st Regt., 992
Hessian Brigade, **Brigadier General Johann Stirn, 2,162**
Leib Regt., 598
Mirbach Regt., 553
Donop Regt., 544

Combined Regt., 467
16th Dragoons (1 Squadron), 119
Queen's Rangers, 398
English Riflemen, 130
Artillery, (200)

American Army, General George Washington, 14,000

1st Division, Major Nathanael Greene, (1,754)
1st Virginia Brigade, Brigadier General Peter Muhlenberg, 850
1st Va., 120
5th Va., 127
9th Va., 391
13th Va., (200)
2nd Virginia Brigade, Brigadier General George Weedon (900)
2nd Va., 182
6th Va., 223
10th Va., 295
14th Va., (100)
Stewart's Pa., (100)

2nd Division, Major General Adam Stephen, (2,000)
3rd Virginia Brigade, Brigadier General William Woodford, (1,200)
3rd Va., 150
7th Va., 472
11th Va., 377
15th Va., (200)
4th Virginia Brigade, Brigadier General Charles Scott (800)
4th Va., 314
8th Va., 157

12th Va., 117
Grayson's Regt., (100)
Patton's Regt., 124

3rd Division, Major General John Sullivan, (1,750)
1st Maryland Brigade, (650)
1st Md., 199
3rd Md., 114
5th Md., (40)
6th Md., 118
Delaware Regt., 79
2nd Maryland Brigade, Brigadier General Preudhomme De Borre, (1,100)
2nd Md. 118
4th Md., 220
7th Md., 95
German Battalion, 305
Hazen's Regt., 393

4th Division, Brigadier General Anthony Wayne, (1,750)
1st Pennsylvania Brigade, Colonel Thomas Hartley, (850)
1st Pa., 335
2nd Pa., 21
7th Pa., (100)
10th Pa., 231
Hartley's Regt., 155

2nd Pennsylvania Brigade,
Colonel Richard
Humpton, (900)
4th Pa, 150
5th Pa., 241
8th Pa., 369
11th Pa., 138

5th Division, Major General
William Alexander
(Lord Stirling), (1,650)
3rd Pennsylvania Brigade,
Brigadier General
Thomas Conway, (950)
3rd Pa., 150
6th Pa., (200)
9th Pa., 193
12th Pa., 231
Spencer's N.j. Regt., 186
New Jersey Brigade, (500)
1st N.J., 184
3rd N.J., 300
Light Infantry Brigade,
Brigadier General
William, 200, Maxwell,
(800)*
Continental Troops, (600)*
Chester County Militia, 200
North Carolina Brigade,
Brigadier General
Francis Nash (800)
Portions of 1, 2, 3, 4, 5, 6, 7, 8 and
9th Regts.
Light Dragoons Brigade, (800)
Bland's Regt., (200)

Sheldon's Regt., (200)
Byrd's Regt., (200)
White's Regt., (200)
Artillery Brigade, Brigadier
General Henry Knox,
(1,600)
Pennsylvania Regt. (Proctor) 251
2 New Jersey Companies, (110)
2 New York Companies, (150)
Continental Regt. (Lamb), 399
Massachusetts Regt., 497
3 Miscellaneous Companies,
(200)

Pennsylvania Militia
Division, Major John
Armstrong 2,973
1st Pennsylvania Brigade,
Brigadier General James
Potter
Moor's Philadelphia Regt.
Mcvaughn's Philadelphia Regt.
Folwell's Bucks Regt.
Watson's Lancaster Regt.
Thompson's York Regt.
Cumberland Regt.
2nd Pennsylvania Brigade
Smith's Philadelphia Regt.
Eranis' Chester Regt.
Greenwalt's Lancaster Regt.
Lowry's Lancaster Regt.
Ballat's Lancaster Regt.
Udree's Berks Regt.

* Maxwell's Light Infantry detachments already reported with parents' units.

BATTLE OF MONMOUTH

British Army, Major General Henry Clinton

Unit strengths of British Army are estimated by the author based on a detailed muster taken at Sandy Hook on 3 July 1778, five days after the battle.

First Division, Major General Charles Cornwallis, 8,400

British Grenadiers, 1,200
1st Battalion, 600
2nd Battalion, 600

Hessian Grenadiers, 1,000
von Liusingen Battalion, 350
von Lengerke Battalion, 400
Minnegerode Battalion, 250

British Guards, 800
1st Battalion, 400
2nd Battalion, 400

3rd Brigade, Major General Charles Grey, 1,500
15th Regt., 300
17th Regt., 300
42nd Regt., 600
44th Regt., 300

4th Brigade, Major General Agnew, 1,400
33rd Regt., 350
37th Regt., 350
46th Regt., 300
64th Regt., 400

5th Brigade, Brigadier General Leslie, 900
7th Regt., 300
26th Regt., 300
63rd Regt., 300

Other Troops, 1,600
16th Dragoons, 300
1st Battalion Light Infantry, 700
Queen's Rangers, 300

Artillery
3 Batteries, 300

Second Division, Major General Knyphausen, 6,500 (Unit not present at battle)

1st Brigade, Major General Vaughn, 1,400
4th Regt., 300
23rd Regt., 400
28th Regt., 300
49th Regt., 400

2nd Brigade, Major General Grant, 1,350
5th Regt., 300
10th Regt., 150
27th Regt., 300
40th Regt., 300
55th Regt., 300

Stirn's Hessian Brigade, Major General Stirn, 1,000
Du Corpe Regt., 500
Combined Regt., 500

Loos' Hessian Brigade, Major General von Loos, 1,150
Donop Regt., 500
Mirbach Regt., 650

Other Regular Troops, 2,250
17th Dragoons, 300
2nd Battalion Light Infantry, 750
Jägers, 600
Royal Artillery, 400
Hessian Artillery, 200

Loyalists, 1,350
1st Battalion Maryland, 300
2nd Battalion Pennsylvania, 150
2nd Battalion New Jersey, 200
Roman Catholic Volunteers, 200
Volunteers of Ireland, 50

Caledonian Volunteers, 50
Pioneers and Guides, 200

Pennsylvanian Dragoons, 200

NOTE: The *Anspach Hessian Regt.* (800) went by sea from Philadelphia to New York.

.American Army-General George Washington

Figures are drawn largely from Samuel Smith's *The Battle of Monmouth.* Many of the brigades at Ponolopon had regiments detached with the advance guard. The exact assignment of brigades to Greene's and Stirling's wings is not known

Advance Wing, Maj. Gen. Charles Lee, 4,800*

New Jersey Brigade, Brig. Gen. William Maxwell, (900)

1st N.J.
2nd N.J.
3rd N.J.
4th N.J.
battery of 2 guns

Riflemen, Col. Dan Morgan, (600)**

11th Va.
Detachments of Continental Regts.

Grayson's Detachment, Col. William Grayson (600)

Scott's Brigade, (300)

Grayson's Additional Continental Regt.
Patton's Additional Continental Regt.
battery of 2 guns

Varnum's Brigade, Brig. Gen. John Durkee, (300)

4th Ct.
8th Ct.
2nd R.I.
battery of 2 guns

Jackson's Detachment, (200)

Jackson's Additional Continental Regt.
Lee's Additional Continental Regt.

Lafayette's Command, Maj. Gen. Lafayette, (2,500)

Wayne's DetachmenT, Brig. Gen. Anthony Wayne (1,000)

3rd N.H.
4th Pa.
13th Pa.
4th N.Y.
9th Mass.
3rd Md.
5th Va.
battery of 2 guns

Scott's Detachment, Brig. Gen. Charles Scott, (1,500)

1st N.H.
4th Md.
9th Pa.
1st Va.
4th Va.
8th Va.
12th Va.
14th Mass.
battery of 4 guns

* 660 Men stayed in camp and not engaged in battle
** Not engaged in battle

Left Wing, Maj. Gen. William Alexander ("Lord Stirling") and

Right Wing, Maj. Gen. Nathanael Greene, 7,824

1st Pennsylvania Brigade, 429
1st Pa.
2nd Pa.
7th Pa.
10th Pa.

2nd Pennsylvania Brigade, 487
5th Pa.
8th Pa.
11th Pa.

3rd Pennsylvania Brigade (Conway's), 438
3rd Pa.
6th Pa.
12th Pa.
Malcom's Additional Continental Regt.
Spencer's Additional Continental Regt.

2nd Massachusetts Brigade (Glover's), 636
1st Mass.
4th Mass.
13th Mass.
15th Mass.

3rd Massachusetts Brigade, Brig. Gen. John Patterson, 485
10th Mass.
11th Mass.
12th Mass.

4th Massachusetts Brigade (Learned's), 373
2nd Mass.
8th Mass.

New Hampshire Brigade, Brig. Gen. Enoch Poor, 754
2nd N.H.
2nd N.Y.

2nd Connecticut Brigade, Brig. Gen. Jedediah Huntington, 632
1st Ct.
2nd Ct.
5th Ct.
7th Ct.

1st Virginia Brigade, Brig. Gen. John Mulenberg, 711
9th Va.
13th Va.
1st Va. State Regt.
8th Va. (German Regt.)

2nd Virginia Brigade, Brig. Gen. George Weedon, 587
2nd Va.
6th Va.
10th Va.
14th Va.

1st Maryland Brigade, 790
Delaware Regt.
5th Md.
7th Md.

2nd Maryland Brigade, 602
2nd Md.
6th Md.

3rd Virginia Brigade, Brig Gen. William Woodford, 475
3rd Va.
7th Va.
15th Va.

McIntosh's North Carolina Brigade, Col. Thomas Clark, 425
1st N.C.
2nd N.C.
3rd N.C.
10th N.C.

Index

Alexander, William (Lord Stirling),
  21, 25-26, 36, 51, 62, 67, 63, 238

Clinton, Henry, 9, 27-28, 118, 197-
  204, 209-210, 213-214, 215-216,
  219, 222, 225, 227, 229, 232-233
Conway, Thomas, 67, 191-192
Cornwallis, Charles, 10, 20, 23, 25-
  26, 40, 43, 48, 61, 66, 118, 123-124,
  144, 160-162, 166, 213-214, 234,
  235

De Borre, Phillipe Hubert Chevalier
  de Preudhomme, 239-240
De Coudray, Phillipe Charles Jean
  Baptiste Tronson, 240
Donop, Emil Kurt von, 120, 130,
  131-132, 133

Fort Mercer, 121-123, 130-135, 143
Fort Mifflin, 123, 127-129, 134, 138,
  139-142

George III, 10, 18, 28, 146, 197
Germain, Lord George, 11, 12, 14,
  16-17, 28-29, 41, 180
Grant, James, 119-120, 183-184
Greene Nathanael, 21, 24, 36, 39, 41,
  51, 57, 113, 115, 127, 178, 237-238
Grey, Charles, 85-89, 90, 92-93, 114,
  118-119, 166, 184

Hazelwood, John, 124, 136, 142-144
Howe, William, 9-10, 11, 12-13, 15-
  17, 19-20, 22-27, 29-30, 33, 37-43,
  47-49, 52-53, 60-61, 63-64, 75, 80-
  81, 83-84, 94-98, 105, 107, 117-118,
  121, 123, 126, 135-138, 150, 152-
  153, 160, 162, 164, 179-181, 185-
  186

Knox, Henry, 238
Knyphausen, Wilhelm von, 30, 43,
  48, 52-53, 55-56, 59, 62, 73-74, 120

Lafayette, Marquis de, 67, 77, 172,
  182-186, 194-196, 207, 218
Lee, Charles, 40, 191, 207-208, 210-
  212, 214, 216-218, 219-222, 223-
  225, 241-243

Maxwell, William, 24, 43, 47, 54, 55,
  58, 62, 108
Mifflin, Thomas, 24, 30
Mischianza, 181-182
Musgrave, Thomas, 105-107, 115

Stephen, Adam, 239
Steuben, Baron Friedrich Wilhelm
  von, 187-190, 230, 243
Sullivan, John, 21, 22, 24, 50, 51, 57,
  60, 62, 63, 65, 68, 113, 165-166,
  238-239

Varnum, James, 129, 142, 143

Washington, George, 13-14, 23-26,
  28-42, 47-51, 57-59, 62, 70-72, 76-
  78, 80-81, 95-96, 99-100, 102-104,
  117, 127, 129, 136, 143, 150-162,
  164-167, 170-171, 174, 182, 191-
  193, 199, 204-207, 219-222, 224-
  225, 228, 231, 233-234, 236-237,
  241-242
Wayne, Anthony, 24, 50, 62, 75, 84-
  85, 86-87, 89-90, 92, 111-112, 113,
  211-212, 214-215, 218, 222-223,
  228, 238